Vulnerability in Police Custody

This book provides a nuanced and timely contribution to the question of vulnerability in police custody. It addresses the implementation of the appropriate adult safeguard in respect of adult suspects and explores police decision-making in this context. Drawing on empirical research carried out in England, the work takes a socio-legal approach to examine how and why police custody officers implement or not the appropriate adult safeguard. The book's core arguments are addressed within three parts. Part I examines how vulnerability is constructed philosophically and practically, firstly within the broader literature, thereafter at common law and in statute, and finally by police custody officers. Part 2 discusses how vulnerability is identified and how decisions are made in response to vulnerability. Part 3 critically assesses the theoretical understandings of police decision-making and criminal justice. Here it is argued that current theories on police decision-making hold explanatory power yet have significant shortcomings in relation to vulnerability and the appropriate adult safeguard. The book thus presents new theoretical insights and, on the basis of these insights, asserts that the current regime of regulation must be reconsidered, while police compliance may only be ensured if vulnerability is radically reconceptualised.

Dr Roxanna Dehaghani is a Lecturer in Law at Cardiff School of Law and Politics, Cardiff University, Cardiff, UK.

Vulnerability in Police Custody

Police decision-making and the appropriate adult safeguard

Dr Roxanna Dehaghani

Routledge
Taylor & Francis Group
LONDON AND NEW YORK

First published 2019
by Routledge
2 Park Square, Milton Park, Abingdon, Oxon OX14 4RN

and by Routledge
52 Vanderbilt Avenue, New York, NY 10017

First issued in paperback 2020

Routledge is an imprint of the Taylor & Francis Group, an informa business

British Library Cataloguing in Publication Data
A catalogue record for this book is available from the British Library

Library of Congress Cataloging-in-Publication Data
A catalog record has been requested for this book

ISBN 13: 978-0-367-66242-4 (pbk)
ISBN 13: 978-1-138-09460-4 (hbk)

Typeset in Galliard
by Taylor & Francis Books

For my family

Contents

Foreword

As the title suggests, Roxanna Dehaghani's book focuses principally on three key areas relevant to fairness and justice: 'vulnerability in police custody', 'police decision-making' and 'the appropriate adult safeguard' for suspects detained in police custody.

As a part of her PhD dissertation, awarded from Leicester University in 2017, Dr Dehaghani spent a total of six months (around 250 hours) in police custody suites across two police forces, observing custody officers booking suspects and detainees into custody. Importantly, she conducted 23 semi-structured interviews with custody officers. She also explored how the courts approach sections 76, 77 and 78 of PACE in cases where the appropriate adult (AA) safeguard was not implemented, and how various pieces of guidance (Code C, College of Policing, Mental Health Act Code of Practice) define vulnerability. The rich material from the semi-structured interviews, which is built on a grounded theory of processing qualitative information, provides an excellent insight into the attitudes, pressures and decision-making of custody officers. This is the most unique feature of the book.

Dehaghani suggests that a 'holistic' approach to the criminal justice process is required if suspects and other detainees are to be adequately safeguarded. This includes a recommendation for completely reconceptualising how we frame vulnerability, which involves widening of the appropriate adult provision to include 'all who undergo police interview under suspicion of committing a criminal offence' and acknowledging that some suspects need more support than others. Dehaghani concludes that 'The resolution is neither simple nor impossible but does require a sea-change in policing practice, police culture, and the structure of the criminal justice process'. These are radical recommendations with huge resource implications.

I have had an interest in the psychological vulnerabilities of police detainees since the early 1980s. Our research for the Royal Commission of Criminal Justice in the early 1990s found that 35% of the suspects were not in a normal mental state due to extreme distress or a mental disorder, which could impair their capacity for rational decision making or coping effectively with the interview and confinement. The study emphasised the importance of situational as well as personal risk factors. We found that 19% of the detainees suffered from an exceptionally high level of anxiety and distress, in large part due to their arrest and confinement. After a brief mental state examination, the researchers found that there were good clinical grounds in about 15% of cases for the presence of an appropriate adult. We considered this to be a very conservative estimate and it increased to above 20% after viewing the detainees' psychometric test results. Only 4% of the detainees were provided with an appropriate adult.

We conducted a similar study 20 years later at Lewisham Police Station and found that in spite of reforms recently made in custodial settings, which included the presence of nurses and risk assessment tools procedures, still only 4% were provided with an appropriate adult. This suggests that risk-assessment tools and healthcare professionals still remained ineffective in identifying vulnerabilities, and when identified these were not acted upon by custody officers. Part of the problem seemed to be the primary focus of health care staff on physical problems and risks rather than mental factors that impairs the capacity for effective decision making relevant to the reliability of testimony. This needs to change.

Dehaghani's research also helps to explain this failure in providing vulnerable suspects with an appropriate adult. It is evident from her research that the decision making of custody officers is complex and involves a number of issues, such as resources issues, the availability of appropriate adults in their area, possible delays in detention, the seriousness of the offence, the demand characteristics of the interview, and the presence of solicitors being seen as substitutes, although legally they are not.

The book advances our knowledge about the issues to do with the definitions and identification of vulnerabilities and the decision-making of custody officers concerning the use of appropriate adults. It has important implications for research, policies and practice.

Professor Gisli Gudjonsson, CBE, PhD

Acknowledgements

The compilation of this book has been full of peaks and troughs and I would like to thank a number of people who contributed to those peaks and enabled me to improve my work. First, thank you to Routledge, particularly Alison Kirk for considering this project and Chloe James for her practical help and patience.

Whilst the book was predominantly produced during my time at Cardiff University, it is a development of my PhD thesis, which was generously funded by the University of Leicester. I am grateful to all who were involved in my PhD journey, particularly my supervisor Steven Cammiss and my PhD examiners Jackie Hodgson and Layla Skinns. During and after my PhD I spent time at Queen's University Belfast and the Vulnerability and Human Condition Initiative at Emory University. Those who provided me with the opportunity to do so – Sally Wheeler, and Martha Fineman, Stu Marvel and Rachel Ezrol, respectively – thank you!

This book, whilst perhaps viewed as a solitary endeavour, was the product of various conversations. It would not have been possible without the support and guidance of a number of people: colleagues at Cardiff and elsewhere, and those who I have had the good fortune of interacting with at various events (practitioners, policymakers, and individuals with lived experience). There are, however, some individuals who deserve a specific mention for providing feedback on individual chapters and for providing advice and guidance throughout my academic career: Vanessa Munro, Layla Skinns, Harriet Pierpoint, Vicky Kemp, Chris Bath, Grev Wallington, Dan Newman (my long-suffering co-author!) and Sam Fairclough. I am also honoured that Gisli Gudjonsson – whose work sparked my interest in this area – agreed to write the foreword for this book. My friends and family must also be thanked for their unwavering encouragement and support: Dad, Granny, Reza, Noosh, Arlene, Ann and Trevor, my Norn Iron companions, my Netherlands vrienden, my Leicester buddies and my Cardiff crew. Additional thanks are reserved for my Mum – Ruth Hill – and the Legal Eagle – Francis Rafferty – for reading multiple drafts of the thesis and the book.

I also owe a debt of gratitude to the custody officers who were involved in my research and showed such enthusiasm for my presence in the custody suite. Without the support of the police and those within the custody suite, this research would not have been possible. I anticipate some disagreement with my research from those quarters, but I hope that I have provided as accurate an account of the topic as possible.

Police Custody: cases

Police Custody: legislation

1 The (vulnerable) suspect in the criminal process

Introduction

When in custody or under criminal investigation, those suspected of committing a criminal offence may feel defenceless, isolated, and apprehensive. The English and Welsh criminal justice system is recognised as being, as with most Anglo-American or common law jurisdictions, adversarial.[1] Within this system, the police are tasked with detecting and investigating crime, and apprehending perpetrators. As part of this process, the police are permitted to detain a suspected perpetrator in police custody for the purposes of questioning and evidence-gathering. Police custody is a pivotal point within the criminal process: it is the gateway to the criminal justice process (Skinns 2011; Her Majesty's Inspectorate of Constabulary (HMIC) 2015). It is also where the case may be discontinued or pursued, where the individual is isolated from family and friends, where the police have utmost control over the individual, and where the 'power of the state [is] most evident' (McConville and Hodgson 1993: 5).

Of course, not every suspect who is questioned is officially detained; there are those who will undergo interview whilst attending 'voluntarily'. Those attending the police station 'voluntarily' do so in order to 'help the police with their inquiries' and are entitled to leave, unless placed under arrest. However, because refusal can result in arrest (Police and Criminal Evidence Act (PACE) 1984 s 29), 'voluntary attendance' is recognised as being far from truly voluntary (see Kendall 2018: 9). Little is known about these voluntary attenders: they are not detainees in the true sense but they may nevertheless be vulnerable, particularly because little is known about their treatment. And although the same safeguards apply to the voluntary interview as they do to the 'detained interview' (see Code C para 3.21),[2] it may be even more difficult to ensure compliance with legal regulations and safeguards in a voluntary interview. This is because the process is not overseen or recorded by the custody officer who will provide the individual with his or her rights and ensure, at least to some extent, that the individual is safeguarded (although see later).

This book is concerned with those who have been detained for the purposes of police investigation. More specifically, it examines how and why the appropriate adult safeguard is (or is not) implemented for adult suspects. This book will connect the practical with the more abstract, addressing what vulnerability means and who could be considered vulnerable. It will also examine the factors affecting the implementation of the appropriate adult safeguard, and the influences on custody officer decision-making. It is contended that conceptually and pragmatically, all suspects could and should be considered vulnerable. The unequal power-play existing between the State and the individual renders the suspect vulnerable. The criminal justice process operates to perpetrate an inequality of arms at all stages. Due process is silenced or, even more worryingly perhaps, serves to meet crime control ends (see Packer 1968; McBarnet 1981). Even something considered fundamental to the protection of the individual and of the process, such as the appropriate adult safeguard, can be very easily side-stepped within the process as it currently operates. This is, at least in part, because the police are both combatants *and* protectors of their opponents. Yet, it is also because the various strands of the State seek to condone police behaviour within a criminal justice process that disadvantages many, if not most, defendants (see Dehaghani and Newman in progress; Newman 2013; Owusu-Bempah 2017; Quirk 2017).

Research rationale

This research stemmed from a broader interest in miscarriages of justice and, more specifically, with what could 'go wrong' during the early stages of an investigation. Through a thorough review of the literature, it was clear that there was still much to be said regarding the implementation of the appropriate adult safeguard, particularly from a socio-legal perspective. Of notable mention is the absence of in-depth observation in many of the previous studies, the lack of attention paid to how vulnerability is defined, and the dearth of analysis in relation to policing and criminal justice theory as applied to police decision-making in reference to the appropriate adult safeguard. In order to fully unpack why the appropriate adult safeguard was often left unimplemented, it was imperative that the social world of the custody officer be observed in-depth. A number of studies were also significantly outdated and a large number were conducted before the ushering-in of the (now disbanded) 'Safer Detention' guidance (ACPO 2012) and (in its place) the College of Policing (2018a) Authorised Professional Practice on Detention and Custody (hereafter APP: Detention and Custody). There have also been regular revisions to the Codes of Practice (although as Skinns (2011: 7) notes, they have never been 'substantially overhauled'). External factors have historically had an impact on the police custody environment such as the decarceration movement[3] that led to, as Bean and Nemitz have noted (1995: 7), changes between 1986 (when PACE was introduced) and 1995 (when their research was conducted):

> In the intervening years, a number of changes have taken place which indirectly affect the workings of the Appropriate Adult Scheme not least being the alleged decarceration movement whereby large numbers of psychiatric patients have been discharged from traditional mental hospitals into the community. One obvious outcome of this decarceration is for an increasing

> number of mentally disordered persons to be prosecuted. Another is that the police have become important agents in the promotion of mental health care.

This study recognised how the socio-political environment has changed since many of these studies were conducted, particularly developments such as austerity and neo-liberalism (the latter of which has 'left an indelible mark on the police custody process' (Skinns 2011: 14)). Neo-liberalism has resulted in new public management (and along with it, efficiency), civilianisation, and privatisation, 'workforce modernisation' of defence lawyering, and the increased involvement of a number of different practitioners (multi-professionalism) (*ibid*.: 13–16. See also Ellison and Brogden 2010). Public finance initiatives have led to a much-improved custody environment, particularly with the construction of new, purpose-built facilities (Skinns *et al.* 2017: 359).

Custody is an interesting environment to study, in part because it is relatively under-researched, and in part because alongside many changes, there have been numerous continuities. As Skinns, Wooff and Sprawson note, these continuities exist because of:

> the unchanging nature of the police role in society including the enduring necessity of discretion and the permissiveness of the law, as well as the enduring features of police occupational cultures, and the unchanging monopoly that the police have over the legitimate use of force.
>
> (*ibid*., references omitted)

There was a question therefore as to how far the implementation of the appropriate adult safeguard had changed since the earlier studies were conducted (although there was a recognition that it would be difficult to properly compare and contrast).

This book draws upon a mixture of doctrinal, socio-legal, empirical and theoretical analyses to provide answers to why the appropriate adult safeguard is often left unimplemented. The qualitative data, collected through semi-structured interviews and non-participant observation[4] conducted at two custody suites in England (see Chapter 3), offers an explanation of how custody officers viewed their navigation of the appropriate adult safeguard and how I believed it to be navigated by custody officers. It could be considered an ethnography; a 'curious blending of techniques' (Denzin 2009: 185 as cited by Newman 2013: 21). Observation across a three-month period at each site provided familiarity with the custody suite and staff, and allowed the custody staff to become familiar with me. A total of 31 custody officers were observed, 20 from Waterside (Site 1) and 11 from Mapletown (Site 2). Of these 31, 23 were interviewed: 15 from Waterside and 8 from Mapletown.[5] I spent from early November 2014 to late January 2015 at Waterside and from early April to mid-late June 2015 at Mapletown. The sample size allowed me to reach saturation point (Charmaz 2006). Interviews were conducted towards the end of this period and lasted an average of 41 minutes (at Waterside) and 43 (at Mapletown). At interview, I was careful to provide participants with the opportunity to ascribe their meaning to the research (Burns 2000: 424–5) and therefore attempted to ask questions in an open conversational manner, using the interview schedule as a reminder or guide rather than a plan (Braun and Clarke 2013: 94). The structure of the schedule commenced with less demanding questions about the role of custody officer. This was followed by questions regarding risk[6] (included because of the significance of risk discourse in policing (Ericson and Haggerty 1998) and conceptual congruence with vulnerability (see Brown 2015)). Thereafter the schedule moved onto the more demanding topics of vulnerability and the appropriate adult safeguard. The structure allowed custody officers to ease into the interview.

Unsurprisingly, there were differences between what was stated at interview and what was overheard during observation. For example, CO21-M was discussing mental health with some detention officers and when I added that it is estimated that one in four people have mental health problems at any given time, he quipped 'everyone has mental health problems these days', chortling as he claimed that 'women are the cause of all mental health problems'. At interview, however, CO21-M took a much more sensitive approach to the issue of mental health. This phenomenon, known as 'audience segregation' (Goffman 1956; 1969), suggests that there are different selves portrayed to different people at different times. Instances such as this reinforce the importance of conducting observation in addition to interviews. Moreover, the rapport built during observation undoubtedly contributed to the ease at which custody officers offered candid responses at interview; very few gave what seemed like 'text-book' or 'professional' answers.

Constructing grounded theory

The research methodology is positioned somewhere between positivism – which 'seeks to apply the natural science model… to investigations of social phenomena and explanations of the social world' (Denscombe 2002: 14) and considers there to be an objective reality that is out there to be discovered (*ibid.*: 15) – and interpretivism (or constructionism) – which focuses on the socially constructed nature of knowledge and argues that it is impossible to gain an objective knowledge of the social world (*ibid.*: 18–20). It has also been informed by the symbolic interactionist perspective. This perspective views reality not as 'out there' ready to be discovered but developed through interaction with others (Blumer 1969). It also recognises that human beings react to and interpret their social world and derive meaning from their interactions and surroundings through an interpretative process (*ibid.*). And, it accepts that meaning is therefore a social product created through how things are defined in interaction between people (*ibid.*: 5). A combination of interviews and observations permit the production of a richer and fuller description of the social world under investigation.[7]

The data were collected employing a constructivist grounded theory approach (Charmaz 2006);[8] an approach that provides the researcher with 'flexible analytical guidelines that enable [them] to focus their data collection and to build middle-range theories' (Charmaz 2011: 360) and thus allows for reflexivity and flexibility. The approach does not demand objectivity and indeed focuses instead on meaning, understanding and interpretation (Gibson and Hartman 2013: 84). Charmaz' approach bridges the gap between Glaser's methodological strategies and Strauss' symbolic interactionist perspective (Charmaz 2011. See Glaser and Strauss 2009; Strauss and Corbin's 2008). Charmaz' approach also 'views knowledge as located in time, space and situation and takes into account the researcher's construction of emergent concepts' (Charmaz 2011: 365), and is thus positioned between positivism and post-positivism. Rather than theory or data being 'discovered', constructivist grounded theory sees data as being co-constructed by the researcher and the researched. Because of the researcher's role in construction, her perspectives, values and beliefs are of importance (see Chapter 3). The researcher must therefore recognise these perspectives, values and beliefs, whilst also recognising the validity of her participant's interpretations. The process of grounded theory involves nine stages, dictating, *inter alia*, data collection, interpretation and writing. The grounded theorist is required to adopt an iterative approach to simultaneous data collection and analysis, analyse action and process rather than theme and structure, constantly compare, and draw on data to develop new conceptual categories. She must also systematically analyse data so as to develop inductive categories, construct theory rather than simply describe or apply current theories, employ theoretical sampling, search for variation (such as negative cases), and pursue the development of theory (Charmaz 2011: 364 citing Charmaz 2010).[9]

Structure of the book and key themes

This book examines, in detail, the implementation of the appropriate adult safeguard, analysing what impacts upon its implementation and explaining the custody officer approach through the application of existing theories *and* through the development of new theoretical insights. The core themes rest upon how vulnerability is defined, how it is identified, what factors influence the implementation of the appropriate adult safeguard, and how we may understand police decision-making in this context. Before exploring the core themes and theoretical insights, I examine, in the chapter that follows (Chapter 2), police powers and procedures, focusing predominantly on PACE. I thereafter place the appropriate adult safeguard in its historic and broader contemporary context. Leading on from this, in Chapter 3 I explore the context the specifics of the research site, how access was obtained and retained, and the ethical dilemmas I faced during the ethnography. I also provide a critical reflection on my positionality within the field. This chapter provides the reader with the frame through which I have produced, or reproduced, the qualitative data. Chapter 4 then provides the theoretical lens through which vulnerability can be understood and seeks to map the key contours of this often ill-defined concept through the use of a diverse literature. This chapter also examines the contributions made by the field of psychology and law to renderings of vulnerability as contained in Code C, focusing particularly on the work of Gisli Gudjonsson. This material is then further built upon in the following two chapters, which provide doctrinal and empirical analyses of vulnerability under Code C. Chapter 5, relying on predominantly doctrinal analysis, examines how vulnerability and the appropriate adult safeguard are couched within PACE, case law, Code C and other sources of regulation. Within this chapter, I illustrate how the law has paid relatively little attention to how vulnerability is defined. Definitions are absent from PACE and whilst Code C provides some definition, it fails to sufficiently explicate the terminology used and is often inconsistent and confusing. The courts have failed to properly engage with the definitions, whilst also condoning police breaches of Code C. The penultimate section of this chapter examines the problematic overlap between fitness for interview and the need for an appropriate adult; here I suggest that greater care should be paid to these provisions. Finally, I map the doctrinal analysis onto the theoretical conceptualisations of vulnerability to illustrate how the law conceptualises vulnerability (something to which I return in Chapter 10).

Chapter 6 is the first of three substantive chapters to explore the qualitative data. In addition to examining the terms 'mental vulnerability' and 'mental disorder' as defined by custody officers, this chapter also explores their conceptualisations of vulnerability more generally. As illustrated through the interview data, custody officers' conceptualisations of vulnerability do not chime with their interpretations of who requires an appropriate adult. Instead, custody officers attempt to determine who is 'appropriate adult vulnerable'. This notion defines adult vulnerability as abnormal and childlike. The 'appropriate adult vulnerable' adult is someone with serious impediments to capacity, comprehension, and/or understanding, and, fundamentally, is someone who performs these characteristics. Like much of the discourse surrounding vulnerability, I argue that, for the purposes of the appropriate adult safeguard, some suspects are recognised as 'genuine' and others are thought to be disingenuous or not actually vulnerable. I argue that the conceptualisation of the 'appropriate adult vulnerable' suspect by custody officers differs quite substantially from the definition contained within Code C, in that it most certainly ignores the 'mentally disordered' category and misconstrues the, then in use, 'mentally vulnerable' category. The analysis of the 'appropriate adult vulnerable' suspect is further bolstered by depictions of the appropriate adult safeguard, contained later in the chapter. Here I illustrate that the appropriate adult safeguard is viewed by custody officers as, first and foremost, a means of facilitating communication between the police and the 'genuinely vulnerable' suspect and, to a lesser extent, a parental figure for the 'genuinely vulnerable' suspect. I propose that custody officers either pay little attention to vulnerability as contained within Code C, are unable to understand, or at least articulate, the definitions, or have interpreted 'vulnerability' for the purpose of the appropriate adult safeguard to suit their own ends. Analysis in later chapters (Chapters 7, 8 and 9) lends greater support to the final explanation.

Chapter 7 explores the issue of identification: what previous studies say about the matter, what was observed, and what was said at interview. There is undoubtedly greater availability of information on or about the suspect, particularly through the development of the risk assessment and the increased use of electronic resources. This *should* facilitate the identification of vulnerability. However, custody officers are still identifying the need for an appropriate adult based largely on observations, as they were in years gone by. They do so because vulnerability, for the custody officer, is based largely on performance and therefore must be observable. Whilst there are, indeed, difficulties in identifying vulnerability, the most significant barrier to the implementation of the appropriate adult safeguard is the custody officer's beliefs regarding who requires an appropriate adult and how to identify this need. In addition, I examine the increased presence of those with physical or mental health expertise – HCPs, FMEs, and AMHPs[10] – and argue that the increased presence could lead to an increase in identification, if only they possessed legal, in addition to medical, knowledge. Finally, I argue that the identification of vulnerability can be conceptualised as an investigation, or at least it is articulated in this manner by custody officers. This theme, amongst others, is revisited in Chapter 9.

Once vulnerability has been identified, the decision of implementation remains. Chapter 8 examines the reasons, both persuasive and dissuasive, given by the custody officers. In addition to examining why a suspect who, by the custody officer's estimation, requires an appropriate adult is not provided with one, Chapter 8 also examines why a suspect who, according to the custody officer, is not in need of an appropriate adult may be provided with one. An analysis comparing decisions on young suspects and adult suspects, and decisions on vulnerability and risk (of death or serious injury) is introduced later in the chapter. These aspects of the decision-making process are considered in Chapter 10.

The various themes and threads from Chapters 4–8 are drawn together in Chapters 9 and 10. These two chapters, taken together, explain the custody officers' approach to the appropriate adult safeguard. In Chapter 9, I explore and then examine the utility of a number of key criminal justice and policing theories. With reference to earlier chapters, these theories may explain what is happening, yet, whilst providing a partial explanation to certain aspects of the custody officer approach, they are somewhat limited when taken in isolation. It is urged that these insights are considered in conjunction with one another. Yet, even when drawn together, these theories cannot get to the heart of the issue. In Chapter 10 it is illustrated that the custody officers' approach is simply one of a path of least resistance; custody officers make decisions for personal and then professional reasons. On the basis of the earlier chapters, a number of recommendations are considered and whilst most of them are deemed unworkable, one – that is a reconceptualisation of vulnerability and reconfiguration of the appropriate adult safeguard – has transformative potential. This approach would remove discretion, more accurately reflect what it means to be vulnerable, may more appropriately safeguard the vulnerable suspect, and may remove the stigma associated with the term 'appropriate adult'.

Notes

1 Although this depiction is certainly not uncontentious.
2 Future references are to that of the 2018 Code, unless stated otherwise.

3 The first closure of a long-stay institution for those with learning difficulties occurred in 1986, and the Government White Paper, Care in the Community was published in 1989 (The Open University undated).

4 I argue that observation is non-participant or non-participating where the researcher is not performing the roles or functions of those she is observing, however immersed in the field she may be.

5 At Waterside, two officers left soon after the research commenced, two could not be interviewed for practical reasons and one did not wish to be interviewed. At Mapletown, one custody officer did not wish to be interviewed and two could not be interviewed for practical reasons.

6 When risk was discussed, this was viewed predominantly as risk to the detainee or risk posed by the detainee, rather than risk to evidence caused by, for example, non-compliance with PACE.

7 This is particularly so given the problems with the stand-alone interview – see Newman 2013: 22.

8 Other forms of grounded theory data collection and analysis include Glaser and Strauss' positivist approach (2009) and Strauss and Corbin's (2008) post-positivist approach.

9 Indeed, the emergent process can often highlight gaps and thus require follow-up data collection, as in this study (see Dehaghani 2017d for more information).

10 Liaison and diversion have an increasing presence in police custody but this was not observed during this study.

2 Police powers and procedures

'Safeguarding' the (vulnerable) suspect

Introduction

Prior to the introduction of PACE in 1986, the Judges' Rules and the accompanying Administrative Directions governed the treatment of suspects in police custody. However, the rules lacked enforceability and thereby failed to adequately protect vulnerable suspects. This became apparent in the landmark pre-PACE 'Confait' case when two youths and one vulnerable adult confessed (allegedly under coercion) to causing the death of Maxwell Confait. The two youths exhibited vulnerabilities beyond their young age – Ahmed Salih (aged 14) spoke English as his second language and Ronald Leighton (aged 15) had a mental age of an eight-year-old and was extremely suggestible. The adult, Colin Lattimore, had an IQ of 75 and was susceptible to succumbing to pressure. Their vulnerabilities were largely dismissed by the police, and evidence pertaining to their vulnerabilities was ignored at trial (see Price and Caplan 1977). The three defendants were convicted of various offences – convictions which were not quashed until some two years later (and after great persistence by Lattimore's father) when the Court of Appeal found that the boys could not possibly have killed Maxwell Confait. An inquiry (Fisher 1977/78) into the police investigation and the subsequent court decisions was established in 1976 (the preliminary hearing was held in 1975).

Allegations of physical assault by the police officers against the three were dismissed. However, it was nevertheless recognised that the Judges' Rules were inadequate in protecting the 'vulnerable' (Brown *et al.* 1992: 70). The findings of the Fisher Report along with the Report of the Criminal Law Revision Committee (HMSO 1972) led to the establishment of a Royal Commission for Criminal Procedure (HMSO 1981) (hereafter RCCP) chaired by Sir Cyril Philips (the Philips Commission). The Report, produced by the Commission in 1981, formed the basis of PACE and the Codes of Practice and sought to achieve 'fairness, openness and workability' (Brown 1997: 1–2) whilst also highlighting the need for better protection of vulnerable suspects. As a result of these developments, the English criminal justice system has been commended for 'taking the lead' (Gudjonsson 2010: 161) in improving the police interview process. One such improvement was the safeguard under investigation: the appropriate adult safeguard. However, a vast number of the due process recommendations suggested by the Philips Commission were not implemented and the safeguards were ushered in alongside increased police powers. To some extent, the increase in powers has indeed outweighed the safeguards (see Reiner 2010; see also McConville *et al.* 1991). Within the discussion that follows, the safeguards are set within their wider and more specific context. Also explored are the nature and role of the appropriate adult safeguard and the various problems with the role, in addition to a brief examination of the role beyond England and Wales.

Safeguarding the (vulnerable) suspect

Prior to the implementation of PACE, suspects could be detained by the police for questioning. However, it was not until PACE that this existed on a statutory footing. Since 1986, custody officers can only permit the detention of a suspect if detention is necessary to 'secure or preserve evidence relating to an offence for which [the arrestee] is under arrest or to obtain such evidence by questioning him' (where there is insufficient evidence to charge) or, where sufficient evidence is available, for the purposes of obtaining a prosecutorial decision from the CPS. Detention can only be granted where the custody officer believes that there are 'reasonable grounds for believing that detention is necessary' for these purposes (PACE s 37). The custody officer can therefore not simply authorise detention because it is desirable, convenient or a good idea (Sanders *et al.* 2010: 216 citing HC Official Report 1984, col 1229); he or she must reasonably believe that detention is necessary for the purposes outlined below. In theory, the requirement for necessity to detain should safeguard the suspect from the power of the state and thus safeguard individual liberty. This is further reiterated in the College of Policing (2018a) guidance (see also Dehaghani 2017a).

Where detention is considered necessary, an individual can be deprived of his or her liberty for up to 24 hours in the first instance (where he or she is not suspected of a terrorism-related offence) (PACE s 41; Terrorism Act 2006 s 23). For non-terrorism related offences and where the offence is indictable (i.e. triable in the Crown Court), the minimum period of 24 hours can be extended, in the first instance, by an officer of rank superintendent or above for an additional 12 hours and thereafter by a magistrate for up to another 36 hours (taking the total detention period to 72 hours or three days) (PACE ss 42 and 43). Special consideration should be given to the suspect's vulnerability and the need to consult and consider the views of the appropriate adult when decisions are being made with regard to the extension of detention beyond 24 hours (Code C: para 15.2A).

When individual liberty is infringed upon – i.e. when a person is detained – he or she has a number of rights and entitlements. These include the right to legal advice and representation (PACE s 58), the right to have someone informed of detention (PACE s 56), an entitlement to read Code C (Code C: para 1.2),[1] and the right not to incriminate oneself (otherwise known as the privilege against self-incrimination). These rights are fundamental to protecting human rights (in particular the right to a fair trial enshrined under Article 6 of the European Convention of Human Rights (hereafter ECHR)) and upholding the integrity of the criminal process. These rights are not, however, without their problems.

The right to have someone informed of your detention, for example, can be delayed on the basis that telling the named person will either result in interference with or harm to evidence connected with the offence, interference or harm to other persons, the alerting of an accomplice, or will hinder the recovery of any property obtained as a result of the offence (s 56 (5) PACE). It can also be restricted where the suspect has benefited from his or her criminal conduct and where telling the named person will hinder the recovery of the value of said property (s 56 (5A) PACE). A delay can only be authorised by an officer of rank of inspector or above and can only be authorised in respect of an indictable offence. The right to legal advice and representation is perhaps even more problematic. Whilst viewed as a safeguard which would 'balance' the police power to detain (Dixon 1997: 283), it is not absolute. Similar restrictions apply in that delay of the exercise of the right can only be authorised in respect of indictable offences where it:

> [W]ill lead to interference with or harm to evidence connected with [the offence], or interference with or physical injury to other persons; or will lead to the alerting of other persons suspected of having committed [the offence] but not yet arrested for it; or will hinder the recovery of [property obtained as a result of the offence]
>
> (PACE, s 58 (8) & (8A)).

As an added protection (at least in theory), delay must be authorised by an officer of rank superintendent (two ranks higher than the inspector). Yet, the right may not be exercised for a plethora of reasons. For example, some suspects (although not repeat suspects (Blackstock *et al* 2014: 275)) may be discouraged from accessing legal advice. They may feel that there is nothing they needed to know, they have done nothing wrong, or do not think legal advice would achieve anything (Kemp and Balmer 2008). Some may be discouraged because they are guilty anyway (*ibid.*), because obtaining legal advice would delay their detention (Kemp 2013; Kemp and Balmer 2008; Skinns, 2009), or because they may believe that making a request for a solicitor is indicative of guilt (Blackstock *et al* 2014: 380). Where a suspect decides to obtain legal advice, there is no guarantee that it will be provided, and, if provided, no guarantee that it will be of good quality, or it may not be in person (see Newman 2013). This matter may be further compounded by the fact that, even though it may be financially beneficial for the legal adviser to attend the police station (Blackstock *et al* 2014: 388), such attendance may be actively avoided (Dehaghani and Newman in progress; Newman 2013). Further, the legal representative is not required to be a solicitor (although he or she must be an accredited or probationary representative) (Code C: para 6.12), may fail to protect the suspect from unfair interrogation tactics (Choongh 1997: 148–64; McConville and Hodgson 1991; McConville *et al* 1994; Newman 2013), and/or may over-identify with the police (McConville and Hodgson 1993). Legal advisers may also be somewhat reliant on the police, particularly for information and safety. As such, the lawyer must carefully navigate his or her relationship with the police if he or she is to, for example, obtain disclosure (Quirk 2017: 92). Recent cuts to legal aid have further fettered-away the abilities of lawyers to offer effective representation for their clients in custody (and beyond) and thus have had a negative effect on the quality of legal advice (see Newman 2013; Dehaghani and Newman 2017).

The diminished position of the suspect *and* of the legal representative is further exacerbated by the developments in the right to silence, which, since the coming-into-force of the Criminal Justice and Public Order Act (CJPOA) 1994, has been chipped-away. The suspect no longer has an uninhibited right to silence: whilst he or she can remain silent during the police interview, the courts are permitted to draw adverse inferences by virtue of s 34 CJPOA 1994 (although they cannot base a conviction on silence alone). Thus, whilst a suspect has the right to remain silent during police interview, he or she must do so in the knowledge that the court can assume that he or she did not have a story that would stand up to scrutiny (and this is providing the suspect understands the consequences of exercising the right to silence). The only instance in which the court cannot draw adverse inferences from the accused's silence is where he or she was not given the opportunity to consult with legal counsel (CJPOA 1994 s 34 (2A)). As Choongh (1997a: 15) highlights, both 'the right to silence and the right to legal advice have been favourite police targets because they are represented as stemming the flow of knowledge'. Indeed, the right to silence became a particular target after PACE was implemented as the police attempted to 'regain authority lost by PACE' (Quirk 2017: 20). By restricting both of these rights, the state is able to diminish the resilience of the suspect, resulting in a treble disadvantage (Quirk 2013: 467). Indeed, the fettering away of the right to silence has, for Quirk (2017), had its most marked effect on the lawyer-client relationship and on the ability of the legal representative to do his or her job adequately. The suspect therefore continues to be in a weak position relative to the state.

A lack of resilience may also derive from the suspect's characteristics. In response to the failure of the Judges' Rules to protect 'vulnerable' suspects, as highlighted by the Confait case, the reforms of the criminal process in the mid-1980s resulted in the introduction of the appropriate adult safeguard. Juveniles (those under the age of 18) and 'vulnerable persons' (see Chapter 5) 'must not be interviewed regarding their involvement or suspected involvement in a criminal offence or offences, or asked to provide or sign a written statement under caution or record of interview, in the absence of the appropriate adult' (Code C: para 11.15. See also Annex E para 8). The only exception to this is where an interview is deemed urgent, i.e. where the time taken to obtain an appropriate adult will lead to interference with, or harm to, evidence or other people; serious loss of, or damage to, property; the alerting of other potential suspects who have not yet been arrested; or will hinder the recovery of property obtained through the offence (*ibid.*: para 11.1). In such instances, an interview with a vulnerable suspect can be conducted where authorised by an officer of rank superintendent or above and where it is believed that conducting the interview without an appropriate adult present will not significantly harm the suspect's mental or physical state (*ibid.*: para 11.18. See also Note for Guidance E3). A record must then be made of the decision not to obtain an appropriate adult (*ibid.*: para 11.20).

It is recognised that vulnerable suspects are 'often capable of providing reliable evidence' but it is similarly recognised that they may nevertheless 'without knowing or wishing to do so, be particularly prone in certain circumstances to providing information that may be unreliable, misleading or self-incriminating' (*ibid.*: Note 11C. See also Note for Guidance E2)[2]. Officers are therefore urged to take special care when questioning vulnerable suspects and an appropriate adult must also be provided where there is any doubt as to the person's age, mental state or capacity. Officers are also encouraged to obtain corroboration of facts when possible (*ibid.*). The inherent focus herein is on the reliability of confession evidence or other forms of evidence. The safeguard could also, however, be seen to contribute to 'reasonable adjustments' under the Equality Act 2010 (Bath 2017b; see also Equality Act 2010 s 28).

In the case of adults, the appropriate adult should be:

i a relative, guardian or other person responsible for their care or custody;
ii someone experienced in dealing with vulnerable persons but who is *not:*

- ~ a police officer;
- ~ employed by the police;
- ~ under the direction or control of the chief officer of a police force;
- ~ a person who provides services under contractual arrangements (but without being employed by the chief officer of a police force), to assist that force in relation to the discharge of its chief officer's functions, whether or not they are on duty at the time.

iii failing these, some other responsible adult aged 18 or over who is other than a person described in the bullet points in *sub-paragraph (b)(ii)* above (Code C: para 1.7. See also Annex E, para 2)[3]

The appropriate adult may therefore be a relative or friend, someone from an organised scheme (either paid or voluntary), a social worker or someone else (subject to certain prohibitions); they may be someone known to the suspect, relatively unknown or completely unknown. The appropriate adult must not, however, be a police officer or someone employed for or engaged in police work (as outlined above). This includes:

> special constables appointed for that area, police cadets undergoing training with a view to becoming members of the police force maintained for that area, and civilians employed for the purposes of that force or of any such special constables or cadets.
>
> (NAAN undated c)

The appropriate adult must also not be a solicitor, an independent custody visitor (Code C: Note for Guidance 1F), or a probation officer (Williams 2000 citing *R. v O'Neill* (1990)). The appropriate adult must also not be a victim, a witness, or be suspected of involvement in the offence (although see *Taylor v Chief Constable of Thames Valley Police* [2004] EWCA Civ 858), involved in the investigation, or someone who has received admissions prior to attending the station as an appropriate adult (Code C: Note for Guidance 1B). Whilst the appropriate adult should be advised of their role (Code C: para 11.17), the courts in *H and M v DPP* ([1998] Crim LR 653 (DC)) have taken the approach that evidence is still admissible where an adult is not informed that he or she is performing the role of the appropriate adult but nevertheless acts in that role.

In addition to their presence at interview, they should also be present for charging decisions and related actions such as cautions, bail, and local authority transfers, when warnings in relation to adverse inferences are given, when ID procedures – fingerprints, photographs and DNA – are conducted, including when consent to ID procedures is given, when the suspect is subject to an intimate or strip search, and when written statements are taken. Appropriate adults should also be present for when rights and entitlements are given. If not present when rights and entitlements are initially given, these rights and entitlements should be re-read in the appropriate adult's presence (Code C; NAAN undated d). This aspect of their role requires that they read and discuss rights texts with the suspect (Rock 2007: 104). Indeed, this latter element is highly important given the difficulty many suspects experience in understanding their rights (Gudjonsson and Clare 1992).

The appropriate adult must also be present when a young person between the ages of 14 and 18 or a 'vulnerable adult' gives their consent to the use of live link (Policing and Crime Act 2017 s 74). According to Code C, if the appropriate adult is present at interview, he or she must not act simply as an observer and must advise the suspect, observe whether or not the interview is being conducted fairly (and inform an inspector if it is not), and facilitate communication between the suspect and the police (Code C: 11.17. See also Annex E paras 2A & 9). Appropriate adults should also make representations regarding reviews and extensions of detention, although they need not be physically present to do so (Code C; NAAN undated d).

The appropriate adult, whilst not destroying privilege, is not him or herself subject to legal privilege. As such, the suspect should be given an opportunity to consult privately with their solicitor in the absence of the appropriate adult if they so wish (Code C: Note for Guidance 1E and 3H; *A Local Authority v B* ([2008] EWHC 1017 (Fam)). See also Bath 2014). Further, surveillance of consultations between the appropriate adult and the suspect, whilst intrusive, are nevertheless permissible (*RE v UK* App no 62498/11 (ECtHR, 27 October 2015)) where such surveillance is in the interests of public safety or the protection of public health. The appropriate adult performs not only a communicative function but also a supportive – or protective (Cummins 2007: 23) – function and advisory function, and is expected to act as more than an observer (Code C: para 11.17). The appropriate adult may also be helpful in reducing anxiety (HMIC 2015: 99).

The most recent version of Code C details that the appropriate adult must support, advise and assist the vulnerable suspect, in accordance with the Code or any other Code, when that vulnerable suspect is asked to provide information or participate in any procedure. The appropriate adult must also 'observe whether the police are acting properly and fairly to respect [the vulnerable person's] rights and entitlements' and must inform an officer of at least rank inspector if the vulnerable person's rights and entitlements are not being respected. Further, the appropriate adult must help the vulnerable person understand his or her rights 'and ensure that those rights are protected and respected' (Code C: para 1.7A). In addition, the appropriate adult must assist communication with the police, whilst, at the same time, respecting the individual's right to silence, should the individual wish to exercise that right. For the first time in the history of PACE, the Codes have broken their silence, albeit only minimally, on the appropriate adult safeguard and its interaction with the right to silence.

Whilst Code C contains very little on the role of the appropriate adult, greater detail can be gleaned from NAAN guidance, which highlights the expectation that the appropriate adult act as an active participant in the process. For NAAN (undated b), the appropriate adult should check whether the suspect's rights and welfare are being complied with, whether the suspect's condition or state has deteriorated, and whether the suspect has understood the significance of the information provided to them (such as rights and entitlements, accusations against them, any cautions given, questions put to them, the various procedures involved and their bail conditions). The appropriate adult should also check whether the police and others have understood what the suspect is communicating to them. The guidance also highlights how advice, support and assistance is required for any procedure under the PACE Codes such as 'rights and entitlements, cautions and special warnings, interviews and written statements, [identification] procedures [and] consent ... strip searches and intimate searches, seeking and giving of consent ... reviews of detention, [and] charging decisions' (NAAN: Information). Advice, support and assistance should also be offered in facilitating effective communication, the understanding, and execution of rights. NAAN guidance also highlights that an appropriate adult should 'inform and intervene' where rights and entitlements are not being complied with and should escalate a compliant through the ranks so as to ensure compliance. They should also inform and intervene where they believe that the suspect's condition has changed significantly or consider that it is in the suspect's best interests to have a legal representative attend the police station (NAAN undated b).

When considering the role of the appropriate adult, the best interests of the suspect are paramount. For example, although it may be more satisfactory that the appropriate adult is someone with experience or training in relation to the suspect's vulnerability/ies, the wishes of the suspect are, if practicable, to be respected, even where the suspect prefers that their appropriate adult is a relative who lacks such qualifications (Code C: Note for Guidance 1D). Moreover, whilst intimate searches should be conducted in the presence of an appropriate adult of the same sex, the vulnerable person can 'specifically request the presence of a particular adult of the opposite sex'; such wishes are to be respected (*ibid.*: Annex E para 12). Further, although the appropriate adult may request that a legal representative attend the police station, the suspect may not be forced against his or her will to consult with said legal representative on their arrival (Code C: Note for Guidance 6.5A).

The appropriate adult safeguard: a distinct advantage?

Not one 'type' of appropriate adult is problem-free. The appropriate adult is often institutional or 'public, formal official and structured' rather than 'private and informal everyday' (Rock 2007: 109–10 citing Barton and Hamilton 1998). In this sense, parents and other relatives (or friends) may be preferable, particularly for the suspect because know the suspect better (see Jessiman and Cameron 2017) and may therefore be better able to provide support, advice and assistance with communication (see Rock 2007: 109). They may, however, be unsupportive or put pressure on the suspect to confess (Littlechild 1995: 542; see also Evans 1993); too readily accept police malpractice, be confrontational or advise the suspect to withhold information (Pierpoint 2000: 386); hold negative attitudes towards the police (Quinn and Jackson 2007: 245); be too emotionally involved or distressed to take an active role (Pierpoint 2000: 385–6); act in a passive manner (Evans 1993: 39; Evans and Puech 2001); and/or fail to intervene when the police are 'haranguing, belittling or threatening' (Evans 1993: 46) the suspect. These criticisms notwithstanding, relatives may be used for expediency (Pearse 1995: 150) and may be preferred as they cost less than someone from a scheme (Pierpoint 2001: 267). The approach of the (parent) appropriate adult towards the police can also have a bearing on how the police treat the suspect: respect and remorse (from the appropriate adult and the suspect) results in more sympathy and less condemnation from the police (Evans and Puech 2001).

Volunteer appropriate adults are potentially more cost-efficient (although there is not necessarily an evidence base to prove this) but, because they are often from affluent areas and may have had little to no contact with the police, they tend to be unrepresentative of the suspect population (Pierpoint 2000: 388–9). Such issues are compounded as many volunteers are retired (ibid). Those who work may be unavailable when called upon (ibid: 388). This may be less likely now that schemes work on a rota, however, no volunteer can be compelled to respond when called and they may not always be available, even if they have agreed to times on a rota (Bath 2018). Volunteers may also have a tendency for being pro-police (and, as such, anti-suspect) (ibid). Volunteers may often be unqualified and not very well trained (ibid; see also NAAN 2015: 12), both with regard to the criminal justice process and/or the needs of vulnerable individuals (Littlechild 1995: 453) and may therefore fail to detect police oppressiveness (White 2002: 64). Even when they detect oppressive tactics, they may be reluctant to intervene (Pierpoint 2000: 389). Appropriate adults may also be ill-equipped to deal with the gravity of what they are dealing with, such as in the case of Janet Leach who acted as an appropriate adult for Fred West (*Leach v Chief Constable of Gloucestershire* [1999] 1 W.L.R. 1421). Issues with training may be less likely amongst schemes which are members of NAAN and utilise its national training pack. However, the question that still remains is: how much training is enough or, perhaps more appropriately, *is* training enough?

Social workers may be better trained than some volunteers but they (social workers) may require additional training to perform effectively (White 2002: 56–7;

see also Hodgson 1997: 786–7). Social workers also tend to make a lesser contribution than that made by parents or other relatives. Moreover, 'the police may incorrectly assume that social workers are familiar with the requirements of the [appropriate adult's] role and, therefore, fail to inform them of the responsibilities' (Pierpoint 2000: 387). Social workers may also be keen to avoid conflict with the police (particularly if their work requires the maintenance of good working relationships), they may be perceived by the suspect as 'part of the system', and they are often torn between welfare and control (ibid). There is, moreover, no consensus on whether social workers known to the suspect are better than those who are not: those with a pre-existing relationship may be over-familiar with the suspect and may struggle to achieve impartiality but by contrast, duty social workers, whilst able to exercise neutrality, may not be familiar with the suspect and may therefore fail to understand him or her (Quinn and Jackson 2007: 247). Confidentiality,[4] trust, and knowledge of individual needs, may also be a concern in relation to professional appropriate adults, particularly from the service user perspective (Jessiman and Cameron 2017).

Some types of appropriate adult services may be better resourced than others: for example, Kemp and Hodgson (2016: 164), when looking at the provision of the appropriate adult safeguard for young people, found that appropriate adults working for Youth Offending Teams (YOTs) 'had access to other YOT workers and mainstream services' whilst volunteer appropriate adults did not. Inequity in resources also made it difficult to address health or welfare issues. This matter undoubtedly places (some) young suspects in a more advantageous position than adult suspects, but it may also be worsened by the inconsistencies in national provision. For example, whilst some appropriate adult schemes are part of NAAN (and will therefore have access to training and professional development and have made a commitment to the NAAN standards), some are not. Moreover, some appropriate adult schemes may be funded by local authorities, some are unfunded, and others may be paid from the police budget (Perks 2010). This latter avenue could raise issues with independence (*ibid.*: 17). The patchy national provision undoubtedly impacts negatively upon availability and response time (see Jessiman and Cameron 2017) but may also influence the general effectiveness of appropriate adults. As Bradley (2009) highlighted, the service someone receives could differ depending on where he or she is arrested (if that service is provided at all). Difficulties in securing the appropriate adult's attendance may lead to delays in the suspect's detention (Pierpoint 2011: 140; Quinn and Jackson 2007: 246. See also Hodgson 1997: 789). This could have a bearing on how the interview is conducted and may influence the outcome of the case (Pierpoint 2011: 139–40; although see Quinn and Jackson 2007: 251). Such delays could mean that an appropriate adult is not provided even when called (NAAN 2015: 11; although see Skinns 2011: 63).

Not only is provision patchy, there may also be ambiguity with regard to the appropriate adult's role (see Pierpoint 2005; 2011; White 2002) and the role can often be contradictory (Pierpoint 2011; 2000). This is arguably in part due to inadequate information provided to the appropriate adult (HMIC 2015: 91) but also, naturally, as a result of the appropriate adult's own interpretation of his or her role (Pierpoint 2006). Question marks remain regarding neutrality and impartiality: should the appropriate adult be independent of the entire investigation or simply independent of the police? In other words, must they be neutral of the entire process or can they side with the suspect? Some appropriate adults may see their role as a safeguard for the suspects, others may believe that they are there to assist the police, and others may view themselves as independent umpires (i.e. neither working on behalf of the police or the suspect) (Kemp and Hodgson 2016: 142). Further, some appropriate adults may not appreciate or understand the nature of their role at all (Hodgson 1997: 789). The role of the appropriate adult may be interpreted as involving due process (ensuring that the suspect has understood his or her rights, can understand the questions posed and what his or her responses are) (Pierpoint 2011: 226–9; Jessiman and Cameron 2017: 3), crime prevention (such as why the suspect has offended without presuming guilt) (Pierpoint 2011: 226–9), providing emotional support (Jessiman and Cameron 2017: 4), and welfare such as ensuring that the suspect has had adequate food and is warm (although this function can operate in a crime control manner (Pierpoint 2011: 226–9)).

Whilst Code C and, to a greater extent, NAAN guidance, contain information on the role of the appropriate adult, the role is nevertheless open to considerable interpretation. For example, although it is clear that support, advice and assistance should be present during the police interview (see *R. v Fogah* [1989] Crim LR 141) and beyond (see *R. v Maguire* (1990) 90 Cr App. R. 115), there is no elaboration on what *type* of support is required and to which other part(s) of the process this should extend. Chris Bath (2017a), the Chief Executive of NAAN, believes that this aspect should be interpreted as widely as possible, i.e. the appropriate adult can do whatever they wish provided they are not expressly prohibited from doing so. This is certainly not problematic, in and of itself, but, as will be examined later, there is a distinct lack of guidance on what appropriate adult are and are not allowed to do. There is also a question-mark over whether the appropriate adult should provide emotional support and assistance in managing physical well-being such as rest breaks and medication, something which the service users in Jessiman and Cameron's (2017) study valued highly.

The requirement that the appropriate adult observe whether or not the interview is being conducted fairly may be difficult to discharge as fairness is a vague and ill-defined concept. Code C fails to elaborate on what is meant by 'fairness' thus undoubtedly making it difficult for the appropriate adult to know when it is appropriate to intervene and when intervention is to be avoided. Bath (2017b) has suggested that it could be considered as something akin to fair trial rights but, given the vagueness of this concept, this analogy does not elucidate, in actuality, what this requirement entails. The appropriate adult can be asked to leave the interview if his or her 'approach or conduct prevents or unreasonably obstructs proper questions being put to the suspect or the suspect's response being recorded' (Code C: para 11.17A). Again, it is unclear what type of conduct or approach would prevent or unreasonably obstruct proper questions being put to the suspect. These rules, and the lack of clarity in their scope, may serve to further undermine the appropriate adult's position and may reinforce the appropriate adult's unwillingness to go beyond mere observation. Indeed, appropriate adults are often discouraged from taking an active role (Hodgson 1997: 790; Quinn and Jackson 2007: 244) and have been criticised for their inactivity or minimal activity during the police interview (Medford *et al.* 2003: 253), to the extent that they have been deemed 'wallpaper' (Hodgson 1997: 790 citing Dixon *et al.* 1990. See also Pierpoint 2011). This is not helped by the fact that Code C is silent on this question of intervention (White 2002: 62). Suspects may pick up on such inactivity: in Kemp and Hodgson's study (2016: 145) they found that young people were not complimentary about the appropriate adult's role: the appropriate adult was seen to be doing nothing or simply making the interview room more crowded. A non-intrusive, passive appropriate adult, whilst not the best form of protection for the suspect, is nevertheless beneficial for the police: by providing an appropriate adult, they have not breached Code C and thus the evidence may nevertheless be admissible (Pierpoint 2000: 386; 2004: 40), and indeed officers may restrict or discourage the appropriate adult from intervening (Kemp and Hodgson 2016).

The appropriate adult's role in 'facilitating communication' (arguably the most important aspect of the role, when looking at the broader context of the Code and its development) also remains unclear. On a practical basis, the appropriate adult, even if trained generally, may be unaware of or unable to adapt to the specific communicative needs of the suspect. Quinn and Jackson (2007: 247) have argued that many appropriate adults do not facilitate communication and indeed do not go far beyond their supportive function. The 'facilitating communication' aspect of the appropriate adult's role is also conceptually problematic as it is undoubtedly co-opted for a police purpose: the appropriate adult is viewed as a means of extracting accurate and, more importantly, admissible evidence from the suspect. A further tension arises when attempting to reconcile this aspect of the appropriate adult's role with the right to silence: the requirement to facilitate communication can contradict the right to silence (Brown 1997) and there was, until the most recent version of the Code (see para 1.7A), nothing in the Code that suggests that facilitating communication also includes the facilitation of the absence of communication. Elsewhere the Code tends to focus on the provision of reliable (and therefore admissible) information. Whilst 1.7A now makes it clear that the appropriate adult must respect the individual's right to silence, the broader context of the Code could still allow for a tension between the appropriate adult's role in facilitating communication and the individual's right to silence.[5] It may be difficult for a suspect to maintain his or her right to silence. Further, given the focus on the provision of reliable information, the suspect may feel unable to provide deliberately misleading information or, indeed, may feel encouraged, by the appropriate adult, to provide only truthful information. Certainly, if the purpose of the appropriate adult is to place the suspect in the position that he or she would be in if he or she were not otherwise 'vulnerable' then it would stand to reason that, if deliberate lies are in the suspect's best interests, that course of action should be permissible. As Fennell (1994: 67) highlights, 'the role of facilitating communication may be over-emphasized to the extent that the adult becomes an agent of the interrogating officers'.

The absence of legal privilege (*A Local Authority v B*) also casts doubt on the assertion or aspiration that the appropriate adult is present to facilitate communication: surely, the appropriate adult needs to know the suspect's side of the story so as to help effectively communicate the narrative. The lack of legal privilege may also undermine the communicative lines between the legal representative and the suspect: if the appropriate adult is required to help the suspect communicate and the suspect struggles to do so with the legal representative then the appropriate adult should be able to sit-in on the consultation without any negative implications for the suspect. If the purpose of the appropriate adult safeguard is to protect the suspect, then Code C is inherently flawed: its emphasis is squarely on the extraction of accurate and admissible information. The NAAN guidance, whilst filling part of the lacuna generated by Code C, does not fully resolve some of these definitional, conceptual, and practical issues.

Questions could also be raised as to the qualities that the appropriate adult is required to possess. For example, in *DPP v Blake* 'it was held that an appropriate adult could not be a person with whom the young person has no empathy' (Pierpoint 2000: 388 citing [1989] 1 WLR 432. See also Nemitz and Bean 2001; Hodgson 1997). Yet, this does not mean that an appropriate adult who criticises and contradicts the suspect will be considered 'inappropriate' (*R. v Jefferson* Times, June 22, 1993 (CA), (1993) Crim LR 880). An appropriate adult may, however, be considered 'inappropriate' where he or she is vulnerable him or herself (*R. v Morse* [1991] Crim LR 195), although not always, as in the case of *R. v W* (Unreported) (CA).

The lack of clarity has resulted in the social construction of the role by the appropriate adult, and, unsurprisingly, by the suspect, the custody officer (see Chapter 6) and other police officers, the courts, legal advisers, Forensic Medical Examiners (FMEs),[6] Healthcare Professionals (HCPs),[7] and also potentially approved mental health professionals (AMHPs).[8] Indeed, Kemp and Hodgson (2016: 142) found that volunteer appropriate adults differed in their interpretation of the role, when compared with appropriate adults from YOTs: a volunteer appropriate adult viewed their role as something which protected the well-being of the person whilst also protecting the police whereas a YOT worker 'considered themselves to be firmly on the side of the juvenile'.

The presence of an appropriate adult may also have some bearing on legal advice. As noted above, the absence of legal privilege can limit the extent to which the appropriate adult performs his or her role. The appropriate adult is also required to provide advice and help communicate rights and entitlements to the suspect but queries could be raised with regard to the appropriateness of advice. Providing legal advice is most certainly out of the question but it may be difficult for the appropriate adult to tread the (often fine) line between general advice and legal advice. It may also be difficult to prevent the appropriate adult from giving what is, or what could be, legal advice. This may present an even greater issue as the appropriate adult becomes more skilled and experienced (Bath 2018), and may be a particular issue because cuts to legal aid mean that legal representatives are spending less time with their clients (see Newman 2013; Dehaghani and Newman 2017).

The advice given by the appropriate adult could also be misleading or detrimental for the suspect, particularly where there is no legal advisor present or where the advice of the appropriate adult is in conflict with the advice of the legal advisor (Quinn and Jackson 2007: 248–9). This particular issue, although more common with relatives, may also arise with professional appropriate adults (*ibid.*). An 'inappropriate' appropriate adult may not only safeguard the evidence; it could also be considered a breach of human rights principles (Pierpoint 2000). Yet, an effective appropriate adult is also not an absolute guarantee that the system will operate fairly: as Nemitz and Bean (2001: 601) highlight, injustices can occur at other stages of the process, particularly because the appropriate adult is only present during the police custodial process and not thereafter. Thus, a vulnerable suspect who is attended by an appropriate adult is not necessarily placed at an advantage over one who is not (Hodgson 1997: 790).

There have been some suggestions for reform. Bradley (2009: 43) recommended that the appropriate adult provision was reviewed so as to 'improve the consistency, availability and expertise of this role'. This recommendation has still not been implemented since the report was published (see Durcan *et al.* 2014) and in 2018 the issue still remains. Pierpoint (2011) has argued in favour of professionalisation, which could bring about consistency, particularly when comparing the contributions made by parents (and arguably other relatives). This could be a costly option, both in terms of time and money, and may therefore deter custody officers from calling appropriate adults (see Chapter 7). It may also be unpalatable to the Home Office who, when addressing the appropriate adult provision in recent months, have sought to cut costs rather than spend more (as gathered from my time sitting on the Home Office Working Group on Vulnerable Adults). Southcott (1999) has proposed making use of mental health nurses. This is, however, a problematic suggestion as, although mental health nurses will have training on mental health issues, they may not (or indeed are unlikely to) be trained in the legal aspects of the appropriate adult role. Moreover, if mental health nurses are embedded within the custody suite, questions could be raised with regard to their independence from police officers and the extent to which they have adopted some of the cultural norms of the custody officers. Further, whilst they have knowledge of mental health, this may not extend to learning difficulty or additional education needs, or indeed other areas that interact with suspect vulnerability such as bereavement, anxiety, or trauma (see Chapter 4). Moreover, the various healthcare professionals in custody should be concerned with the health of the individual and should not be required to deal with other matters (Bath 2018).

The term 'appropriate adult' also results in some problems, conceptually and practically. Whilst it may be less offensive when used in relation to young suspects, the term 'appropriate adult' when used as a safeguard for adults, can be interpreted as meaning that the adult is neither 'appropriate' him or herself, or an 'adult'. This can cause conceptual incongruence – it may be difficult for custody officers to accept that an adult, particularly one who behaves in an 'adult' manner, requires help from another (see Chapter 6) and it may be unpalatable, degrading, or offensive for adults to be told that they need another adult to attend their interview, an adult who is 'appropriate'. This may also deter custody officers from using the appropriate adult and may discourage adult suspects from engaging with the appropriate adult. This contention will be re-examined in Chapter 9 (see also JUSTICE 2017).

Notwithstanding the myriad of issues, the appropriate adult may have a positive impact on the custody process. For young suspects in particular, the presence of the appropriate adult can increase the likelihood that a legal representative will be present (although note that this positive effect did not exist for adults (Pierpoint 2004 citing Robertson *et al.* 1996)).[9] It may decrease interrogative pressure and may encourage the legal representative to take a more active role (Medford *et al.* 2003: 253) (that is, provided the appropriate adult does not undermine the advice given by the legal adviser). Moreover, whilst unable to adequately facilitate communication, the appropriate adult is particularly useful in its supportive function (see Quinn and Jackson 2007).

Implementing the appropriate adult safeguard: potential pitfalls

The implementation of the appropriate adult safeguard is the responsibility of the custody officer (although it can be facilitated by others – see Chapter 6). In addition to deciding whether the arrestee should become a detainee, the custody officer is also responsible for 'supervising custodial interrogation' (Irving and McKenzie 1989: 5), for ensuring compliance with the Act and Codes (PACE s 39), and for providing information to the detainee or suspect (usually upon detention) such as the reason for detention and legal entitlements. The custody officer must also decide, 'in consultation with the officer in charge of the investigation and appropriate healthcare professionals as necessary' (Code C: para 12.3), whether the suspect is fit for interview. Suspects should not be interviewed 'if the custody officer considers [that interview] would cause significant harm to [their] physical or mental state' (*ibid.*). In particular, vulnerable suspects should always be treated as 'being at some risk during an interview' (*ibid.*). Where the suspect is unable to 'appreciate the significance of questions and their answers [or] understand what is happening because of the effects of drink, drugs or any illness, ailment or condition' an interview must not be conducted unless authorisation is given by an officer of rank superintendent or above (*ibid.*). As will be explored in Chapter 5, whilst there is some overlap in the legal guidance regarding fitness for interview and the requirement for an appropriate adult, a suspect can be deemed fit for interview but with the requirement that an appropriate adult be present.

This role of the custody officer has not escaped criticism. As McConville, Sanders and Leng have noted, the custody officer is a *police officer* and remains part of the police culture with both 'institutional and collegial ties with other officers'

(1991: 42). The custody officer is mindful not to undermine the authority or question the judgement of his co-workers (*ibid*.: 43) and acts as a 'facilitator, not simply a doorkeeper' (*ibid*.: 55). Not only do custody officers lack independence through sharing police objectives and values, they also lack independence from the cases (Choongh 1997: 173). Custody officers may also be undermined by the pressures of the custody suite and the influences of senior command (Dehaghani 2017a; Kemp 2014). Their independence, or lack thereof, impacts upon the implementation of the appropriate adult safeguard for vulnerable adult suspects (see Chapters 5–9). Not only may custody officers lack independence, they too may lack training – as Coppen (2008) has highlighted, training may be minimal or entirely absent in some forces (see also CJJI 2014). This too may impact upon his ability to understand the terms contained within Code C and, connected with that, his ability to identify vulnerability. The custody officer may also face practical constraints in the form of CPS Charging Guidance and procedures contained within the Mental Health Act (MHA) 1983, both of which may impact negatively on the time available to perform other aspects of his role (Coppen 2008: 85–8). Other aspects of his role, such as the booking-in procedure – often conducted when the detainee or suspect arrives at the custody suite – is time-consuming and can take around 40–50 minutes per individual (*ibid*.: 85). Whilst most custody suites are staffed with permanent custody officers (and this was certainly the arrangement in the Waterside and Mapletown), the custody officer is not required to perform his functions over a specific period of time. Therefore, whilst some custody officers may perform their roles over weeks, months or even years, another may not know of his role until he starts his shift (Zander 2005: 136).[10]

Custody officers are also not trained in mental health, mental disorder, learning difficulties, and so on. Put simply, they are police officers and not mental health workers, social workers, or doctors. The custody officers lack of knowledge may operate as a barrier to implementing the appropriate adult safeguard for vulnerable adult suspects (see Palmer and Hart 1996; Gudjonsson *et al.* 1993; Irving and McKenzie 1989. See also Bucke and Brown 1997; Phillips and Brown 1998; Medford *et al.* 2003). Similarly, they may be able to identify whether someone is vulnerable but may be unable to make sense of the information and how this translates to the implementation of the appropriate adult safeguard (Bean and Nemitz 1995: 48). This may then mean that a vulnerable adult suspect passes through the criminal process unaided.

Yet, even those who are considered 'experts' have been criticised for various reasons. HCPs have been subject to criticism, particularly their tick-box approach to the risk assessment (Adebowale 2013: 21–2), their inadequate training (NAAN 2015: Paper A6), and their insufficient competency in meeting the suspect's healthcare needs (HMIC 2015: 97). FMEs have also been criticised for lacking specific training and failing to trigger the AA safeguard even where it was recognised that the suspect had a learning disability (CJJI 2014: 5). For example, the CJJI highlighted an instance of an FME deeming that no appropriate adult was needed in the case of a suspect who had 'complex problems including Asperger's, anger management problems, suicidal thoughts, self-harm, self-inflicted head injury' (*ibid.*: 19). Medical professionals may have medical knowledge, but this does not translate to legal knowledge (and this medical knowledge does not necessarily translate to knowledge of mental health problems). This would not necessarily be problematic for the purposes of the appropriate adult safeguard if it were not for the fact that custody officers have been found to delegate the appropriate adult decision to HCPs (NAAN 2015: Paper A6) and FMEs (see also Chapters 6 and 7).

'Remedies' for non-implementation of the appropriate adult safeguard

Despite all the practical and conceptual difficulties with the implementation of the appropriate adult safeguard, all is not lost: the trial court may decide to throw the case out of for breach of the appropriate adult provision or may rule the evidence inadmissible. For example, s 76 of PACE allows for a confession – that is 'any statement wholly or partly adverse to the person who made it; whether made to a person in authority or not and whether made in words or otherwise' (PACE, s 82 (1) – to be excluded at trial where the confession has been obtained through oppression or as a consequence of something said or done which was likely, in the circumstances existing at the time, to render it unreliable. The exclusion of such evidence covers the confession only; any evidence gathered as a result of an excluded confession remains admissible (PACE s 76 (4)) unless it can be considered to 'have such an adverse effect on the fairness of the proceedings that [it ought not to be admitted]' (PACE s 78). These rules apply to trials held summarily (i.e. in the magistrates' court) and trials held on indictment (i.e. in the Crown Court) and may be applied by the trial court or may be used on appeal. In *Miller*, for example, evidence was excluded after expert evidence, given by Professor Gisli Gudjonsson, was adduced to highlight that the suspect was vulnerable (see *R. v Paris, Abdullahi and Miller* (1993) 97 Cr App R 99; [1994] Crim LR 361).

Defendants who are considered 'mentally handicapped' – that is, suffering from an 'arrested or incomplete development of mind which includes significant impairment of intelligence and social functioning' (PACE s 77 (3)) – and who have confessed in the absence of an 'independent person' (i.e. an appropriate adult, a social worker, or a solicitor (see Chapter 5)) may avail of a s 77 jury direction. For this direction to apply, the prosecution case must rest wholly or substantially on confession evidence. If such criteria are met, the court must warn the jury that the confession was given in such circumstances. By virtue of being a jury direction, s 77 is only available in a trial on indictment. Moreover, the rules are limited to mentally disordered and mentally vulnerable suspects who are considered 'mentally handicapped'; the Royal Commission on Criminal Justice (1993: 49) (hereafter RCCJ) recommendation to extend this to the mentally ill or otherwise mentally disordered was ostensibly ignored.

However, these remedies apply only when the case reaches the courts. The unfortunate reality is that many cases are effectively 'tried' at the police station

(Cape 2013: 16). A number of factors may prevent the case from reaching the courts. Firstly, the English criminal justice system is known for employing a system of plea-bargaining, otherwise known as the 'Sentence Discount Principle' (see Criminal Justice Act (CJA) 2003, s 144 (1)). This means that many defendants, rather than entering a plea at court, enter an early plea so as to obtain a sentence discount. As Darbyshire (2000) has highlighted, rather than being of benefit to those who plead guilty, the plea-bargaining system is actually of detriment to those who maintain their innocence. Cases may also fail to reach the courts where out-of-court disposals, such as fines and cautions (CJA 2003, s 23), are used. To avail of these disposals, individuals must admit guilt, however, it should be recognised that some individuals be induced into 'admitting' guilt (whether they are guilty or not) so as to avoid the (arguably traumatic) criminal trial. Thus, vulnerability may be undetected.

Although there may indeed be cases where confession (and other) evidence is challenged, similarly there are cases where it is not. Supposing that an individual has been convicted, the case must successfully reach the appeal stage for the courts to consider whether evidence should have been admitted. Magistrates' court appeals typically go to the Crown Court; in such appeals, the grounds are unrestricted, fresh evidence is allowed, and the case is heard anew. However, there is a 21-day time-limit, public funding is means and merits tested, and the defendant risks being handed a longer sentence (Magistrates Court Act 1980 s 108; Legal Aid, Sentencing and Punishment of Offenders Act 2012; Ministry of Justice 2015: part 34). For appeal from Crown Court to Court of Appeal (such as those cases discussed in Chapter 5), the individual requires leave for appeal and must illustrate that the conviction is 'unsafe' (Criminal Appeals Act 1968 as amended by the Criminal Appeals Act 1995). Fresh evidence may also be admitted but this is rarely allowed. The deprivation of liberty associated with the Crown Court is much higher than that in the magistrates' court (although any conviction is worthy of attention, whether serious or otherwise – see McBarnett 1981; see also Chapter 8) and yet it is inherently more difficult to appeal from the Crown Court to Court of Appeal. If the individual's appeal is not successful, then questions surrounding admissibility will not be ventured into and the non-implementation of the appropriate adult safeguard will not be rectified. And, even where the case reaches the appeal stage, a breach of Code C may be condoned by the courts, as will be illustrated in Chapter 5.

Avoiding the reliance on 'faulty' remedies

Early identification of vulnerability in police custody may ensure that costly proceedings are avoided and that the individual's case is removed from the criminal process – a process which is, of itself, punitive (Feeley 1992). It can ensure that justice is delivered (or at least not delayed) and protects the integrity of the individual and the process. Even where confession evidence is not in dispute or where a prosecution is not pursued, the identification of vulnerability may be important to protect the individual from any risk of harm or ill treatment within custody, in so far as is possible.[11] It also increases the likelihood that the vulnerable suspect can understand and assert his or her rights (Rock 2007), particularly where, as in England and Wales, the right to legal advice is triggered by a positive request (PACE s 58; McConville *et al.* 1991: 50). The presence of an appropriate adult, as noted above, has a positive impact on the provision of legal representation and the use of interrogative pressure. Timely identification may also alert the police to behavioural or healthcare issues. For example, some vulnerable suspects may exhibit uncooperative behaviour due to issues with capacity, confusion about the process, or simply due to a feeling of suspiciousness or helplessness. This is particularly problematic as being uncooperative leads to police suspicion (McConville *et al.* 1991: 29). Detention in police custody could potentially heighten the risk that an individual may pose to him or herself (see Angiolini 2017). Early identification of mental health issues or otherwise may then alert the custody officer to other risk factors. Identification of vulnerability may also be significant in ensuring diversion from the criminal process (CPS 2010) and may also feed-into decisions on the public interest stage of the Code for Crown Prosecutors (see Bradley 2009; see also Cooper and Gerry 2017). The Confait case attests to how vital timely identification of vulnerability (and implementation of the appropriate safeguards) can be.

The appropriate adult safeguard beyond England and Wales

By virtue of Code C to the Police and Criminal Evidence (NI) Order 1989, the appropriate adult safeguard is also available in Northern Ireland (see Department of Justice 2015). The Northern Irish Code largely mirrors that used in England and Wales. The appropriate adult safeguard is also available for young and adult suspects in Scotland (see Thomson *et al.* 2007). Whilst the role in Scotland somewhat mirrors that of the appropriate adult in England and Wales (and Northern Ireland), unlike the safeguard in England and Wales (and Northern Ireland), the Scottish appropriate adult has no legal standing (Police Scotland 2017). Safeguards akin to the appropriate adult are also available for young suspects in Australia, New Zealand, Denmark (see Pierpoint 2008) and Ireland.

Providing additional rights and entitlements of those who are considered vulnerable is also a recognised, or recognisable, ideal on a European Union level. In 2009, the European Commission (2009) developed a 'Roadmap' on strengthening procedural rights for those accused of a criminal offence and, in doing so, outlined a measure for strengthening safeguards for the vulnerable. Measure E urges that special attention is paid to those 'who cannot understand or follow the content of the meaning of proceedings, owing, for example, to their age, mental or physical condition'. The Commission Recommendation (2013) seeks to further strengthen the procedural rights of those suspects and accused who can be considered vulnerable. It further highlights the importance of identifying and recognising vulnerability, and the need for an initial assessment of vulnerability by police officers, law enforcement or judicial authorities. It also emphasises the need for independent expert advice on 'the degree of vulnerability, the needs of the vulnerable person and the appropriateness of any measures taken or envisaged against the vulnerable person' (*ibid.*: 8). The suspect or accused person or their lawyer is permitted to challenge the assessment of their potential vulnerability, particularly where the assessment would 'significantly impede or restrict the exercise of their fundamental rights' (*ibid.*).

The term 'appropriate adult' is also introduced and is described as 'a relative or person with a social relationship with the vulnerable person who is likely to interact with the authorities and to enable the vulnerable person to exercise his or her procedural rights' (*ibid.*). Such a definition differs somewhat from the definition of the appropriate adult provided under Code C. As in England and Wales, the appropriate adult must be informed of the nature of the accusations against the suspect and of the procedural rights available to the suspect. The appropriate adult or legal representative must also be notified that the suspect has been deprived of his or her liberty and the reasons for deprivation, unless doing so would be contrary to the suspect's best interests. The Recommendation urges that professionals who come into contact with the vulnerable are adequately trained so that they are aware of the specific needs of the vulnerable person.

The Recommendation requests that vulnerable persons are given access to medical examination. Suspects are deemed 'particularly vulnerable' if they are unable to follow and understand the proceedings against them. There is an assumption of vulnerability in relation to those with 'serious psychological, intellectual, physical or sensory impairments, or mental illness or cognitive disorders' (*ibid.*: 10) which may hinder the person in understanding or being able to effectively participate in the proceedings against them. Vulnerable individuals are not entitled to waive their right to a lawyer and interviews should be audio-visually recorded to 'avoid any contestation of the content of an interview' (*ibid.*: 9). These measures, particularly the latter, are undoubtedly geared towards the safeguarding the evidence rather than protecting the individual.

It appears that the Recommendation has borrowed heavily from England and Wales' approach to vulnerability, yet it leaves much to be desired. It does not provide as comprehensive a definition of vulnerability when compared with Code C, nor does it elaborate on the role of the appropriate adult to the same extent. It is, moreover, considerably shorter than the other Roadmap provisions (which have been implemented as directives) and, unlike a directive, it is non-binding upon Member States. There is therefore great flexibility in how the recommendations are implemented and, indeed, whether they are implemented at all.

In Belgium, for example, the Code of Criminal Procedure (*Wetboek van Strafvordering*) simply requires that account be taken of the suspect's vulnerability when rights are being communicated (Art 47bis). A public prosecution (*Openbaar Ministerie*) circular has provided notification of this. Yet, as Mergaerts (2017) discovered, some lawyers are entirely unaware of this circular. Moreover, the Belgian position seems to accept innate vulnerability and does not therefore take account of situational vulnerability (*ibid.*). In the Netherlands, as in Belgium, vulnerable suspects are protected with no other safeguard than, in some circumstances, compulsory consultation with a lawyer (Designation for legal assistance during police investigation (*Aanwijzing rechtbijstand politieverhoor)* 2010; See

Blackstock, Cape, Hodgson, Ogodrodova and Spronken 2014: 215). For young suspects, as compared with adults, there is ostensibly more protection. In Belgium and the Netherlands, for example, a young suspect may have a 'trusted person' (*vertrouwenspersoon*) – a parent, guardian, sibling or friend – present during interrogation. However, this role does not equate to that of the appropriate adult (see van Oosterhout and Meese 2015: 99; van Oosterhout and de Vocht 2015: 285. See also Blackstock *et al.* 2014: 244). In Italy, young suspects are entitled to an appropriate adult (Cesari 2015: 225) and in Poland, interviews should take place in the presence of a parent, guardian, or defence lawyer or, failing that, someone chosen by the young person (Stańdo-Kawecka and Kusztal 2015: 351). Outside of England and Wales, therefore, the safeguards seem to rely heavily on defence lawyers or parents and guardians, apply more so to young suspects than adults, and (with the exception of Northern Ireland) do not exist on a statutory footing.[12] Yet, in light of the translation of the law in books into law in action, even were these safeguards to be contained, in considerable detail, in a Code of Practice, this would not necessarily ensure protection of those considered 'vulnerable'.

Conclusion

This chapter has explored PACE safeguards and the historical context leading to the introduction of the appropriate adult safeguard. It is important that the appropriate adult safeguard is not viewed in isolation; indeed, it must be seen within the broader context of other PACE safeguards particularly because vulnerability can be exacerbated by the absence of ineffectiveness of other legal protections. These protections have also been herewith explored, such as the various safeguards on the authorisation of detention, the right to have someone informed of one's detention and, perhaps most fundamentally, the right to legal advice. The right to silence and the adverse inferences that have been introduced by the CJPOA 1994 too have a bearing on vulnerability and the appropriate adult safeguard, particularly because there is little said on the right to silence and the appropriate adult's task of facilitating communication. This chapter has also examined the vulnerability provisions and the scope of the appropriate adult safeguard. The operational realities of the appropriate adult safeguard in combination with the definitional ambiguities will be a recurring theme within this book. It is important to recognise that the shortcoming of various legal protection including, but not limited to the appropriate adult safeguard as the safeguard is not a soiled provision but impacts upon and is impacted upon other provisions. The realities of police custody must too be recognised – custody officers are police officers and undoubtedly find it difficult to separate themselves and their decisions from their ties with other police colleagues. They may also face pressure from the various dimensions of their role and may lack knowledge and training. These issues also extend to other individuals within the custody suite such as HCPS and FMEs. Remedies to some of these issues may be sought through the exclusion of evidence at trial. Such a 'remedy' is not infallible as the remedies exist within a broader system that is fraught with various impediments to trial. As such, it is imperative to establish as early as possible if the individual suspect is sufficiently vulnerable to require the presence of an appropriate adult. England and Wales, whilst not without its problems, seems to have provided other jurisdictions with a framework through which to protect vulnerable suspects. It remains to be seen how these provisions operate in practice and whether they encounter similar problems to that explored later in this book, but their mere precedence could be viewed as a positive development.

Notes

1 Code C was often referred to by custody officers as their 'rule book'.

2 Note for Guidance E2 replaces the word 'wishing' with 'wanting'. This is the first and only time that 'wanting' appears in place of 'wishing'.

3 The 2017 version of the Code (and the version in place at the time of the custody suite research) contained the terms 'mentally disordered' and 'mentally vulnerable'. These have been replaced with the term 'vulnerable persons', although the reference to mental disorder has been retained. The 2018 iteration of the Code will be referred to solely as 'Code C', whereas the year of publication will be denoted when reference is made to earlier versions.

4 Social workers trained by NAAN have raised the issue of conflicts between duty of confidentiality and professional duties (Bath 2018).

5 Through my involvement in the Working Group on Vulnerable Adults, the public consultation, and the individual consultation that followed, I was able to raise this issue with the Home Office therefore leading to the inclusion of (some) consideration of the appropriate adult safeguard and the right to silence.

6 The term FME refers to those who are typically on call-out and assist the HCP. Their role is much broader than that of the HCP and, in addition to many of the HCPs duties, it also involves: '[providing] telephone triage for both police and HCPs; [examining] victims and perpetrators of sexual offence cases; [attending] scenes of sudden and suspicious deaths to confirm life extinct' (Group 4 Securicor undated b).

7 The term HCP refers to those who are embedded within the custody suite. They are required to: '[assess] patients and advising custody on their fitness to be detained, charged, transferred, interviewed and released; identify vulnerable patients and advise on the necessity of additional support whilst in custody e.g. appropriate adults etc.; take blood and other intimate forensic samples for analysis for cases such as drink driving; document injuries and attend court for cases which require your representation; manage and advise on chronic and acute conditions' (Group 4 Securicor undated a).

8 An AMHP is a social worker trained to implement elements of the Mental Health Act 2007 in conjunction with medical practitioners. They have a pivotal role in assessing individuals and in deciding whether they meet the criteria to detain them without their consent and were formerly known as Approved Social Worker (Criminal Justice Joint Inspectorate 2009: 5) (hereafter CJJI).

9 It should be noted that this is an old study and it would be hoped that the presence of an appropriate adult would also have a positive impact on the provision of legal representation for adults.

10 Whilst in both research sites in this study custody officers worked on a permanent basis as custody officers, from time to time they were moved between suites within the same force (but they were, nevertheless, permanent custody officers).

11 Although the risk assessment (as discussed in Chapter 7) may ensure that risk is identified, even if vulnerability is not. Ill-treatment is subjective (*Ireland v UK* [1978] ECHR 1).

12 Although there are discussions in Scotland of introducing a statutory duty to provide appropriate adults for all suspects (Scottish Government 2018). This, if introduced, would develop the appropriate adult provision beyond what exists in England and Wales, where a statutory duty only exists in respect of young suspects (Crime and Disorder Act (CDA) 1998 s 38(4)(a)).

3 Police custody

Getting inside, being inside, getting onside and being onside

Introduction

Qualitative research is, by its very nature, uncertain and messy, just like the contours of vulnerability. Where such research involves participants, it requires access and where these participants work within an organisation, it is not simply the consent of the participants that is required, and their employers must also provide access to the research site. Thus, the researcher must negotiate the access requirements of the employer and then, once inside, must also obtain consent of the employees. In this study, that meant the individual police force agreeing to grant access and the custody officers agreeing to be observed and interviewed. The negotiation of access does not end there, however; the researcher must then continue to negotiate access, whether that be to the physical building – such as asking security to 'buzz' her through – or to the participant's thoughts and feelings.

As part of the ethical requirements of qualitative research, the researcher must provide participants with an opportunity to withdraw at any point. If this should happen, the researcher would be required to delete any data collected in respect of this participant. The researcher must therefore be careful not to upset or irritate her participants, whilst also remaining true to her own convictions. At the start of the research period, the researcher may be concerned about the 'Hawthorne effect', i.e. that participants would alter their behaviour as a result of knowingly being observed, but after time the researcher must also be careful not to alter her own behaviour and 'go native'. The researcher may also be aware that her presence disturbs the field (even where her participants do not alter their behaviour) and must reflect on how she is regarded by her participants and others in the field.

The job of a qualitative researcher is far from easy and is, at times, anxiety-inducing, confusing, unclear and exhausting. But, along with these negative emotions, being able to penetrate the field and answer previously unanswered questions is fundamentally and most importantly exciting and rewarding. For the reader to fully understand the empirical data, it is important to gain a sense of the context and environment within which this research took place. This chapter provides such context through the exploration of 'getting inside' (gaining access to the sites), 'being inside' (a description of the research sites), 'getting onside' (gaining access to the participants once in the field), and 'being onside' (the challenges of being in the field, in particular, the phenomena of 'going native').

Getting inside: accessing the research sites

As I was researching the police and would be based at a police custody suite, I required the permission of a senior police officer. Formal access was obtained at Waterside through a former colleague of a family member. This former colleague was a senior officer in the Police Service of Northern Ireland and had, during his time at a senior officer, attending numerous training days with senior officers in England and Wales (amongst other jurisdictions). He put me in touch with an Assistant Chief Constable of Garwoodshire who granted access almost immediately. He then put me in touch with a Chief Inspector based at Waterside who would greet me on my first day and introduce me to the staff; I simply had to advise the Chief Inspector on when I wished to start. Access to Mapletown in Smithshire, although granted within a few weeks, was subject to vetting, as this had not been conducted for my time at Waterside. Through negotiation, I managed to overcome this stumbling block and instead was 'assigned' to a custody officer each day until the staff became familiar with me. This arrangement proved useful as I was not granted formal access until two weeks before (what was to become) my end date. Unlike at Waterside where I was permitted to speak to whomever I pleased, the Inspector at Mapletown wanted to 'cherry-pick' participants, suggesting that some officers may be difficult to work with. I made it clear from the outset that every officer who was willing to take part should be given the opportunity to do so and I did not mind interacting with someone who was considered 'difficult' (see Loftus 2009: 204). At Waterside, I was not provided with an access card but simply asked to be buzzed through by the security guard on reception. Once inside, I would not leave the building for the whole day (or night and morning, in the case of a night-shift). At Mapletown, the intention was that I would be provided with an access card and collar number, however, the delay in granting formal access meant that these never materialised. Instead, I gained access through a phone call to the custody suite or the Custody Inspector upon my arrival.

Being inside: knowing the research site

Waterside and Mapletown shared similarities and differences. Both were city-based, although Mapletown was situated further from the city than Waterside. Both also encountered a similar number of detainees per custody officer per day (around five to 10). However, Waterside was substantially larger than Mapletown (approximately twice the size with well-over 50 cells, whereas Mapletown had less than 50). At Waterside, custody officers and detention officers worked 7am–7pm or 7pm–7am (although staff would often come in 15 minutes ahead of shift); at Mapletown shifts were arranged in (somewhat flexible) eight to 10-hour slots, with three shifts across a 24-hour period. This meant that 'handovers' were less rushed at Mapletown than at Waterside. Whilst lamenting about the busyness of the custody suite, custody officers at Waterside would also take great pride in working at one of the biggest and busiest custody suites in the country, if not Europe (see also Choongh 1997). Each shift at Waterside was staffed by four or five custody officers and between 10 and 15 detention officers. Mapletown had smaller staffing numbers: there were typically between one and three custody officers on each shift, accompanied by usually two to four detention officers. Custody and detention officers were then overseen by a PACE Inspector: at Waterside, there were four PACE Inspectors (one for each team), whereas at Mapletown, there was a Custody Inspector who worked Monday to Friday 8am to 5pm and outside of these hours a range of Inspectors would frequently visit the custody suite.

Detention officers at both sites were employed by the police but were not police officers (although this was set to change as, at both sites, detention officers were soon to move to private contracts (see Skinns 2011)). By virtue of their position as police staff, they could take fingerprints, photographs, footwear impressions, conduct intimate and non-intimate searches, and conduct searches so as to ascertain identity (see Police Reform Act 2002; Skinns 2011). Although booking-in was conducted by the custody officer, detention officers would assist with this by measuring the detainee, physically searching the detainee and their property, and assisting with the recording of information. At both sites, detention officers were mainly responsible for detainee welfare, ensuring that detainees were fed and provided with adequate hydration; visiting the cells and checking up on the detainee as per the principles of 'Safer Detention' (ACPO 2012. See College of Policing 2018a); monitoring the screens of the 'CCTV cells', the intercom, and the buzzer; removing the detainee from his or her cell and taking him or her back from interview; and handing the detainee over to court staff. Although detention officers were also responsible for close-proximity observation at both sites, given relatively low staffing numbers, this was often left to a 'beat' police officer, particularly at Mapletown. 'Beat' officers would also assist with the CCTV observation when staff numbers were low.

Detention officers at both sites worked within the same team of custody officers (although the distinction between teams was more obvious at Waterside than at Mapletown) and tended to do the same task all day. The only exception here was at Waterside where one team refused to do the same tasks and were instead placed on two-hourly task rotations. Their refusal to do the same tasks throughout the day caused great annoyance to the custody officers with whom they worked. One custody officer (CO17-W) felt that this undermined the management of risk (of death or serious injury) as

> if they go and check somebody at nine o'clock and then go check them again at eleven, they can personally see if the person's got any worse or deteriorated in any way. So if they pass it onto somebody else, somebody's opinion of how they are may differ.

He felt that this problem was caused, in part, by the fact that detention officers in Waterside were civilians and not police officers and could therefore not be told exactly what to do. He also felt that the situation would worsen after the private company took over, stating that there would be 'some shuddering changes' (CO17-W Interview). As Skinns highlights, accountability may become an issue when civilians and/or private companies are introduced to police custody (Skinns 2011: 152–3. See Skinns 2011: 157–8).

Waterside had a (seemingly unsuccessful) in-house duty solicitor scheme (solicitors were often overheard complaining about the lack of clients); the scheme was not available in-house at Mapletown. Both sites had privately employed 'in-house' embedded HCPs and on-call FMEs. The prior experience of HCPs was varied: some had worked as nurses previously whereas others were paramedics. The experience of nurses was widely varied: some had worked in general nursing, accident and emergency nursing, or mental health nursing. One had worked as an army nurse, in addition to other types of nursing. HCPs were available 24/7 at these two sites (although officers did comment on how, at the smaller suites within the force, HCPs were 'shared' between the small suites) and were responsible for safeguarding the welfare of detainees (to include assessing fitness for interview), prescribing and administering medication, and examining injuries. At Mapletown, AMHPs were available 24/7; at Waterside, this provision was adopted prior to my departure (although my return to custody in July 2015 allowed me to discuss this development with custody officers). AMHPs are responsible for making decisions in relation to the MHA 1983; at Waterside, much to the annoyance of custody officers, AMHPs did not weigh-in on the implementation of the appropriate adult safeguard or on other aspects of detainee welfare. This was in stark contrast to Mapletown, where AMHPs would assist with the decision on the appropriate adult, in addition to advising on more general detainee welfare (thus overlapping with the role of HCP). Appropriate adult services for adults were provided by a private company on a 24/7 basis at both sites and were therefore, with the exception of family and friends, professionals. However, rather confusingly, many officers at each site often referred to the appropriate adults as volunteers. At both sites it was recognised that it was quite difficult to secure an appropriate adult after 5pm and extremely difficult after 8pm and before 9am. Indeed, some custody officers seemed to think that the provision was unavailable after 5pm.

The buildings also differed: Mapletown was purpose-built whereas Waterside had been remodelled into a custody suite some 20–30 years ago. Mapletown therefore appeared to be a less busy custody suite. At Waterside, police officers did not have to 'buzz' to get in, which meant that custody officers, in their own words, were unable to 'stem the flow' (CO9-W Interview). The holding cells were positioned directly opposite the booking-in desk and custody officers therefore seemed to be under constant pressure to deal with the queues. It also meant that the custody suite was rarely quiet. The design problems did not end there: the samples rooms and the CCTV monitor room were located quite far away from the booking-in desk and there were different wings of cells in different directions.

Muffled sounds and loud bangs seemed to travel from the cells to the booking-in desk. Custody staff at Mapletown, by contrast, had control over who entered and when. Holding cells were located on a wing either side of the booking-in desk, which meant that the custody suite had (at the very least) the appearance of being less busy than Waterside and it was most certainly less noisy. This meant that custody officers were able to more clearly explain rights information to detainees and were able to have clear (and largely uninterrupted) conversations with others in the custody suite. The samples room was located opposite the booking-in desk and the cells were contained in two corridors, one on each side of the booking-in desk. The CCTV monitors were located in a 'pod' between the booking-in desks and, from here, detention officers could take and make calls and answer the buzzer and intercom.

At Mapletown, Police National Computer (PNC) checks were conducted by the arresting officer prior to their 'prisoner' being booked-in. Due to the layout of the custody suite, custody officers also seemed to have ample opportunity to check PNC and custody records before the suspect/detainee was brought to the desk. At Waterside, by contrast, arresting officers were not encouraged to check PNC prior to bringing their 'prisoner' to the booking-in desk and these checks were seemingly either not done or hurriedly done by the custody officer at the point of booking-in. Although it did not seem to take markedly more time, the booking-in process most definitely appeared more leisurely at Mapletown than at Waterside. Seemingly in response to a post-release death (as discussed by CO3-W), the pre-release risk assessment was much more detailed at Waterside where there seemed to be as many questions on pre-release as on booking-in (at Mapletown where detainees were simply asked how they were feeling and whether they wished to speak to the HCP). There were also some minor differences in how risk was managed: for example, shoes and coats had to be left outside the cell at Mapletown, yet these items were secured in a 'prisoner belongings bag' at Waterside.

Getting onside: participation with the custody officers

Access through the formal channels did not equate to an access carte blanche: consent was required from each individual custody officer. There were no opportunities for a group de-brief so attempts were made to disseminate information on the project via email. Upon arrival, however, it transpired that not one custody officer at Waterside and only one at Mapletown had read this email. Consent was obtained through ad-hoc individual conversations (I grabbed the chance when I had it), which also helped to build rapport and provided a dialogue through which custody officers could ask questions. Observations were conducted at various times, for between six and 12 hours a day, and for around four days a week. Often the excitement of conducting ethnography or the desire to follow-through on a case would spur me on to stay far beyond my planned departure time. Some custody officers were much more receptive to the research than others and took the time to explain their decisions, ask about the research, and offer insights into the project (such as discussing recent cases, offering views on policy, and giving opinions about their role and police work in general). Some treated the research as an opportunity to learn and, from time to time, let-off steam. Others, whilst happy to take part, did not wish to spend quiet interludes discussing the research. Of course, there were occasions, at both sites, when the demands of custody would override the needs of the project. Undoubtedly, the rapport built during observations, in addition to the custody officer's personality, impacted upon the interview. Some Inspectors were also more interested than others: at Waterside, one PACE Inspector took a keen interest in the research and often made time for informal chats. Upon leaving the field, this Inspector would update me on changes in the custody suite and was more than accommodating when I requested access for additional interviews (see Dehaghani 2017d).

The layout at Mapletown meant that I could sit beside the custody officer – I had my own work-station and, as such, I could follow the observation much more comfortably and was able to ask questions with minimal interruption. At Waterside, by contrast, I hovered behind the booking-in desk, moving between custody officers, observing one interaction at a time. Whilst I experienced enhanced comfort at Mapletown, neither approach was 'better' than the other in terms of data collection – in both, I was able to view the entire interaction. The practical knowledge gained at Waterside also proved useful when chatting with custody officers at Mapletown, thus enabling further rapport-building. Custody officers at Mapletown also expressed an interest in the findings from Waterside. I permitted superficial discussion but was reluctant to divulge much information as I did not wish to influence the behaviour or responses at Mapletown. This seemed to cause some disappointment; custody staff also took this as an opportunity to poke fun at me for being a stickler for the rules.

Conducting overt observational research (compared with covert research – see Holdaway 1983) may potentially undermine the openness and honesty of research participants; police research poses an additional challenge because of the tendency for police officers to be suspicious (see Reiner 2010: 121–2). Of particular concern is the potentiality for the 'Hawthorne effect' i.e. that knowingly being observed results in an altering of participant behaviour. Such concerns were unfounded as custody officers had become accustomed to being observed and/or monitored – CCTV (see Newburn and Hayman 2002) and audio-recording were in operation at both sites and records were audited monthly. Moreover, whilst initially aware of my presence, after a few days it seemed that the demands of custody had taken precedence. Assurances of confidentiality also ostensibly alleviated concerns. Custody officers would, however, lament about being constantly monitored, and in particular being criticised for swearing or making jokes. Thus, whilst making it clear that scrutiny was likely, I also stressed that my intention was not to 'catch them out'. Most custody officers seemed comfortable with this, as they felt that they were nevertheless used to being monitored, and appeared to trust me (although it is always difficult to know for sure).

Being onside: 'going native' and personal identities

All research projects experience difficulties of some sort. One particular challenge for those conducting ethnography or observation is that of 'going native'. Within the research setting, the researcher can absorb the values and beliefs of the community or group under investigation. Researchers who are made to feel like an insider and are adopted as 'part of the team' may feel flattered at having been accepted but may also experience conflict. My experience was no different: not only was I informed that I would be missed on the day I left Waterside, I was also referred to as 'one of the family' at Mapletown. Greater challenges arose, however, not simply in relation to mere acceptance but with regard to being seen as an 'expert': my advice was often sought on charging decisions or for feedback on the risk assessment. To avoid an ethical conundrum, whilst being mindful to maintain good will, I would explain that my expertise was limited and that, in any event, I was an academic and not a practitioner (see also Loftus 2009: 205). The experience of 'going native' affected me in other ways: there were moments in the field when I would adopt the custody officer construction of vulnerability: I began to think that a number of suspects who were vulnerable according to Code C did not actually require protection (see Chapter 6). After an hour or two away from the field, I would reorient myself and the custody officer definition of vulnerability began to emerge as an important and interesting aspect of the research. With the passage of time came the ability to know when I was 'going native', thereby making it easier to rectify. That said, whilst 'out of the ordinary' activities (at least, for me as a non-police officer) – such as suspects being arrested in peculiar circumstances; detainees or suspects singing, shouting, or banging on the custody desk or cell doors; and alleged or actual illicit drug-consumption – were initially the cause of excitement or anxiety, over time they merged into the mundane.

A researcher's personal biography, and in particular characteristics such as age, class, gender, and ethnicity, can have an impact upon how he or she is perceived by the police and how the researcher positions him or herself in the field (Loftus 2009: 206). Policing is a male-dominated field, with custody being even more so: of those working on a full-time and permanent basis at Waterside, there was only one woman (CO15-W); there were no women custody officers working at Mapletown. Questions most certainly arose as to how far being a woman 'prevented me from accessing the dominant male and sometimes heterosexist culture' (Loftus 2009: 206), and, whilst I was not obviously excluded from conversations or interactions, the male researcher may well have experienced the field much differently (see Westmarland 2001a: 9–10). Gender most certainly had a role to play in perceptions of me as an undergraduate student, particularly at Waterside. On one occasion I was mistaken for the PACE Inspector's daughter (see Dehaghani 2017d). There were also mentions of whether I was being well 'looked-after' and whether I had yet been placed on tea-making duties. My presence did not seem to cause any notable discomfort to those in the custody suite, particularly once I had reassured them that I was not a Home Office official, a custody visitor, an HMIC Inspector, a 'government mole' (see also Loftus 2009: 304), or someone from human resources.[1] As a young woman, I was viewed as non-threatening and trustworthy (*ibid.*: 206. See also Westmarland 2001b), and found that officers confided in me (which undoubtedly led to richness and depth in the interview data). My relationship status proved to be a source of interest and both probationers and detention officers made advances towards me. Indeed, on my last day in Waterside, one male detention officer asked for my phone number on behalf of another male detention officer. At Mapletown, I also received a few requests for my phone number, although from non-custody staff. Such experiences were, however, infrequent and atypical.

Accessing the dominant culture was made easier by my outside interests – going to the gym, weightlifting, and listening to punk rock and heavy metal. Such interests, in addition to my presence in the custody suite over Christmas time and through nightshifts, seemingly challenged any preconceptions of the dossing or 'out-of-touch' academic (Loftus 2009: 207), as did my family connection with policing. These familial connections enabled me to empathise with police officers and understand some of the jokes and quips. In addition to influencing formal access, it is also possible that this fact facilitated access to the individual custody officers. My relative lack of knowledge in relation to realities and practicalities of custody proved useful as custody officers, assuming the role of expert, would answer all manner of questions. The knowledge gained at Waterside proved useful in Mapletown and would act as a source of conversation: custody staff were eager to know about my experiences of Waterside. Whilst being careful so as not to influence the field but without seeming dismissive, I would avoid these conversations by explaining that I was not assessing each suite and that, in any case, each suite was different.

Custody staff, as noted above, were initially suspicious of my presence. My taking of field notes was often a source of interest and I was frequently asked about what I had written. My principal concern was not to disturb the field by raising suspicions further whilst also avoiding censorship. I explained that whilst I was happy to have conversations and answer questions, my notes were for my own purposes and would probably be of little use or interest to custody staff (see Loftus 2009: 208–9). As part of the consent exercise, custody officers were also able to request a write-up of my findings. Despite signage explaining my presence, detainees often mistook me for social worker, mental health worker, or a legal advisor. An explanation as to my actual identity was usually met with little resistance or suspicion, but on one occasion a suspect demanded that I assess him under the MHA 1983 and refused to interact with custody staff until I did so. It took repeated explanations for him to accept that I was not a nurse but a researcher (Interaction 16-W). On another occasion, a young suspect remarked that I 'looked too posh' to be a police officer and asked whether I was a legal advisor. I remained unconvinced that custody officers had fully understood the purpose or focus of my research, as they would often discuss self-harm within NHS policies or deaths in police custody, and would frame the discussion as 'something that you're looking at' (Chat with CO4-W). Such interactions raise ethical questions regarding, in the case of custody officers, the digestion of information provided or, in the case of third parties, the adequate provision of information.

One thing that was taken for granted was my ethnicity, which arose as a topic of conversation at both suites. On a number of occasions, I decided to challenge the suggestion that it was 'easy' to correctly identify someone's ethnicity. The custody staff would each take turns to guess my ethnicity and I would confirm if they were correct or incorrect. After various combinations of 'White' (White-British, White-Irish, White-Northern Irish, White-Scottish, White-European), I disclosed that I am actually of mixed ethnicity. The decision to challenge this pre-conception was taken so as to illustrate that it is not always easy to identify something on the basis of appearances alone. Whilst passing for White allowed me to '[fit] in with the dominant ethnicity of the organisation' (Loftus 2009: 207), my true ethnic background, once it was known, allowed me to establish common ground with minority ethnic officers.

Conclusion: reflections on research

Empirical research is not without its challenges. Qualitative research, by its very nature, raises numerous issues. The researcher must negotiate access to the organisation, the physical building, and the research participants. She must build and maintain rapport with her participants without going native. She faces questions of identity: both making herself known to those she encounters, whilst also reflecting on how her own experiences and identities may shape the world around her. She must also remain flexible as, in research as in life, there are constraints and constants. She must recognise that she is responsive to her environment and that her environment is responsive to her. She must recognise that research rarely goes according to 'plan': research questions shift, emerge, and are jettisoned or altered. Getting the seat of one's trousers dirty means getting involved in the messy and complicated. Along with the many challenges of qualitative research is the excitement and reward. The socio-legal researcher obtains a unique insight into an often un- or under-explored research site, is provided with the opportunity to explore the reality of the law, and is able to answer many unanswered questions about the law in action (and construct and deconstruct valuable knowledge of the law in books). The reward most certainly outweighs any obstacle. The researcher does not simply learn about the field, by having the opportunity to reflect on her experiences, she may also learn about herself. But the researcher must be mindful that, whilst the research experience may be pleasant for her, it is far from pleasant for the suspect or detainee.

Note

1 This was unsurprising as at both sites the detention officers were being moved onto private contracts and many were fearing redundancy.

4 Constructing vulnerability – the concept

Introduction

'Vulnerability' is a term that is both lauded and regarded with suspicion; it can serve to empower or disempower (Munro and Scoular 2012: 189). The disempowering nature of vulnerability can be particularly problematic where the individual does not self-identify as vulnerable (Dunn, Clare and Holland 2008; Asquith and Barthowiak-Théron 2015). According to the Oxford Dictionary, vulnerability is defined as 'expos[ure] to the possibility of being attacked or harmed, either physically or emotionally' (Soanes and Stevenson 2008: 1621). As Misztal highlights:

> dictionary definitions stress that vulnerability refers to human liability to being wounded, susceptibility to wounds or external injuries, or to being mistreated, exploited, taken advantage of. They also point to such characteristics of an individual as weakness, defencelessness, helplessness, exposure and liability.
>
> (2013: 1)

The dictionary definition lacks nuance and depth, and, moreover, neglects the positive connotations associated with the term. As Levine (2004: 395–6) has noted, vulnerability is not simply something negative such as 'being at risk' but can also denote a positive characteristic, i.e. 'being in touch with one's feelings'. The problems with the concept do not end there, however. As Misztal (2013: 2) notes, vulnerability more typically gives rise to notions of exposure to risk, a lack of control, or difficulty responding to or overcoming adversity. The term 'vulnerable' is applied in different ways, on the basis of different characteristics to different groups or individual: the contrasting approach between the vulnerable suspect/defendant and the vulnerable victim is one example (see Chapter 4).[1]

Vulnerability is intangible and can possibly only be deeply understood through one's own lived experience. It is socially constructed and clouded by the lens of one's social world and influenced by one's own understanding, conceptions, and experiences. As such, each individual may have his or her own way of 'being vulnerable' or of 'feeling vulnerable'. Similarly, that which makes one person feel vulnerable may not trigger the same feelings in another. And, of course, it depends on what one *means* by 'vulnerable'. Recognition must therefore be given to the subjective and constructed nature of vulnerability. Despite – or because of – the problematic nature of this concept, vulnerability has attracted growing interest within the academic community and beyond. Vulnerability has been hijacked within neo-liberal discourses to justify the restriction of resources to some (see Dehaghani and Newman 2017; Munro and Scoular 2012) and within policy circles, it has become a 'zeitgeist' (Brown 2015: 5). These various constructions of vulnerability will be explored herewith. Discussion will centre on how it has manifested within various threads of literature, then more specifically within legal psychology, and thereafter how constructions differ depending on subject and purpose. Finally, there will be some exploration of how vulnerability could be reconceptualised within the context of police custody.

Principal manifestations of vulnerability

Vulnerability can have a plurality of meaning; however, Brown (2015) has identified five main manifestations. First, it may be tied to social disadvantage and space whereby the concept, on a macro level, can be used to describe 'social exposure to natural or environmental hazards, or more broadly as a way of bringing social and economic disadvantage and "coping capacity" into focus' (*ibid.*: 33. See also 33–6). Second, vulnerability may also be viewed as conceptually intertwined with risk, although vulnerability has 'more pronounced ethical connotations' (*ibid.*: 42), is more successful in disguising its 'controlling undertones' (*ibid.*), is 'more remote in terms of potential harm' (*ibid.*: 15) when compared with the probabilistic calculation associated with risk and has behavioural dimensions, whereby it denotes the performance of weakness and frailty. Third, intrinsic qualities and 'aspects of the life-course' (*ibid.*: 29) may also make someone vulnerable – that is, innately vulnerable. Such vulnerability is bound-up with characteristics such as young age, old age, physical, mental or sensory impairment, and mental health problems. It can also be connected with temporary biological states such as acute illness or pregnancy. Theories of innate vulnerability posit 'individuals as "at risk" in a way that can be modified by action, but where some risk will always remain' (*ibid.*).

Fragility may also be elevated due to circumstance. This fourth manifestation of vulnerability is something which Brown has labelled 'situational vulnerability'; it tends to result from political, personal, social, economic, or environmental factors but may also 'contain elements of individual agency or choice' (*ibid.*: 31). The situationally vulnerable – such as Roma people, homeless people, women involved in prostitution, asylum seekers, drug users, poorer people and prisoners – may be viewed as 'victims' or 'victims of circumstance' and may therefore be owed a statutory duty. Anyone detained in police custody could also fall under this categorisation (see Chapters 5 and 9). However, as vulnerability is inextricably linked with deservingness (Brown 2015: 32), there is a question as to how one can reconcile situational vulnerability with transgression. Situational vulnerability may also be gendered: women are, for example, often more likely to be accepted as vulnerable because they are 'more inclined to behave with deference and accept dependence' (*ibid.*: 33 [footnote omitted]), and as Holdaway (1983: 77–9) highlights, women may be considered 'disarmers'. However, those who have failed to take advantage of opportunities to avert harm to themselves may be apportioned all, if not at least some, of the blame for the circumstances which befall them (Goodin 1985: 129).

Finally, vulnerability can also be considered as a characteristic possessed by all, something which 'defines our humanity' (Turner 2006: 1). Whilst Turner argues that such vulnerability is 'common and uniform' (*ibid.*: 9), Fineman (2013a: 20–1) points to two distinct forms of difference: our embeddedness and our embodiment. The latter of which 'carries with it the imminent or ever-present possibility of harm, injury, and misfortune' (Fineman 2013a: 20–1. See also Fineman 2013b; Fineman 2009), whereas the former results from 'the social and constructed ... [and] overlapping and complex webs of economic and institutional relationships' (Fineman 2013a: 21). Vulnerability can therefore be something that all we possess by virtue of being human. Yet, innate and situational differences interact to make some individuals more vulnerable, or, perhaps more accurately, less resilient – than others. Vulnerability may manifest through our interdependence on others (Herring 2016), particularly on those who one '[does] not know and may never know' (Butler 2004: xii). Misztal has categorised our dependency on others as the first manifestation of vulnerability, arguing that we are vulnerable because of our dependence on others for our self- realization, and thus our development of self- confidence, self- respect, and self- esteem. This dependence, as Butler (2004) highlights, is on those who are currently (and may continue to be) unknown. Such notions are tied to what Misztal recognises as the second manifestation of vulnerability – a fear of the uncertain future (and the potentiality for unknown individuals to do harm) – which she terms the predicament of unpredictability. Misztal further highlights how the actions by others cannot be undone – the predicament of irreversibility – i.e. vulnerability that occurs as a result of having been wronged or harmed in the past (2013: 47–9). As Goodin has suggested, an individual may be vulnerable, or less resilient, because he or she is unfit or unable to play in games of advantage, has renounced playing advantage for themselves, is no match for the other person, or is in a position of grave misfortune (Collins 2013: 33–7 citing Goodin 1987). Due to our limited to no control over others, our lives are rendered precarious and unpredictable.

Within this book, these various manifestations of vulnerability will be examined within the context of the appropriate adult safeguard and the broader context of police custody. As will be seen in later chapters, tensions may arise between these different manifestations. For the purposes of the appropriate adult safeguard, vulnerability arises through both situational and innate factors, although the law in action does not always take account of this (see Chapter 5).

Legal psychology and vulnerability

The field of legal psychology has heavily contributed to how vulnerability is framed for the purposes of the appropriate adult safeguard. Whilst there is no 'generally agreed definition' of psychological vulnerability (Gudjonsson 2010: 166 citing Bull 2015: 1), in the context of police custody it is understood as 'psychological characteristics or mental states which render a [person] prone, in certain circumstances, to providing information which is inaccurate, unreliable or misleading' (Gudjonsson 2006: 68). These vulnerabilities, rather than being 'definitive markers of unreliability' are viewed, instead, as potential risk factors (Gudjonsson 2010: 161); indeed, vulnerability can exist along a continuum (Gudjonsson and Joyce 2011: 18). The vulnerable are viewed as such 'because they may not fully understand the significance of the questions put to them or the implications of their answers [or] are unduly influenced by short-term gains (e.g. being allowed to go home) and by the interviewer's suggestions' (Gudjonsson 1993: 121). Those with less than average intellectual ability 'may feel intimidated when they are being interrogated by people in authority' (St-Yves 2006: citing Gudjonsson and MacKeith 1994; Gudjonsson 1995) and 'are often more willing and open to suggestion' (St-Yves 2006: 98 citing Clare and Gudjonsson 1995). They may be suggestible, compliant or acquiescent. In other words, they may be more likely to change their behavioural response on the basis of communication, regardless of the questions asked answer 'yes', or, whilst disagreeing with a statement, nevertheless go along with the idea (O'Mahony *et al.* 2012) in order to avoid conflict or maintain a level of self-esteem (Gudjonsson 2003).

When compared with the general population, those with a low IQ (between 57 and 75) are more likely to acquiesce, confabulate, and be suggestible to leading questions (Clare and Gudjonsson 1993b: 295).[2] Individuals with even a mild learning disability may experience difficulty communicating with others or may be awkward in doing so and have to make an effort in order to be sufficiently well-understood, particularly in unfamiliar situations. Their limited communication skills may make it challenging for them to easily interpret questions and statements from others. They may also have problems handling information such as understanding and memory, and problems with regulatory functions such as attention, inhibition and planning. Their problem-solving abilities such as self-regulation and being able to take perspective may also be lacking (Moonen *et al.* 2011: 235–9). Behavioural problems such as attention-deficit/hyperactivity disorder (ADD/ADHD) may also make individuals particularly susceptible to giving false confessions (O'Mahony *et al.* 2012: 302). Some individuals are, in essence, less resilient than 'others'.

The capacity of the suspect to cope with police interviews, as Gudjonsson and MacKeith have argued, depends on the 'circumstances (the nature and seriousness of the crime, pressure on the police to solve the crime) … interactions … personality, and health (physical and mental health), mental state' (Gudjonsson 2010: 167 citing Gudjonsson and MacKeith 1997. See also Gudjonsson and Joyce 2011). Gudjonsson's later work has categorized vulnerability in a different manner. Here he has identified four 'types' of vulnerability relevant to suspects (Gudjonsson 2003: 61–75): mental disorder, abnormal mental states, intellectual functioning, and personality. The first category encompasses mental illness, learning disability, and personality disorder; the second includes anxiety,[3] phobias, bereavement, intoxication, withdrawal and mood disturbance; and the fourth includes traits such as suggestibility, compliance and acquiescence.

Whilst the first category – mental disorder – is contained explicitly within Code C, the second, third and fourth are arguably encapsulated, albeit implicitly, under the 'mental vulnerability' category in previous iterations of the Code. The 2018 version[4] instead includes the term 'mental health condition' in addition to the term 'mental disorder',[5] which may or may not encapsulate the latter of Gudjonsson's three categories (see Chapter 5 for discussion on the 'new' definition of vulnerability). The traits, as highlighted by Gudjonsson, are 'regularly admitted as evidence to challenge admissibility and the weight of the confession evidence' (*ibid.*: 3), although this, of course, requires that the case reaches the courts (and, as Gudjonsson (1993) notes there are issues with expert evidence at trial). Some conditions, such as personality disorder, may raise complications, as little is known, scientifically, on how it effects reliability in police interviews (Gudjonsson 2010: 167). Moreover, the interaction between personality disorder and vulnerability is yet further complicated due to the connections with 'criminal propensity, dishonesty, and disregard for others' (*ibid.*). Thus, even innate vulnerabilities may be challenged by transgression, whether actual or perceived.

Negative life events[6] have also 'been found to impact considerably upon interviewee susceptibility to misleading information and negative feedback incorporated within an interview' (Drake *et al.* 2008: 306). This means that 'interviewees with a high number of negative life-events may more easily accept any misleading information put forward to them, as well as be more prone to shifting their initial answers in response to interrogative pressure' (ibid). Many suspects detained in police custody will undoubtedly fall under this category. Some suspects may fall outside of the prescribed criteria but may nevertheless falsely confess. Gudjonsson and MacKeith (1990: 329) have detailed how a 17-year-old youth falsely confessed to two murders during police interview. Initially, he did not have legal representation, yet also later confessed during a second interview when assisted by the duty solicitor. These misleading admissions were also made to prison staff and a fellow inmate whilst on remand. The authors noted that:

> The confession elicited by the police appeared very detailed and apparently convincing. The confession subsequently by chance proved to be false. It appears to have resulted from persistent pressure and psychological manipulation of a man who was at the time distressed and susceptible to interrogative pressure.

A detailed psychological assessment 'indicated a clear improvement in the man's ability to assert himself and to cope with interrogative pressure' (*ibid.*). What was most striking about this case was that this man was of 'average intelligence, suffered from no mental illness and his personality was not obviously abnormal' (*ibid.*). Whilst this suspect would now be provided with an appropriate adult as a 'juvenile' (see Dehaghani 2017c), it is not unconscionable to think that a similar situation could arise in relation to someone above the age of 18.

Vulnerability does not simply materialise as a result of mental conditions; physical conditions may too create or exacerbate vulnerability. Illnesses such as epilepsy, diabetes, and heart problems have been known to lead to heightened agitation and distress, and may therefore impair the accuracy and reliability of a confession (Gudjonsson *et al.* 1993: 16). Whilst physical illnesses are recognised as creating or exacerbating vulnerability for the purposes of a criminal trial (see Chapter 4), they are not included within the definition of vulnerability for the purposes of the appropriate adult safeguard in police custody. It is also important to recognise that neurological conditions (which are not categorised as a mental health problem or psychiatric condition), such as, inter alia, Parkinson's disease, stroke, and dementia can impact on an individual's cognitive abilities and thus render them vulnerable (JUSTICE 2017: 15).

Although not all vulnerable suspects may falsely confess, possession of a vulnerability can lead an individual to do so. False confessions may arise for a range of reasons and may be either voluntary, coerced-compliant, or coerced-internalised (Gudjonsson 2003: 194–242). Voluntary false confessions are offered in the absence of police pressure and may arise from an unhealthy longing for notoriety, a need to redress guilt from a previous transgression, an inability to tell the difference between fantasy and reality, an expectation of leniency, a desire to safeguard or assist the actual offender, or to take revenge on another (*ibid.*: 194–5). Such false confessions are not confined to those with mental health problems, and may occur when suspects are above average intelligence (*ibid.*: 218–24). Coerced-compliant confessions occur where as a result of police and where the suspect seeks to gain something, such as being able to go home 'earlier', having the interview brought to an end, or avoiding being locked-up in police custody (*ibid.*: 196). Such false confessions can arise in the absence of mental disorder, but where the suspect is prone to anxiety and abnormally succumbs to interrogative pressure, or where the suspect has a learning disability (*ibid.*: 224–233). As Gudjonsson (*ibid.*: 196) highlights:

> The suspect's perceived immediate instrumental gain of confessing has to do with an escape from a stressful or an intolerable situation. The suspect may be vaguely or fully aware of the potential consequences of making a self-incriminating confession, but the perceived immediate gains outweigh the perceived and uncertain long-term consequences.... Suspects may naively think that somehow the truth will come out later, or that their solicitor will be able to sort out their false confession.

Coerced-internalised false confessions may occur when the suspect believes that they have committed the crime without any memory of having done so (*ibid.*). The suspect may have no memory of what he or she was doing at the time of the alleged offence from the outset of the police interview or may come to distrust his or her memories as a result of 'subtle manipulative influences by the interrogator' (*ibid.*: 197). These false confessions can arise where the suspect suffers from blackouts due to heavy alcohol consumption, where the suspect has poor self-esteem and easily succumbs to pressure, or where the suspect is eager to please (*ibid.*: 233–42).

Vulnerability is also significant beyond the issue of false confessions: it is important because those who are 'vulnerable' may be unable to participate effectively in their own case, provide best evidence, and be able to act in their own best interests (whether that means providing information or obstructing the evidence gathering procedures).

Conclusion

Vulnerability is not an unproblematic notion: in addition to having both positive and negative connotations (Levine 2004), it can also be used for the furtherance of both supportive and coercive agendas. Munro and Scoular (2012: 189) have highlighted how, in the case of sex work, vulnerability can be used to further improve social justice or can be used as a form of neoliberal governance through which individuals are constructed as 'risk managers' and required to behave responsibly (see also Brown 2015). Vulnerable individuals are therefore constructed as either 'dangerous' and 'risky' or deserving of additional support (Brown 2015: 33). The varying definitions of vulnerability permit policymakers to 'convey legitimacy on different types of policy towards vulnerable groups' (Misztal 2013: 32 citing Beckett 2006). Vulnerable individuals may also be considered unable to 'negotiate and transcend the problems of contemporary social and political life' (McLaughlin 2012: 127) and thus are viewed as 'sick and irrational'. McLaughlin (*ibid.*) argues that 'government, campaign groups and many mental health professionals ... have a vested interest' in viewing the vulnerable as such. Such an approach serves to 'other' the vulnerable individual, thus resulting in a stigmatisation, which 'marks them as lesser, imperfect, and deviant, and places them somehow outside of the protection of the social contract as it is applied to others' (Fineman 2013a: 16). This view is problematic for two core reasons: it may call into question the vulnerable person's autonomy (see Herring 2016; Diduck 2013) and it suggests that there is such a thing as invulnerable. On this latter point, Fineman notes:

> [P]erhaps the most insidious effect of segmenting society and designating only some as constituting vulnerable subpopulations is that such a designation suggests that some of us are not vulnerable. Those who stand outside of the constructed vulnerability populations are thus fabricated as invulnerable.
>
> (2013a: 16)

It may, as Fineman (2009; 2013a; 2013b) has suggested, be more appropriate and accurate to conceptualise all individuals as vulnerable and instead to focus on the lack of, or limited, resilience that an individual may have. Vulnerability continues to generate 'continuing confusion' (Misztal 2013: 5), to the point where it is an 'unclear, catch-all concept' (*ibid.*). It can be either a force for good or a term through which to permit state encroachment; it can be something negative or something positive; it can, in essence, mean many things or not very much at all. Not only is vulnerability a complex concept, but people are also far from homogenous. As will be evident in the following chapter, the problematic manner in which vulnerability manifests itself extends also to Code C.

Notes

1 Misztal (2013: 31) also argues that vulnerability differs depending on geographical location, citing the example of the United States – where vulnerability discourse addresses issues around natural disasters and 'risk to basic needs and terrorism' and the United Kingdom – where, particularly in the social sciences, vulnerability is used as a 'yardstick' by which to disentangle 'problems and feelings connected within experience of uncertainty, fragility and a lack of agency'. This does, however, seem a rather simplistic comparison, particularly given the important emerging vulnerability scholarship in the United States.

2 Gudjonsson (2010) has highlighted how a high proportion of suspects have a low IQ.

3 Gudjonsson (2010) has highlighted that there are high levels of anxiety amongst suspects. Anxiety correlates highly with suggestibility (Gudjonsson *et al.* 1995).

4 The 2018 version refers to the version dated 2018. The commencement date is 21 days after the Order has been signed by the Minister. The change in 2018 is substantial and therefore reference is made generically to 'pre-2018' Codes to refer to the Codes in force during the empirical research (2014–15) and the earlier stages of writing. It should be noted, however, that there are differences between each version of the Code. For example, the 1991 version contained the term 'mentally handicapped' (see Bean and Nemitz 1995: 6).

5 The Home Office were intending to remove this term. They decided to retain it after I highlighted that, based on Gudjonsson's research, the presence of a 'mental disorder' presented a particular risk and so it ought to be retained as a distinct category.

6 Such as threatened death or serious injury, bereavement, stressors such as divorce or financial problems and daily stressors (see Kraaij *et al.* 2002).

5 Constructing vulnerability – PACE, Code C and the courts

Introduction

The concept of vulnerability is difficult to define and in relation to the appropriate adult safeguard it is no different. There are two main legal sources through which vulnerability for the purposes of the appropriate adult safeguard may be defined: soft law (Code C) and case law (themes arising from appeals in the Court of Appeal). Statute is somewhat limited in this regard: beyond the exclusionary rules on evidence (under ss 76 and 78 PACE) and the jury direction (s 77 PACE) not much is mentioned within PACE proper. Other sources of guidance also assist in elucidating how vulnerability is, or may be, defined, such as the College of Policing Authorised Professional Practice (APP) on Detention and Custody (2018a) and the MHA Code of Practice (Department of Health 2015). Other aspects of the criminal process may assist in the exploration of vulnerability, particularly definitions contained under the Youth Justice and Criminal Evidence Act 1999 (YJCEA 1999). Such constructions seek to promote the rights of the individual concerned. This can be contrasted with constructions beyond the criminal process, particularly within mental capacity law, where the discourse of vulnerability emerges and is utilised in a way that restricts, rather than promotes, individual liberty. Vulnerability, for the purposes of the appropriate adult safeguard, also has rather baffling overlap with the fitness for interview criteria. Key legal actors play an important part in determining whether an individual's rights should be promoted (in the case of the appropriate adult safeguard or special measures) or an individual's autonomy be restricted (in the case of mental capacity law). However, in the instance of the appropriate adult safeguard, the courts are not necessarily required to engage with the definition of vulnerability in any meaningful manner. Nevertheless, the courts are key to reprimanding the police for breaches of PACE and the Codes of Practice, and for encouraging future compliance. These aspects will be examined in this chapter, with the aim of reaching a deeper understanding of how vulnerability is defined by the law, particularly in reference to the appropriate adult safeguard. Through the course of this chapter, it will become evident that hard law, soft law, and the courts each engage minimally with how vulnerability is defined for the purposes of the appropriate adult safeguard. Questions are then raised as to whether these sources can do more to explicate vulnerability in reference to the appropriate adult safeguard.

Code C and PACE: constructions of vulnerability and the appropriate adult safeguard

PACE proper is devoid of any mention of vulnerability, however, s 77 provides a part-definition in its reference to the (offensive) term 'mentally handicapped'. This term is elaborated on as being 'a state of arrested or incomplete development of mind which includes significant impairment of intelligence and social functioning' (PACE s 77 (3)). This same definition is used under the MHA 1984 to describe a learning disability (s 1(4)); it could therefore be suggested that those with a learning disability would fall under this category. A jury direction under s 77 will not apply to some of those who are caught under the Code C definitions. Under previous versions of Code C, it was evident that someone who was 'mentally handicapped' was most certainly 'mentally vulnerable' and may have been 'mentally disordered' (if the definition is taken to mean 'learning disability' (see Department of Health 2015)). Similarly, under the 2018 version of the Code, someone who is 'mentally handicapped' could have a 'mental disorder' or 'mental health condition'. However, not every individual with a 'mental vulnerability', 'mental disorder' or 'mental health condition' is necessarily 'mentally handicapped'. As such, this definition, and the associated protection of a jury direction, could be criticised for its restrictiveness. The term 'mentally handicapped' was also present in previous versions of Code C, such as the 1991 Code of Practice (see Bean and Nemitz 1995: 6) where it stated:

> If an officer has any suspicion, or is told in good faith that any person of any age may be mentally incapable of understanding the significance of questions put to him or his replies, then that person shall be treated as a mentally disordered or mentally handicapped person for the purposes of this Code.

Whilst removed from Code C, this archaic and offensive term remains in s 77. Recommendations made in 1993 to extend the remit of s 77 were ostensibly ignored (RCCJ 1993: 49). Such a change would make the jury direction applicable to someone who has a 'mental disorder' or 'mental health condition' (under the 2018 version of the Code) but who falls 'short' of being significantly impaired. Therefore, whilst more recent versions of Code C could include issues such as, for example, limited educational attainment or additional education needs, a jury direction under s 77 would not.

In previous versions of the Code, those who were 'mentally disordered' or 'mentally vulnerable' were recognised as 'vulnerable' and thus in need of an appropriate adult (see Code C 2017: para 3.5). These definitions were detailed in the Note for Guidance para 1G of pre-2018 versions of the Code, where it stated:

> *'Mentally vulnerable' applies to any detainee who, because of their mental state or capacity, may not understand the significance of what is said, of questions or of their replies. 'Mental disorder' is defined in the [MHA] 1983, section 1(2) as 'any disorder or disability of mind'. When the custody officer has any doubt about the mental state or capacity of a detainee, that detainee should be treated as mentally vulnerable and an appropriate adult called.*

Although these categories were contained separately, a suspect could have been both mentally disordered and mentally vulnerable, whether that be mentally vulnerable independently of or as result of the mental disorder. The concern was, and continues to be, that vulnerable suspects 'may, without knowing or wishing to do so, be particularly prone in certain circumstances to provide information that may be unreliable, misleading or self-incriminating' (Code C: Note for Guidance 11C).

The most recent version of the Code contains a more detailed explanation of why an adult may be 'vulnerable'. According to Code C para 1.13d, a 'vulnerable person' is an adult who, because of a mental health condition or mental disorder:

i may have difficulty understanding or communicating effectively about the full implications for them of any procedures and processes connected with:

- their arrest and detention; or (as the case may be)
- their voluntary attendance at a police station or their presence elsewhere, for the purpose of a voluntary interview; and
- the exercise of their rights and entitlements.

ii does not appear to understand the significance of what they are told, of questions they are asked or of their replies.

iii appears to be particularly prone to:

- becoming confused and unclear about their position;
- providing unreliable, misleading or incriminating information without knowing or wishing to do so;
- accepting or acting on suggestions from others without consciously knowing or wishing to do so; or
- readily agreeing to suggestions or proposals without any protest or question.[1]

This updated definition (or, perhaps, explanation) of vulnerability recognises that a suspect may be vulnerable due to issues with communication and/or understanding, and/or through tendencies towards acquiescence and suggestibility.

Whilst it is recognised in the most recent version of the Code that a suspect may be vulnerable because of his or her mental disorder or mental health condition, a cautionary note explains that simply being in possession of a mental health condition or mental disorder does not render someone vulnerable. Similarly, an individual who 'does not have, or is not known to have, any such condition or disorder' (Code C: Note for Guidance 1G) could nevertheless be vulnerable for the purposes of the Code.[2] Rather, the functional test, as detailed above, must be considered and decisions must be made on a 'case by case basis'. Whilst para 1.13d would suggest that someone is vulnerable if they possess innate characteristics and appear to be vulnerable, the cautionary note would allow for a recognition of vulnerability even where the individual does not possess an innate vulnerability (e.g. where that person could present as vulnerable because of the situation within which they are placed). This therefore allows for a recognition of both innate and/or situational vulnerability.

The officer must also 'take into account the particular circumstances of the individual and how the nature of the investigation might affect them' (Code C: Note for Guidance 1G). This also provides recognition of situational vulnerability. For the first time in the history of the Codes, there is now a warning in relation to the effect of drugs or alcohol on the appearance of vulnerability (*ibid.*: Note for Guidance 1GC). Those who are under the influence of drink and/or drugs, are not automatically treated as vulnerable and therefore in need of an appropriate adult unless there is other information to indicate that they may be vulnerable. The Code also urges that the individual is reassessed once they have recovered from the effects of drugs and/or alcohol.

Investigating officers are urged to exercise special care when questioning vulnerable suspects and must seek to corroborate facts wherever possible (Code C: Note for Guidance 11C). An appropriate adult should be called where there is 'any doubt about a person's ... mental state or capacity' (*ibid.*). This is further reiterated in the main body of the 2017 Code:

> If an officer has any suspicion, or is told in good faith, that a person of any age may be mentally disordered or otherwise mentally vulnerable, in the absence of clear evidence to dispel that suspicion, the person shall be treated as such for the purposes of this Code.
>
> (Code C 2017: para 1.4)

And is again later reiterated in an Annex:

> If an officer has any suspicion, or is told in good faith, that a person of any age may be mentally disordered or otherwise mentally vulnerable, or mentally incapable of understanding the significance of questions or their replies that person shall be treated as mentally disordered or otherwise.
>
> (Code C 2017: Annex E para 1)

The most recent version of the Code (para 1.4) contains a similar warning in relation to both detained persons and those attending 'voluntarily':

> If at any time an officer has any reason to suspect that a person of any age may be vulnerable in the absence of clear evidence to dispel that suspicion, that person shall be treated as such for the purposes of this Code.[3]

Yet the Code now also requires that a custody officer (in the case of a detained person) or an investigating officer (in the case of someone attending 'voluntarily') establish vulnerability or cause vulnerability to be established. To do so, they must make reasonable enquiries as to the information available that could indicate that the individual is vulnerable, make a record of the 'factors that appear to apply and provide any reason to suspect that the person may be vulnerable or (as the case may be) may not be vulnerable' and make this information available to police officers, police staff, or others who are entitled to communicate with the person concerned. The Code includes in this latter category solicitors, appropriate adults and HCPs (para 1.4). The approach taken in the 2018 version of Code C differs from previous Codes in that it requires that the custody officer (or investigating officer, if the individual is attending 'voluntarily') take steps to establish or dismiss that the person is vulnerable. The detail contained in para 1.4 is further reiterated in Annex E.

In previous versions of the Code, the officer need only have had suspicion that the individual was mentally vulnerable, mentally disordered or, in the case of Annex E, mentally incapable; he was not required to know with absolute certainty. The term 'mentally incapable' (Code C 2017: Annex E para 1) is also seen in the older version for the first and only time in the Code. The reason for the inclusion of this term, at this point, is unclear, although it has since been removed. The various peculiarities and anomalies in Code C will, however, be examined in greater detail later.

Additional constructions of vulnerability

Code C does not elaborate further on definitions of vulnerability, beyond that explored above. Yet, this does not mean that custody officers are not provided with further definitions (although whether they consult this guidance is another matter (see Dehaghani 2017b)). For example, custody officers may consult the College of Policing APP on Detention and Custody (2018a) and/or the College of Policing APP on Mental Health (2018c). The Mental Health APP guidance does not provide a definition of 'mental disorder' but rather 'mental ill health' – a term which 'is used broadly to refer to all those matters relating to mental health problems' (*ibid.*). This term can include 'mental disorders, mental illness, mental health needs and many of the issues that fall within the MHA 1983 of mental disorder and the … Code C definition of mentally vulnerable' (*ibid.*).[4] Mental ill health 'also covers people who are experiencing mental distress at the time they come into contact with the police, whether or not they have been formally diagnosed or have previously received mental health services' (*ibid.*). The guidance also mentions 'mental vulnerability' and contributes to the Code C guidance by cautioning that a suspect may be 'mentally vulnerable' but 'not be considered to be experiencing a mental illness by an HCP' (*ibid.*). Thus, a medical or healthcare diagnosis is not required for an appropriate adult to be called.

In addition, the guidance includes information on 'learning disabilities or difficulties', citing the definition of the former, as per the MHA 1983 s 1(4), as 'a state of arrested or incomplete development of the mind which includes significant impairment of intelligence and social functioning' (*ibid.*). It also explains how a learning disability may affect the person concerned in that it:

> [M]ay be mild, moderate or severe and affects the way a person learns and communicates. It results in a reduced ability to learn new skills, adapt to and cope with everyday demands, understand complex information or, in some cases, to live independently. Most people with a learning disability look physically the same as the general population, although some may have clear physical characteristics, for example, people with Down's syndrome (which is classed as a learning disability).
>
> (*ibid.*)

It is made clear that suspects with learning disabilities or difficulties must be provided with an appropriate adult when in police custody and that learning disability can exist in varying degrees, yet the guidance does not distinguish between a learning disability and a learning difficulty.

Prior to 2018, the Code C definition of 'mental disorder' merely referred to the definition contained within the MHA 1983 (see Code C 2017: Note for Guidance 1G) and it went no further in its explanation of what constituted a mental disorder. A comprehensive (although not exhaustive) list of 'mental disorders' is found within the Code of Practice of the MHA 1983 (Department of Health 2015: 26) which cites the following clinically recognised conditions:[5]

- Affective disorders, such as depression and bipolar disorder
- Schizophrenia and delusional disorders
- Neurotic, stress-related and somatoform disorders, such as anxiety, phobic disorders, obsessive compulsive disorders, post-traumatic stress disorder and hypochondriacal disorders
- Organic mental disorders such as dementia and delirium (however caused)
- Personality and behavioural changes caused by brain injury or damage (however acquired)
- Personality disorders
- Mental and behavioural disorders caused by psychoactive substance use
- Eating disorders, non-organic sleep disorders and non-organic sexual disorders
- Learning disabilities
- Autistic spectrum disorders (including Asperger's syndrome)
- Behavioural and emotional disorders of children and young people

The MHA 1983 Code of Practice also provides a definition of learning difficulty: 'a state of arrested or incomplete development of the mind which includes significant impairment of intelligence and social functioning' (*ibid.*: 206) or a 'significantly reduced ability to understand new or complex information, to learn new skills, and reduced ability to cope independently which starts before adulthood with lasting effects on development' (*ibid.*; see also Department of Health 2001: 14). The 2018 version of the Code now contains a link to the MHA Code of Practice (Note for Guidance 1GB).[6]

Vulnerability in the courts

If a custody officer fails to implement the appropriate adult safeguard for a vulnerable adult suspect, he will not be liable to civil or criminal proceedings (s 67 (10) PACE), however, the evidence gathered may be rendered inadmissible at trial (ss 76 and 78 PACE). This therefore requires some interaction on behalf of the courts: they must hold that a breach has occurred and that this breach renders the confession 'unreliable' (s 76) or that the admission of evidence renders the proceedings, as a whole, unfair (s 78). Even where the requirements of s 76 are discharged, the evidence gathered as a result of the confession is still admissible (s 76 (4) PACE) unless it can be excluded under s 78. Here the courts would consider 'all the circumstances, including the circumstances in which the evidence was obtained' (*ibid.*) and would make a decision on the basis of their discretion; however, as Sharpe (1997: 10) has noted, the term 'fairness' is open to judicial interpretation. The courts may also consider, in line with s 77 PACE, whether the jury, in a trial on indictment, should have been advised that a 'mentally handicapped' confessed in the absence of an independent person. In some instances, the courts have condemned a police failure to provide an appropriate adult for a vulnerable adult suspect, yet in other instances, they have held that neither s 76, 77 nor 78 apply and have therefore condoned the absence of an appropriate adult (for ss 76 and 78 PACE) or independent person (s 77 PACE). Such instances will be examined below.

The courts: condemning the breach

The case of *R. v Lamont* ([1989] Crim LR 813) concerned an appellant (A), who was considered 'mentally subnormal', had a reading and comprehension ability comparable to that of an eight-year-old child, and an IQ of 73, and was appealing his conviction for attempted murder and assault occasioning actual bodily harm. At his Crown Court trial, his defence sought to have his interview evidence excluded under ss 76, 77 and 78 PACE. The grounds were such that A had been interviewed after 18 hours in which he refused food, and had cried and was emotional during the interview. No appropriate adult was present and A refused the assistance of a solicitor. His appeal was successful on the basis that the trial judge had omitted to give a s 77 direction to the jury, despite indicating that he would do so. Further, the trial judge had, contrary to the PACE Codes, indicated that the presence of an appropriate adult was of little importance. A's conviction for attempted murder was regarded as neither safe nor satisfactory and was quashed (although A's conviction for assault occasioning actual bodily harm was recorded).

In *R. v Bailey* (*Times*, January 26, 1995 (CA)), the appellant (A) appealed against her convictions for manslaughter and arson. A suffered from a severe personality disorder and mild mental handicap, and had confessed and retracted on numerous occasions, some of which her solicitor and social worker were present for. On one occasion, officers had given her information regarding the seat of the fire. The defence unsuccessfully applied for an exclusion of evidence under s 78 PACE. At appeal it was submitted that the judge had (1) wrongly refused to exclude the confessions or withdraw the case from the jury, (2) failed to give the jury a clear warning regarding the dangers of relying on an unsupported confession of a mentally handicapped person, and/or (3) failed to warn the jury pursuant to s 77 PACE. The Court accepted the latter two submissions, A's appeal was allowed, her conviction was quashed, and a retrial ordered.

The case of *R. v Aspinall* ([1999] 2 Cr App R 115) also concerned a challenge under s 78 where the appellant (A), who was diagnosed with schizophrenia, had been convicted of conspiracy to supply a Class A controlled drug. A had advised the custody officer of his condition who then arranged for A to see the police surgeon. The surgeon noted that, whilst A suffered from schizophrenia and was on regular medication, he was lucid in thought and oriented in time and space. Upon request by A, the custody officer arranged for a second assessment to be conducted by another police surgeon who confirmed the probable diagnosis of paranoid schizophrenia and that A was adhering to his medication regime, was not in need of further treatment, and was probably fit to be interviewed. A was interviewed without an appropriate adult present. Evidence was adduced at trial attesting to A's mental illness, that he had been held in a secure unit for six months in 1993, and had been admitted to hospital during an acute psychotic episode in 1996. Yet, the psychiatrist, upon an examination of A sometime after the police interview, indicated that A was 'likely to have understood the nature of the procedure and questions, and would have been able to answer questions' (at 118) but 'might have been less able to cope with questions about his role, with the possibility that he might have given answers which he thought were likely to result in his early release from custody' (*ibid.*). He also had 'a degree of passivity and lack of assertiveness' (*ibid.*). In considering the appeal, the Court noted that, as per Code C para 1.4 combined with Note 1G, A had a mental illness and the custody officer was aware of this, thus requiring that A was attended by an appropriate adult. The court also noted that the absence of legal advice, with the exception of a brief conversation with the duty solicitor, 'compounded the unfairness arising from a breach of the Code of Practice' (*ibid.*; see also *R. v Glaves* ([1993] Crim LR 685). They held that trial court had erred by wrongly assuming that the lucid state of A removed the need for an appropriate adult to be present and had further erred by '[justifying] the actions of the police by reason of the presentation of the appellant, instead of considering the significance of the safeguards' (*ibid.*: 123). The question the trial court should have considered was whether, in line with s 78 PACE, the admission of the evidence would have rendered the proceedings, as a whole, unfair. A's appeal was therefore successful.

A similar outcome occurred in the case of *R. v Cox* ([1991] Crim LR 276) which concerned an appellant (A) who was deemed 'mentally handicapped' with an IQ of 58 and who had been charged with burglary. A admitted at interview, in the absence of an appropriate adult, of being involved in two burglaries. The trial judge allowed the confession to be admitted on the basis that it was likely to be true in light of the confession that A made in court. A's appeal was allowed and conviction quashed as the trial judge should have asked himself not whether the confession was true but whether it was made in consequences of anything which was likely to render it unreliable.

When considering whether evidence should be excluded, the court will consider the difference made by the appropriate adult. This approach was explicit in *R. v Haroon Ali* (Court of Appeal (Criminal Division) 24 November 1998, unreported cited in Ventress *et al.* 2008). The appellant (A), who had an IQ between 66 and 72, had made exaggerated and boastful statements during interview. The appropriate adult, had one been present, would have been able to intervene to establish whether A was saying what he really meant to say. Whilst the trial judge excluded some interview evidence on the basis of 'mental handicap' and the absence of the appropriate adult, A was still convicted. The Court of Appeal quashed his conviction, accepting that whilst some of A's evidence was reliable, his admissions were exaggerated and thus likely to be unreliable.

In another successful appeal, *R. v Kenny* ([1994] Crim LR 284), the appellant (A) was unable to read or write and was convicted on his own admission (and on a *voir dire*) of burglary. A was deemed to have the mental age of a child aged nine and a half or between nine and ten and was, moreover, considered 'illiterate', with a reading age between six and six and three-quarter years. It was submitted, and accepted, that A was 'mentally handicapped' for the purposes of s 77 and that, given his 'mental handicap', his confession, given in the absence of an independent person, was unreliable. In allowing the appeal, the court noted the guidance provided by Lord Lane CJ in *Cox* (Unreported 12 November 1990. See [1991] Crim LR 276) where he stated:

> It seems to us that the true question was not whether the confession was unreliable or untrue so much as whether the confession, true or not, was obtained in consequence of anything done which was likely to render any confession unreliable, the burden being on the prosecution to prove beyond reasonable doubt that it was not so obtained. One emphasises as well as the word 'likely' the words 'in the circumstances existing at the time'.

The court was, by their own admission, 'reluctant' to rule that the learned judge in the case had erred. However, the confession, considering its reliability, should not have been admitted. As there was no other evidence against A, the conviction was quashed.

Similarly, in *R. v Dutton* (Unreported case no. 4627.G1/87 cited by Ventress *et al.* 2008: 374), the appellant (A) successfully appealed his conviction for sexual offences where the admission was made in the absence of an appropriate adult. A was born in a psychiatric ward, attended a residential school for 'retarded' pupils and had a mild mental handicap. The trial judge, whilst recognising that the police should have requested an appropriate adult, nevertheless allowed evidence to be put to the jury. Further, in *R. v Ham* ((1997) 36 BMLR 169) the appellant (A), who was 'mentally handicapped', made an admission in the absence of an appropriate adult. In addition to being 'mentally handicapped', A was deemed to be 'at serious risk of being "easily led" or suggestible in a police interview', had an IQ above 70 but below 80 (at 174), had a reading age of seven years, with an average intelligence of a child of 11 (at 175), and was aged just 18 years and 2 months at the time of the alleged offences. A was interviewed twice – the first interview was not tape-recorded and A did not want a solicitor present; the second, where he made more extensive admissions, was tape-recorded but again A declined legal advice. A challenge as to the admissibility of the confession evidence was made on the basis of s 76 (2) and a direction under s 77 was sought. The appeal was allowed as the trial judge had erred in his approach. The detective constable had described A as 'streetwise', 'quite cocky', 'unremorseful' and not possessing any difficulty answering questions. However, the court highlighted that 'the prohibition in para C: 11.4 applies to juveniles as to persons who are mentally handicapped [sic], and a juvenile may well be capable of answering questions and "streetwise" or "cocky"'. The court (Waterhouse J at 177) went on to state that an objective test is required:

> It was not what the police officers here thought, if they gave any thought to it at all, about the mental condition of the person they were asking the questions of which was material, but, as was subsequently ascertained from doctors, what the mental condition of the appellant actually was.

The conviction was therefore quashed (see also *R. v Everett* [1988] Crim LR 826).

In the (quite recent) case of *R. v W* ([2010] EWCA Crim 2799), the Court of Appeal, citing *R. v Gill* (at 11), held that the trial judge should have considered whether the appropriate adult would have made a difference and whether the appropriate adult's absence would have rendered the admission unreliable, rather than considering how well the interview was conducted. The Court of Appeal concluded that the appellant (A) could be considered 'mentally vulnerable' and that the appropriate adult might have secured legal advice for A, which would have resulted in no admission.

In the most recent case, at the time of writing, to consider exclusion of the non-implementation of the appropriate adult safeguard – *Miller v DPP* – the High Court considered that the appellant (A) should have his conviction for failing to provide a specimen of blood in breach of section 7 of the Road Traffic Act 1988 set aside on the basis that he was not provided with an appropriate adult. A who had learning difficulties and Autism and suffered, by his own admission, from Asperger's Syndrome. He had also been behaving erratically and aggressively in police custody. An FME assessment could not be conducted because he was acting aggressively, yet, on previous occasions in police custody had been provided with an appropriate adult and he had, on this particular occasion, requested an appropriate adult. The court highlighted how the appropriate adult would have had a calming influence on A and would have enabled him to understand the purpose of obtaining the specimen and the consequences of failing to comply with the request. The conviction was quashed.[7]

The courts: condoning the breach

Whilst the courts have excluded evidence where the appropriate adult safeguard was not implemented, they have likewise found that the failure to obtain an appropriate adult should not result in evidence being held inadmissible. One such case was that of *R. v Law-Thompson* ([1997] Crim LR 674) where the appellant (A) had Asperger's Syndrome (now diagnosed as falling under the umbrella term of an Autism Spectrum Disorder), high performing autism, and an IQ of 150, and was convicted of the attempted murder of his mother. A was interviewed without an appropriate adult present. His counsel argued that, where a mentally disordered defendant was interviewed in such circumstances, the court's discretion could only be exercised one way, i.e. by excluding the evidence. The appeal court, however, considered not the apparent unlawfulness or irregularity of the evidence but rather 'its effect, taken as a whole, upon the fairness or unfairness of the proceedings' (citing Lord Nolan in *R. v Khan (Sultan)* [1997] AC 558 at page 301g) – it was necessary to illustrate how the mental disorder resulted in unreliability.

A similar approach was taken in the case of *R. v Brown* ([2011] EWCA Crim 1606). Here the appellant (A), who had an extremely low IQ of 58, was not provided with an appropriate adult and sought to appeal against his conviction. The Court of Appeal considered that A was 'able to give "reasonably clear and comprehensible answers" and had "apparently had no major problems with understanding the questions"' (at 41) and was also able to 'maintain a high level of concentration and "hold a story"' (at 34). Further, whilst A had made 'it clear that he did not read very well and would need help reading documentation', he had declined the help of an appropriate adult when offered one (at 39). A had also been provided with a solicitor who had 'played a comparatively pro-active role' (at 40). Whilst the appropriate adult would have been there to provide support and non-legal advice, it was stated that the appropriate adult would not have had much impact on the interview, particularly because A was 'a confident, assertive and strong-willed man'. In line with *Law-Thompson*, the absence of an appropriate adult where a solicitor is present will unlikely fulfil the requirements for exclusion of evidence (at 40).

The courts also disputed that the appellant (A) was 'mentally vulnerable' or 'mentally disordered' in *R. v Foster* ([2003] EWCA Crim 178). Here, A, who, on the basis of evidence submitted by Professor Gudjonsson, was deemed to be abnormally suggestible and of limited intelligence (at 88), sought to appeal his conviction for murder.[8] The courts were to consider whether the evidence should have been excluded under ss 76 or 78 of PACE and whether a jury direction under s 77 of PACE should have been provided. The court did not believe that abnormal suggestibility and/or limited intelligence meant that A was 'mentally handicapped' or 'mentally disordered' as required under Code C (at the time Code C did not contain the criteria 'mentally vulnerable'). Further, the court held that an independent person – in this case a social worker – had been present (at 89). The appeal was thus unsuccessful.

In contrast with *Bailey*, in *R. v Campbell (Oliver Keith)* ([1995] 1 Cr App R 522) the appellant (A) sought to appeal against his conviction for conspiracy to rob and murder. A had implicitly confessed twice in the absence of an appropriate adult or solicitor, later declined to answer but made comments suggestive of involvement in the presence of a solicitor and appropriate adult, and then, in the presence of his foster-mother as appropriate adult, confessed but said the killing was accidental. In respect of the submissions relating to PACE, the Court held that the judge was right to exercise his discretion as the admission of evidence would not have had such an adverse effect on the fairness of the proceedings that the court ought not to admit it (s 78 PACE). The Court also held that s 77 warning was not necessary as the case against A did not depend wholly or substantially on confession evidence.

In *R. v Gill* ([2004] EWCA Crim 3245), the appellant (A) who had low intelligence (and could therefore be considered mentally vulnerable under the Code C definition as existed at the time) and had confessed in the absence of an appropriate adult sought to appeal his conviction. The appeal was unsuccessful: the courts stated that the absence of the appropriate adult does not lead to automatic exclusion of confession evidence, rather each case must be taken on its own merits. The courts should question what had been lost as a result of non-compliance with the requirement to provide an appropriate adult. The court considered that the trial judge was correct to consider that the absence of the appropriate adult did not adversely affect A's evidence.

A similar approach was taken in *Stanesby* ([2012] EWHC 1320 (Admin) 2012 WL 1469169) where the appellant (A), who suffered from depression, had been breathalysed without an appropriate adult present (see also *R. (on the application of DPP) v BE* [2002] EWHC 2976 (Admin); *R. (on the application of DPP) v Preston* [2003] EWHC 729 (Admin)). It was found that the breath-test had been properly administered, the custody officer had acted in good faith, A was coherent and understood what he was being asked, and the presence of an appropriate adult would have made no difference to the administration of the breath-test.[9] The administration of a breath-test also presents a particular problem as it is time sensitive.

In the very recent case of *R. v Rashid (Yahya)* ([2017] EWCA Crim 2), the court seemed to dismiss the suggestion that the appellant (A) was vulnerable. A appealed against convictions for offences under Terrorism Act 2006. He was interviewed without an appropriate adult after being deemed fit for interview by the FME. His solicitor, present during interview, also did not request the attendance of an appropriate adult. Part of A's appeal rested on the failure of the court to exclude the confession on the basis of his vulnerability. He had argued at trial that his confession was inadmissible because, whilst entitled to an appropriate adult on the basis of his mental vulnerability, he was interviewed without one. Expert evidence adduced at trial suggested that A had a low IQ, although experts were divided on the issue of whether A required an appropriate adult at interview. The trial judge had watched videos of A's police interview and concluded that A understood what was being put to him and his replies. The Court of Appeal held that the confession, considering the evidence before them and before the trial court, was reliable and therefore admissible.

In *R. v Beattie* (considered in the Northern Ireland Court of Appeal (NICA)),[10] the appellant (A), who had been charged with perverting the course of justice, sought to have evidence excluded under Article 74 of the Police and Criminal Evidence (NI) Order 1989 (the equivalent of s 76 PACE). A reported being frightened and was visibly upset. He also had advised the FMO (the equivalent of an FME in England and Wales) that he suffered from depression. The FMO deemed him fit for detention and fit for interview and he was interviewed without an appropriate adult present. A made a straightforward admission at interview, in the presence of his solicitor. At trial, one FMO (called on behalf of A) deemed A to be 'mentally vulnerable' whereas the FMO who had assessed A at the custody suite was satisfied that A was not 'mentally vulnerable'. The arresting officer was also satisfied as such (the custody officer was not called as a witness). His appeal was dismissed: the Court noted that the custody officer had illustrated care for B and had further noted that the solicitor had not requested an appropriate adult.[11]

The courts and the appropriate adult safeguard

Although they have engaged little with the definition of vulnerability, the courts have addressed the purpose of the appropriate adult. The case of *Weekes* ([1993] 97 Cr App R 222), whilst concerning a young suspect, provides insight into how the appropriate adult safeguard is constructed by the courts. In this case, the courts stated that young suspects may 'sometimes say things they do not mean' either through fear or an inability to adequately express themselves. This is why, the courts argued, young suspects require 'the presence of a more experienced person to assist them' (at 225). It seems, from this, that the court is principally concerned with the veracity and reliability. Yet, the court neither explains from where this fear derives nor refers to the supportive or welfare function of the appropriate adult. For the appellant in *Weekes*, he had '[entered] into the realm where fairness demanded that [he] was supported by somebody older who could assist him in answering the questions or advising him if he could not' (at 227). The appropriate adult, in the case of a young suspect, is someone older but also, and alluding to the communicative function of the appropriate adult, someone who can answer questions or provide advice. Whilst not entirely clear from the statement, it is likely that this 'realm' could be custody (or the criminal process, more broadly) and one could, on this basis, suggest that the vulnerability arises from detention in custody or from contact with the criminal process. More recently, in the case of *R. (on the application of HC) v Secretary of State for the Home Department* ([2013] EWHC 982 (Admin)), where the courts considered extending the appropriate adult provision to 17-year-olds, Moses LJ had indicated how vulnerability could manifest 'in the face of an intimidating criminal justice system' (at para 93). In *R. v Campbell (Oliver Keith)*, the court suggested that, in line with Code C, the function of the appropriate adult was 'to minimise the risk of the accused giving unreliable information by seeing that the interview is properly and fairly conducted and by facilitating communication between the police and the suspect' (Crim LR 159).

The courts have also, ostensibly, suggested that a solicitor can act as an appropriate adult. In the case of *R. v Lewis* ([1996] Crim LR 260) the court held, when considering s 76 PACE, that there was nothing said or done to render the confession unreliable, when considering s 78 PACE, that the admission of the evidence did not render the proceedings unfair, and that, for the purposes of s 77 PACE, a solicitor could be considered an independent person. The courts were correct in their interpretation of s 77: a solicitor, in this instance, can be considered an 'independent person' (although their discussion most certainly seemed confused). However, they had erred in their application of ss 76 and 78: whilst prior to a change to Code C in 1991, a solicitor or independent custody visitor could act as an appropriate adult, this principle had changed at the time of *Lewis* such that a solicitor or independent custody visitor could not act as an appropriate adult (see Palmer and Hart 1996: 63. See also Code C: Note for Guidance 1F). The court also reasoned that the solicitor and the appropriate adult performed 'very similar' roles, although it accepted that the solicitor may be devoid of experience in assisting those with a 'mental handicap' (*Lewis* at 261).[12] The courts discussed the admissibility of evidence but did so in the same vein as discussing the purported 'similarities' between the solicitor and an appropriate adult. As Ventress, Rix and Kent (2008: 377) highlighted, '[the court's approach] suggested that the role of the appropriate adult could be incorporated into that of the solicitor, potentially negating the need for their presence at all'.

Critiquing the courts' constructions

It is evident that the courts have not really considered what vulnerability means. The issue, however, lies with the fact that they are not required to engage in any meaningful way with how vulnerability is constructed. Rather, pre-2018 they had to consider whether the defendant could be considered 'mentally vulnerable' or 'mentally disordered' and then consider whether the confession could be considered reliable (when considering s 76); whether the defendant could be considered 'mentally handicapped' and confessed in the absence of an independent person (when considering s 77); or whether the admission of evidence had an adverse effect on the fairness of the proceedings (in relation to s 78). The courts will, as of the implementation date in 2018, now have to consider whether the defendant is 'mentally disordered' or had a 'mental health condition' and whether he or she met the functional test (as contained under Code C para 1.13d). It remains to be seen whether the new definition of vulnerability will alter the approach of the courts. As can be seen from the preceding discussion, the mere absence of an appropriate adult does not constitute automatic grounds for exclusion. Instead, each case is to be considered on its own merits (*Kenny; Gill*). Some difficulty thus arises in assessing exactly how the courts interpret vulnerability, however some general conclusions can be drawn. The courts have, for example, highlighted the importance of the suspect's *actual* vulnerability (i.e. whether he or she could be considered 'mentally vulnerable' or 'mentally disordered') rather than the police *perception* of vulnerability (*Ham*).

The courts have also held that evidence is inadmissible where legal advice, in addition to the appropriate adult safeguard, was absent. Such an approach was taken in *Aspinall*, where there was a 13-hour delay in arranging legal advice and A was interviewed with neither an appropriate adult nor legal representative present. This could, at least superficially, be contrasted with *Lewis* where the presence of a solicitor obviated the need for an appropriate adult. Further, possessing the mental age of a child and being considered 'mentally handicapped' pursuant to s 77, as in both *Kenny* and *Ham*, could encourage the court to exclude the evidence, as could the absence of any other evidence. The existence of other 'evidential issues' could also lead to the exclusion of evidence, as was the case in *R. v Reid* (unreported). According to an appropriate adult with whom I spoke at the NAAN Professional Development Day (PDD), the case of *Reid* concerned a defendant who had depression and was not provided with an appropriate adult when in police custody. The case was thrown out of the magistrate's court.

As the courts are assessing reliability and fairness, rather than 'mere' absence of the appropriate adult, there are, as explored above, cases where the conviction stood even where there had been a breach of Code C, as explored above. By contrast with *Kenny* and *Ham*, confession evidence was not excluded where it was given by a 'mentally handicapped' suspect as in *Foster* (the defendant had an IQ of 72, which indicated a mental age of 10; he was on the borderline of being a 'mental defective'; and was highly suggestible with a strong tendency to contradict himself (at para 29)). In *Foster*, as with *Kenny* and *Ham*, A's admissions at interview constituted the main prosecution evidence (they also relied on certain circumstantial evidence which, alone, would have been insufficient to prove guilt). The defendant's ability to understand the significance of what he or she says seems paramount when assessing reliability. This can be further illustrated by the approach taken in *Law-Thompson* where, instead of excluding evidence, the trial judge thought it apt to highlight A's 'quite exceptional intelligence', 'apparent and obvious ability' for coherent and lucid self-expression, and the absence of issues with comprehension on the basis of his 'peculiar condition' (he was deemed to understand the importance of the questions put to him and the consequence of his answers). Such factors meant that there was nothing 'that might be said to render his answers unreliable'. Whilst this may indeed be true (i.e. that the accused knew what he was saying), the appropriate adult is not simply present to facilitate communication; the role also encompasses a supportive provision. Therefore, whilst A was mentally disordered as per the definition contained within the MHA 1983 and Code C, he presented no issues with capacity or comprehension. His appeal was also arguably not helped by the fact that he was provided with a solicitor. Indeed, in *R. v Brown* it was stated that '*R. v Law-Thompson* … makes it clear that the absence of an appropriate adult from interviews where a solicitor was present is unlikely, in itself, to justify excluding the interviews' (at para 40).

Although the courts were arguably correct in their application of the PACE provisions, these cases highlight a flaw in the admissibility criteria: it matters not whether the police approach was unlawful but instead whether the confession is rendered unreliable (pursuant to s 76) or whether the evidence jeopardises the fairness of the proceedings (pursuant to s 78). The courts are not necessarily concerned with the absence of an appropriate adult where there should have been one, but rather the effect that the lack of an appropriate adult may have had, taking into account the nature of the interview and those present (see NAAN 2015: Case law review citing *DPP v Cornish* [1997] *The Times*, 27 January). The courts have, however, gone further than merely refusing to exclude evidence and have excused the police approach: in *Glaves*, Owen J stated that it is 'not always easy… to have every item of the Code in mind… It is of no consolation to the public at large that the police may be criticised' (although in this case the conviction *was* quashed). A similar statement was made in *R. v W*: the Court quashed the conviction but reiterated that 'we attribute no fault to the officers in the case for not appreciating the true situation' (at 25).

The courts are, in some senses, bound by the instructions provided by ss 76, 77 and 78. This is not to say that they could not use their discretion to interpret such provisions more broadly, but rather that their decisions are guided by the legislation. In relation to s 78, rather than applying certain principles, Zander argues that the courts determine breach on a case-by-case basis. The courts have also, as Zander highlights, been seemingly reluctant to exclude evidence under s 78 and the Court of Appeal, more often than not, dismisses the appeal. This is not simply a practice found commonly in cases where the appropriate adult was not provided in breach of Code C but also arises in other areas where PACE and/or the Codes of Practice have been breached (Zander 2015: 442–3). For example, the courts have allowed evidence to be admitted where a caution was not provided but was needed, such as in the cases of *O'Shea* ([1993] Crim LR 951, CA), *Weekes* (Unreported, Case No. 90/859/Y4, January 11, 1991. CA), *de Sayrah* (Unreported, Case No. 89/5270/Y3, June 25, 1990. CA), *Allison and Murray* (Unreported, Case No. 1731/A1/88, October 25, 1988), *Pall* ([1992] Crim LR 126, CA), *Nelson and Rose* ([1998] 2. Cr App R 399; [1998] Crim LR 814, CA), *Slater and Douglas* ([2001] EWCA Crim 2869), *Armas-Rodrigue* ([2005] EWCA Crim 1081), *Devani* ([2007] EWCA Crim 1926), and *Senior and Senior* ([2004] EWCA Crim 454, [2004] Crim LR 749).

The courts have also condoned breaches where access to legal advice was wrongly refused pursuant to s 58 PACE, such as in the cases of *Alladice* ((1988) 87 Cr App.R 380; [1988] Crim LR 608, CA), *Dunford* ((1990) 91 Cr App R 150; [1991] Crim LR 370, CA), *McGovern* ((1991) 92 Cr App R 228; [1991] Crim LR 124, CA), and *Oliphant* ([1992] Crim LR 40, CA), or where procedural formalities were not complied with, such as in the cases of *Langiert* ([1991] Crim LR 777, CA), *White* ([1991] Crim LR 779, CA), *Hoyte* ([1994] Crim LR 215, CA), *Walsh* ((1989) 91 Cr App R 161, CA), *Dunn* ((1990) 91 Cr App R 237, CA), *Bedford* ((1991) 93 Cr App R 113, CA), *Wright* ([1994] Crim LR 55, CA), *Duffy* ([1997] N.I.J.B. 228), and *Dures, Dures and Williams* ([1997] 2 Cr App R 237, CA; [1997] Crim LR 673).

Hodgson (1997: 794) has argued that the different approach toward breach of PACE or the Codes is simply 'the adoption of a less robust interpretation of the appropriate adult provisions and the need to comply with them strictly' and reflects the courts' approach to other aspects of PACE such as the right to legal advice. Rather than condemning police breaches of PACE and its accompanying Codes, the courts have sought mitigating factors that permit admission of evidence.

Thus, whilst accepting that PACE and/or the Codes had been breached, the courts may nevertheless hold that the admission of evidence does not render the proceedings, as a whole, unfair. An s 78 challenge, whilst helpful in some instances, does not always provide an effective remedy to breach of PACE and/or the Codes because the courts are not considering whether the evidence is unfair but rather whether the admission itself is unfair (Sharpe 1997: 38). The same issues can also arise with s 76 – the courts may consider that, in light of the circumstances, the confession is nevertheless reliable and should not be excluded; they are not considering mere breach of the Code but rather, whether the anything said or done is likely to render the confession unreliable (s 76 (2) PACE).

Given the approach the courts take to the breaches of Code C, as evidenced by the discussion of case law, it is possible that the introduction of a functional test under Code C will result in no changes to court practices. Indeed, it seems that the court already consider how the suspect was functioning at the time that he or she was when in police custody.

Whilst some common themes have emerged from the discussion of case law on non-implementation of the appropriate adult safeguard, the reality is such that cases may thus hinge on the minutiae of the facts. Given the predominance of guilty pleas and the use of summary trial (where admissibility challenges are rarely heard), reliance on s 78 (or ss 76 and/or 77) for rectifying a breach of the requirement to implement the appropriate adult safeguard for a vulnerable adult may thus be a fruitless exercise.

Unfit to be interviewed or fit with an appropriate adult?

Decisions made in relation to fitness for interview are worthy of discussion here, given the potential overlap with the requirements for the appropriate adult safeguard.[13] When considering whether a suspect is fit for interview, the custody officer must consider whether the suspect could suffer significant physical or mental harm as a result of the interview or whether because of their physical or mental state the information provided by the suspect regarding their involvement or suspected involvement in the offence might be considered unreliable in court (Code C: Annex G para 2). When assessing whether a suspect should be interviewed, Code C requires that the custody officer consider how the suspect's mental or physical state could impact upon their understanding of the nature and purpose of the interview or of what is being asked, their appreciation of the significance of their answers, or their ability to make a rational decision about whether they should say something. They should also consider whether the replies given represent a 'rational and accurate explanation of their involvement in the offence' or whether such replies may be affected by the suspect's physical or mental condition; and the effect that an interview may have on a suspect, particularly the use of probing questions. The HCP must consider the 'functional ability of the [suspect]' (Code C: Annex G para 4) rather than whether he or she has a medical diagnosis.

Fitness for interview, by incorporating physical as well as mental state, provides a much broader construction of vulnerability when compared with the appropriate adult safeguard (which focuses on mental state only). When looking at the mental state requirements solely, it is difficult to establish a distinction – a suspect who may fail to understand the implications of interview due to his or her mental state could be considered unfit for interview – but, similarly, he or she could be deemed fit to interview but with an appropriate adult present. The focus on functional ability (rather than medical diagnosis) for fitness for interview also corresponds with the requirements for appropriate adult, which, according to the College of Policing guidance (2018a), does not necessarily demand a medical diagnosis. The parallels do not end there: both fitness for interview safeguard and the appropriate adult safeguard are entwined with references to reliability. There are only two clear distinctions: that a suspect is unfit for interview if there is potentiality for physical or mental harm arising from interview and if the suspect's physical state could potentially impinge upon the reliability of evidence. An interview must, therefore, not be conducted if it were to result in physical or mental harm to the suspect or if the physical state of the suspect could render the evidence unreliable. However, where it is felt that the suspect's mental state could impinge upon the reliability of evidence, the suspect may be deemed unfit for interview *or* fit for interview but with an appropriate adult present. The similarities between the fitness for interview criteria and the criteria for the appropriate adult safeguard seem ever more pertinent given the functional test that has been introduced into Code C.

Code C and manifestations of vulnerability

As noted in Chapter 4, there are various manifestations of vulnerability and the way in which the term is deployed often serves to designated some as vulnerable and others as invulnerable. Code C is not unproblematic in this sense – whilst the appropriate adult safeguard is used to provide something to vulnerable suspects rather than to legitimise an encroachment on their lives (see Chapters 2 and 4), much of the wording of Code C lends itself to notions of weakness and defectiveness (although note Code C: Note for Guidance 11C). It clearly conceptualises vulnerability as the risk of or exposure to self-incrimination or, perhaps more accurately, the provision of unreliable or misleading information (*ibid.*). Individual factors such as age, ethnicity, gender, mental state and previous convictions or confessions; the nature and seriousness of the alleged offence; access to legal advice; the presentation or strength of the 'evidence'; and the amount of interrogative pressure may further increase the vulnerability to falsely confess (see Gudjonsson 2003: 140–51). But if a suspect is to fall outside one of the 'vulnerability' categories (see Chapter 2 and Chapter 5) then he or she deemed, by law, as not requiring protection. Yet, detention in police custody can be, for a plethora of reasons, detrimental to an individual's physical and mental state (see Gudjonsson *et al.* 1993: 16). Many individuals entering police custody may have recently experienced a bereavement or relationship breakdown. Being arrested and then detained can create or exacerbate feelings of precariousness, unease, or discomfort; the physical space is far from welcoming or pleasant (see Chapter 4). Suspects may be 'over-awed' by what is going on (Rock 2007: 111) and, whilst in custody, the suspect must contemplate the possibility that they face criminal sanction. Even where the police have no intention of pursuing the case beyond custody, the process nevertheless serves as the punishment (see Choongh 1997; 1998; Feeley 1992).

When the suspect is 'locked-up', it is not what is actually happening but rather what the individual *perceives* to be happening that may exacerbate his or her feelings of isolation, desperation, and despair. Police detention results in the restriction of liberty, constrained contact with friendly forces (i.e. family and friends) and limited control over everything but the most intimate bodily functions (although see s 55 PACE). The dynamics of the relationship between the police – who have 'the upper hand through information, physical and territorial control' (Hodgson 1997: 90. See also McConville *et al.* 1991) – and the suspect could result in an inescapable vulnerability for even the most articulate, steadfast and strong-willed individual. The nature of custodial detention has an adverse effect on the suspect's ability to make decisions pursuant to his or her own interests (Irving and McKenzie 1989: 24). As Gudjonsson (2003: 25) has noted, even with markedly improved legal provisions, any type of custodial interrogation is coercive when viewed in terms of police power and control[14] and one must not forget that the suspect is firmly on police territory. Vulnerability arises because of the power that the police, whether implicitly or explicitly, exercise over the suspect.

In the context of daily life many individuals can make choices that are advantageous to their long-term well-being (placing long-term implications over short-term gains) but the coercive nature of the custody and the criminal process significantly undermine this. Therefore, whilst the notion of a shared, universal vulnerability is useful in highlighting the precarious nature of human existence and is capable of transforming society through theoretical (re)-conceptualisation (Brown 2015: 36), it is the notion of the vulnerability of circumstance – or a lack of resilience through this situation – that provides the basis through which to broaden the provision of the appropriate adult safeguard. This argument will be returned to in Chapter 10.

Vulnerability can be conceptualised in a plethora of ways and can mean a number of things; it can be innate, situational, or inherent, or may be linked with space or notions of risk. Code C recognises the innate nature of vulnerability and also, albeit less explicitly, acknowledges the situational vulnerability of a suspect in police custody. Both conceptualisations of vulnerability, under Code C, are, however, limited: whilst Code C recognises physical factors for fitness for interview, it ignores the potential physical impact on the suspect for the purposes of the appropriate adult safeguard. Such factors, whilst ostensibly unimportant for the vulnerable suspect, may be taken into account for the vulnerable victim/witness or defendant[15] at trial under s 16 of the Youth Justice and Criminal Evidence Act

(YJCEA) 1999 (although see s 33A YJCEA).[16] Most of the YJCEA, whilst only applying to witnesses (i.e. not defendants), also recognises how fear or distress can make an individual vulnerable, and it takes account of, inter alia, the nature and alleged circumstances of the offence, the social and cultural background and ethnic origins of the witness, the domestic and employment circumstances of the witness and the political or religious beliefs of the witness (see Fairclough 2017; 2018). The CJPOA also allows for a defendant's physical or mental condition to be taken into account where he or she is silent at trial (s 35 (1)(b)).

Some of the dimensions of vulnerability under the YJCEA are also recognised by the HMIC (2015: 17); the report defined vulnerability as including mental health problems, learning difficulties, physical illness or disability, alcohol and/or substance misuse, age and race. The definitions contained under the HMIC guidance and the YJCEA more accurately accord with what vulnerability can mean; for adults, they are not limited only to mental elements. The YJCEA has additional force, at least symbolically, as it is on a firmer statutory footing than the appropriate adult requirement for vulnerable adults (although see CDA 1998 s 38 in respect of young suspects).

Outside of the criminal process, it is recognised that vulnerability is much more *restrictively* conceptualised (see, for example, the Mental Capacity Act 2005). A vulnerable adult[17] has been defined as

> someone over the age of 18 who is or may be in need of community care services by reason of mental or other disability, age or illness and who is or may be unable to take care of him/herself or unable to protect him/herself against significant harm or exploitation.
>
> (Dunn *et al.* 2008: 239 citing Lord Chancellor's Department 1997)

This definition is used in a context where an individual's autonomy is restricted and whereby he or she is prevented from making certain decisions. This more restrictive deployment of vulnerability is justified on the basis that it interferes negatively with the individual's autonomy and, in doing so, takes something away from the person (such as whether to maintain contact with her father (*Re G (An Adult) (Mental Capacity: Court's Jurisdiction)* [2004] EWHC 2222 (Fam)) or whether she is permitted to marry (*Re SA (Vulnerable Adult with Capacity: Marriage)* [2006] 1 FLR 867)).

Within the criminal process context, the label of 'vulnerability' does not prevent an individual from doing something but instead provides them with something additional. Whilst the appropriate adult safeguard, at least to a certain extent, interferes with autonomy, the individual who is attended by an appropriate adult is still permitted to make decisions, such as whether to consult with a legal representative, and as such, still retains control over his or her own decisions. Thus, the appropriate adult safeguard, rather than being paternalist (see Cummins 2007), could be more accurately conceptualised as 'parentalist' (see Buchanan 2005). Further, as Sanders and Young (2000: 242) have highlighted:

> It is true that, in normal circumstances, people do not have things foisted on them against their will simply because someone else thinks it will be good for them. But suspects are not in normal circumstances. If they can be held in stinking conditions against their will, their mouths and hair invaded against their will, and questioned against their will why shouldn't they be given something that does some good against their will?

A lack of clarity and consistency?

Pre-2018, Code C recognised two distinct but potentially overlapping categories of adult vulnerability. These definitions were not elaborated on any further, aside from the superficial information as to why a vulnerable suspect may require an appropriate adult. The provisions largely leant themselves to capacity or comprehension-based understandings of vulnerability. Code C did not, for example, explain that whilst individuals with mental disorder may or may not have issues with capacity or comprehension, they may nevertheless be prone to providing misleading or false information. Instead it suggested, or stated, that the vulnerability must render the individual 'at risk' of providing unreliable, misleading, or falsely incriminating evidence. It did not say *how* this may come about, neither did it explain that failing to 'understand the significance of what is said' (Code C: Note for Guidance E1; see also Note for Guidance 3H) did not necessarily equate to issues with capacity or comprehension. The word 'significance' here was of paramount importance: a suspect may be influenced by short-term gains or may fail to appreciate the long-term implications of interview (see Gudjonsson 1993: 121). In other words, the suspect may understand what is being said but wants to be released as soon as possible and will say anything to be released. He or she, in such circumstances, may fail to recognise the significance of the statements made or may, misconstrue the *mens rea* elements of the offence, as the following example (McConville *et al.* 1991: 70–1) illustrates:

> *CC-A002* – The defendant was alleged to have damaged a mini-cab windscreen in the course of an argument with his girlfriend. Both had been drinking heavily and the defendant had to sleep off the effects of the drink before being fit to be interviewed. He said that, in the course of the row, he had swung his arm out 'and hit the windscreen and it broke'. The police then turned their attention to the question of *mens rea*:
>
> *Police:* 'Did you intend to smash the windscreen?'
> *Defendant:* 'No.'
> *Police:* 'So you just swung your hand out in the *reckless* manner?' (emphasis supplied)
> *Defendant:* 'Yes, that's it, just arguing.'
> *Police:* 'Why did you hit the window in the first place?'
> *Defendant:* 'Just arguing, *reckless*, it wasn't intentional to break it …' (emphasis added)

Here, the defendant did not understand the significance of the word 'reckless' for the purposes of the offence of criminal damage. As McConville, Sanders and Leng highlight (1991: 71), 'A002 was not using the term in the technical sense, but rather using the term colloquially to support a plea that the breakage was *accidental*'. Even where officers do not intend to manipulate the suspect, it may be easy to lead someone, particularly if that individual is in a fragile mental state (which could, arguably, be any suspect). A failure to understand the significance of what is said, in the example provided by McConville, Sanders and Leng, may be utilised the police to get what they want (i.e. a detection). However, even where there is no such intention, it may nevertheless be difficult, if not impossible, to ascertain whether someone is easily led or manipulated short of an in-depth psychological assessment (see Gudjonsson *et al.* 1993). This scenario, as presented by McConville, Sanders and Leng, illustrates that those who do not have or are not known to have a mental disorder of mental health condition may nevertheless misunderstand the significance of what they are saying.

The most recent version of the Code clears up one very obvious inconsistency – the term 'mentally incapable' (Annex E para 1) has been removed. This term appeared only once in the Code and was ostensibly contained within the (previously existing) 'mentally vulnerable' category – i.e. those who were 'mentally incapable' were, by virtue of being mentally incapable, also 'mentally vulnerable'. This was therefore not an extension of 'mentally vulnerable'. Yet, if someone was mentally *incapable*, they then surely should not have been interviewed, as they would have been entirely unable to understand what they are being asked and/or what they are saying. This term has, however, since been removed from the Code.

The 2018 version of the Code contains a fuller explanation of how someone may be vulnerable but does not explain the broader context of this. Further, whilst Note for Guidance 1G makes it clear that a suspect can be considered vulnerable even if he or she is not known to have a mental disorder or mental health condition provided he or she meets the functional criteria set out in para 1.13d, this is nevertheless tucked away in a Note for Guidance and may not be consulted by custody officers (see Dehaghani 2017b). Prior to 2018, the category of 'mental disorder' was problematic in that there was no explanation of what it meant, short of the fact that it derived from the MHA 1983 and constituted 'any disorder or disability of the mind'. This issue has been (at least somewhat) remedied in the most recent version of the Code, which contains a reference to the MHA Code of Practice.[18]

Problems are also evident with the College of Policing guidance. For example, by explaining that the term 'mental ill health' includes 'mental disorder' and those suffering from 'mental distress', it potentially suggests that 'mental distress' is distinct and independent of 'mental disorder' and thus potentially excluded from the Code C definition. The more accurate explanation is that those who are suffering from mental distress may also be considered 'mentally vulnerable'; the relationships between these terms could be better explained. The guidance could also benefit from further discussion of learning difficulty – whilst it explains what a learning difficulty is, it does not explain the difference between learning disability and learning difficulty.[19] To do so may serve to further demarcate learning difficulty from what is required for the appropriate adult safeguard. A more explicit explanation of how these terms relate to the Code C definitions could improve custody officer's knowledge. The guidance should also clarify that learning difficulties, although potentially distinct from learning disabilities (and therefore mental disorder), are caught under the 'mental vulnerability' category of Code C. Whilst the APP cautions that 'those with mild learning disabilities may not receive any formal support and their needs and disability may not be obvious' (College of Policing 2018c), it goes on to state that, 'other people have profound and multiple learning disabilities and their needs may be considerable' (*ibid.*). Whilst it is undoubtedly the case that some individuals require more support (although whether the appropriate adult can provide this additional support is up for debate), such phrasing may suggest to custody officers that those with mild learning disabilities do not require the assistance of the appropriate adult. The guidance is certainly less problematic than the older version(s) of Code C in one respect – unlike Code C (2017), it explains that those who may fit the definition of 'mentally vulnerable' may 'not be considered to be experiencing a mental illness by an HCP' (College of Policing 2018c). It does not, however, go any further to suggest, for example, that vulnerability can be brought about by circumstance.

Conclusions: clearing up Code C?

Ambiguities within the Code could be removed or lessened. The most recent version of the Code better conceptualises 'vulnerability': it makes clear that it can be connected to a mental health condition or mental disorder but may not necessarily be so. It also references the MHA Code of Practice.[20] This is a slight improvement on the previous versions of the Code where the MHA was simply referred to (i.e. that the definition 'mental disorder' is derived from the MHA). At the time that the observations were conducted (in 2014 and 2015), I neither saw a copy of the MHA Code of Practice in either of the two sites nor heard the Code mentioned on any occasion in custody. Only since 2018 have custody officers been advised to consult the MHA 1983 Code of Practice (Code C: Note for Guidance E6. See also Note for Guidance 1GB).[21] This change is, of course, based on the assumption or hope that custody officers will consult the guidance, be able to understand it, and then use such guidance when making their decisions.

The Code does not, however, go far enough. There is no mention of learning difficulty: this is something that is distinct from a learning disability (see Mindroom undated) (learning disability is caught under the definition of 'mental disorder). There is also no recognition of the fact that a cognitive impairment, additional educational need or simply a temporary issue with understanding and communication could render someone 'vulnerable'. Undoubtedly, these aspects may be caught by the functional test but, despite the caveat in Note for Guidance 1G, the focus of custody officers (and others who assist in the identification of vulnerability) may be squarely on the terms 'mental health condition' or 'mental disorder'. In this sense, the new Code is actually worse than the previous versions (as 'mental vulnerability' could, albeit implicitly, be seen to include learning difficulty, cognitive impairment, additional educational need, and temporary issues with capacity and/or comprehension). It also needs to be highlighted that the word 'significance' is of relevance: it is not simply that the individual does not understand what is said, but rather the individual does not understand the significance of what is said. The interaction noted by McConville, Sanders and Leng (1991: 70–1) is a clear example of this.

Because their focus is squarely on reliability and/or fairness, the courts have engaged sparsely, at best, with the meaning of vulnerability. How they react to breaches of Code C can have an (implicit or explicit) impact on police practice. At present, their approach can be seen to have done little to promote compliance with the vulnerability provisions. Providing further information to custody officers may facilitate their understanding of these categories and may thus improve implementation of the appropriate adult safeguard, as may a more critical approach by the courts. Both approaches are not, however, without their flaws: the former supposes that clearing-up the ambiguities in the law will facilitate and therefore improve practice; the latter supposes that the case reaches the courts.

Notes

1 I suggested to the Home Office that compliance also be included as a category. The response indicated that compliance was too similar to suggestibility and acquiescence to be included as a distinct category.

2 I suggested this latter sentence to the Home Office as not including such a caution could preclude custody officers from implementing the appropriate adult safeguard where they believe that the suspect has met one or more of the requirements of the functional test in para 1.13d but where the suspect does not have or is not known to have a mental health condition or mental disorder.

3 The term 'reason to suspect' is seen as preferable to the term proposed ('reason to believe') – see NAAN (2017) for a discussion.

4 This has not been updated since the Code C changes were implemented.

5 Only the information required has been contained within this list.

6 This was a suggestion that I made to the Home Office when asked to further comment on the proposed changes to Code C.

7 For a fuller discussion, see Dehaghani (2018).

8 Whilst PACE was in force at the time of trial, Foster's interview had occurred during the period of transition between the implementation of PACE and the coming into force of PACE.

9 These cases were distinguished from *Miller* (above) on the basis that the presence of an appropriate adult *would have* made a difference to Miller's situation.

10 Cases heard in Northern Ireland are not binding upon English and Welsh courts (but are nevertheless persuasive).

11 For a fuller discussion, see Dehaghani (2018).

12 The role of the solicitor can be considered very different from that of an appropriate adult; the solicitor may be unable to cope with suspect vulnerabilities – see Dehaghani and Newman 2017.

13 The fitness for interview criteria also lack clarity (Jacobson 2008).

14 Gudjonsson also suggested that coercion in police interviews may lead to Post-Traumatic Stress Disorder, however, a direct link has yet to be established.

15 Special measures do not automatically apply to the accused but they can be implemented at the discretion of the trial judge (see *R. (on the application of C) v. Sevenoaks Youth Court* [2009] EWHC 3088 (Admin); [2010] 1 All ER 735. See also *R. v Cox (Anthony Russell)* [2012] EWCA Crim 549).
16 For a defendant to avail of live-link, he or she must suffer from a mental disorder or significant impairment of intelligence and social functioning (s 33A YJCEA as inserted by s 47 Police and Justice Act 2006). For defendants, therefore, physical disability is therefore omitted as a category of vulnerability, as is anything that would fall within s 17 YJCEA.
17 The Home Office considered changing the Code C guidance so as to contain the term 'vulnerable adult'. It was highlighted in my response (Dehaghani 2017e) to the consultation and by NAAN (2018) in their response that this would be problematic.
18 As previously note, this was a suggestion that I made to the Home Office when asked to further comment on the proposed changes to Code C (see Dehaghani 2017b).
19 Previous versions of the College of Policing guidance did not include a definition of learning difficulty – see Dehaghani (2017b).
20 The suggestion to introduce a reference to the MHA Code of Practice was included in previous drafts of this book and in Dehaghani (2017b).
21 This amendment was made by the Home Office after I had suggested the possibility of referencing the MHA Code of Practice within Code C.

6 Constructing vulnerability – the custody officer approach

Introduction

The contours of vulnerability must be constructed before it is identified: is vulnerability something which is innate, situational or inherent to all suspects? The definition of vulnerability for the purposes of the appropriate adult safeguard has thus far been afforded scant attention. One could assume that custody officers defined vulnerability in the same way as Code C defines it: an adult suspect was 'vulnerable' if he or she had a mental disorder or was mentally vulnerable (as were the terms when the observations and interviews were carried out). Yet, that would be too simplistic an assumption. Therefore, whilst the law provides some guidance on what is required for the appropriate adult safeguard, this guidance is subject to some form of interpretation by custody officers. These legal actors may adopt their own construction of the law or may ignore the law's definitions entirely. The definition of vulnerability, as negotiated, unpacked and constructed by custody officers, must be understood if one is to appropriately examine why the appropriate adult safeguard is often left unimplemented. Vulnerability has many dimensions and is a term used for different purposes. It may also mean different things to different people (even those performing the same role within the same organisation). This holds true in the context of police custody. These various uses and constructions have implications for how safeguarding is deployed. The safeguard itself may also be subject to construction: how this is interpreted will undoubtedly have a bearing on why the safeguard is used and for whom. These various elements will be explored in this chapter.

Expounding the general contours of vulnerability

Vulnerability was 'difficult to put it into words' (CO9-W Interview) owing, at least in part, to the fact that it had a plurality of meaning, i.e. it 'could mean literally lots and lots and lots of things' (CO22-M Interview). It could thus be broad and/or ill-defined and, as such, there was 'no straight answer' (CO29-M Interview). Vulnerability could also be inherent: 'there's a certain vulnerability for everybody' (CO9-W Interview) and 'anyone could be vulnerable at any given time' (CO17-W Interview). It could also relate to victimisation, thus exhibiting some parallels with the dictionary definition and the characteristics identified succinctly by Misztal (2013). For example, one custody officer, when asked what 'vulnerable' meant to him, stated:

> I tend to think that that's in the 'too difficult' box to deal with because of the complexities of the thought process and their understanding and in terms of how they are as a victim and these things going on to court, if they're making a complaint ... you're almost in the situation where you're dealing with the ten year olds.
>
> (CO10-W Interview)

Here, vulnerability was compared to childhood, parallels are made with thought-processes and understanding, and it was perceived to create some difficulty for those interacting with the vulnerable individual. That a vulnerable individual required a different response is reiterated by a separate quote:

> Let's say for example a rape victim, I would suggest is vulnerable.... So, for an example of vulnerable, I would say that that person would probably be vulnerable and say you'd avoid any issue that sort of might upset them.... So, certain sensitive, sensitivity, needs, they're the vulnerable types.
>
> (CO21-M Interview)

Those who conformed to the 'ideal victim' type (Christie 1986) were recognised as being vulnerable. Being a victim had much greater congruence with vulnerability than being a suspect or defendant (see for example, Kemp and Hodgson 2016: 163), particularly because a victim was not to 'blame' for the difficulties he or she was facing. Because suspects may have behaved problematically, or be perceived to have done so by custody officers, their vulnerability could be challenged – they may be seen as 'to blame' for 'landing themselves' in custody.

Vulnerability was also linked with helplessness and, interestingly, addiction. Some of those considered that the 'vulnerable' are not 'at fault' for their vulnerability. Rather, they are vulnerable to others who may exploit their vulnerability (see Goodin 1985). The transgression of the person who was addicted to alcohol or drugs did not, in this case, challenge his or her vulnerability because 'their addictions can make them vulnerable when they need money or drugs or drink or whatever, their addiction makes them vulnerable to people who can prey on them' (CO29-M Interview). Bound-up with notions of helplessness, vulnerability was also viewed in terms of exposure or liability (Misztal 2013). Those whose exposure was greater were viewed as having a greater sense of vulnerability. However, being in possession of some experience could reduce one's exposure to harm thus challenging vulnerability:

> Someone who lives in a criminal fraternity family, used to criminality going on around them and everything else, not working, not going to have a social impact being arrested, anything else and they come into custody for the first time and [they] can just glide through the process as if nothing's wrong. But ... somebody else who comes into custody for child sex offences, first

> time in custody as well, going to have a massive social impact with them and family personal impact with them and, yeah, they're going to be vulnerable at some point through that process, aren't they?
>
> (CO27-M Interview)

Having knowledge of the criminal justice process ostensibly negates vulnerability. By contrast, having no knowledge (i.e. being a 'first-timer') can exacerbate one's vulnerability.[1]

An individual may also be vulnerable as a result of the offence for which he or she is under investigation (arguably in spite of the current moral panic in relation to paedophiles and 'predators'):

> Some people can be vulnerable, particularly coming into the custody area, simply by the crime that they've been accused of. A perfectly respectable middle-class, middle-aged gentleman with a good job: if he's accused of a sexual offence involving young boys for instance, the very nature could make him vulnerable to what he perceives the outside world to think.
>
> (CO29-M Interview)

In addition to bolstering the claim of CO27-M (i.e. that paedophiles can be vulnerable), CO29-M's quote also indicated other reasons as to this heightened perception of vulnerability. Characteristics such as class ('perfectly respectable middle-class'), age ('middle-aged'), and employment status ('good job') may be seen to place an individual at greater 'risk' or heightened vulnerability. Thus, vulnerability may be understood to have class and age dimensions, in addition to being understood as something relating to the individual's alleged conduct. Vulnerability thus arose as a result of the predicament of unpredictability (i.e. not knowing what to expect from the criminal process) or the predicament of irreversibility (i.e. criminalisation that results in stigma which, even if found not guilty, cannot be retracted) (see Misztal 2013). This latter predicament came across in CO1–1's interview:

> Somebody could be charged for a relatively minor offence, to you or me or somebody who's not been in much trouble it might not mean anything [but] to somebody who's previously been to prison that could make them vulnerable because all of sudden they could think, 'What's going on in the future?'... They could be going to prison; they therefore could risk harming themselves and things like that.

In addition to illustrating the conceptual congruence of vulnerability and risk, this quote also highlights how vulnerability can relate to the irrevocability of the past (see Misztal 2013).

The situational, rather than innate, nature of vulnerability was explicitly recognised: '[v]ulnerability isn't necessarily somebody suffering from a condition but of something that's happening to them either then or has happened to them previously, which is causing them stress, anxiety, depression' (CO4-W

Interview). The situational nature extended to the act of being detained in custody (see Gudjonsson 2010: 122) – vulnerability could be affected by 'all [sorts] of external triggers ... obviously one of them being in custody' (CO30-M Interview). Although it was recognised that custody was a 'stress factor' (CO18-W Interview), unsurprisingly, custody officers did not recognise the power dynamic between themselves (the detainer) and the suspect (the detainee) as something which could contribute to the suspect's vulnerability. The situational nature of vulnerability was also viewed as variable: '[p]eople arrive fine but because you're not interacting enough with them, you're not answering their questions, things escalate or deteriorate or whatever. And that's when these issues arise and they become more and more vulnerable' (CO16-W Interview). Yet, just as vulnerability could be increased, so too can it be lessened: '[a]nd once they've been here for a while, that sort of vulnerability has gone because they've come off whatever they've had and they're just normal, sane people sometimes' (CO17-W Interview). Here, vulnerability was viewed as the antithesis of 'normality' and therefore attributed to a negative characteristic (see Levine 2004).

The discussion above suggested that vulnerability was used as a synonym for risk (Brown 2015: 15). Suspects or other detainees with physical or mental health problems were viewed as 'vulnerable' but such vulnerability did not render them in need of an appropriate adult. Rather they were at potential risk of self-harm, suicide, injury or death as a result of their vulnerability. Custody officers had 'to act in that person's best interests, if we feel they're vulnerable in any way, be it mental health, self-harm, whichever way, medically' (CO24-M Interview). For the duration of the detainee or suspect's time in custody, officers had to ascertain 'whether or not there are any vulnerability issues, whether from a medical point of view, mental health point of view or just vulnerable in general' (CO30-M Interview). Similarly, risk factors or 'vulnerabilities' could also include 'drug dependency or mental health issue or learning difficulty, or whatever it might be' (CO18-W Interview) – the aim was to 'flag up vulnerabilities [when] looking at risk' (*ibid.*). Observations also seemed to highlight the conceptual congruence between vulnerability and risk:

> Suspect seems distressed and anxious – she has been using an inhaler, is swaying from side to side and is visibly upset. She is being charged with domestic assault. She has dyslexia but the decision was taken to interview her without an appropriate adult. She was booked-in last night [CO3-W had not made this decision]. The decision is not criticised (suggesting that he would have made the same decision or indicating an unwillingness to criticise his colleagues). A police officer is asked to escort suspect home as she lives far away and is 'slightly vulnerable in a general sense but not for interview purposes'.
>
> (Interaction 73-W)

> Suspect arrives handcuffed and is placed in a holding cell (handcuffs are later removed). Suspect is angry, agitated and her speech is slurred. She has been arrested under suspicion of criminal damage and for threatening behaviour. She reports no difficulty reading or writing but she suffers from fits and anxiety. She is also alcohol dependent and suffers from withdrawal symptoms.
>
> CO12-W discusses timing of interview with the investigating officer. He raises his concerns in relation to intoxication on the one hand and alcohol withdrawal on the other. He advises that the interview will have to be conducted when the suspect is sober but before alcohol withdrawal sets in. A fitness for interview assessment, on account of her 'vulnerability', is requested. An appropriate adult is deemed unnecessary as suspect 'does not have mental health problems'. Suspect asks to make a phone call, CO12-W agreed. She lifts her own phone from the 'Prisoner Belongings' bag and calls her parents. CO12-W tries to explain that she should be calling from the custody phone but she does not seem to understand this and replies, 'I'm using my own credit, not yours'. CO12-W makes a comment that 'At least this saves the taxpayer some money'. She is asked if she knows her rights and she replies 'Yes'. She reads the screen and thinks 'misc.' is 'music'. This makes me question her ability to read, although this may be as a result of alcohol consumption/intoxication. CO12-W does not query this, neither does he make any connection between this and the suspect's ability to rea.
>
> (Interaction 116-W)

Whilst these dimensions of vulnerability facilitate understanding of how custody officers conceptualise this term more generally, they do not explain what determines or undermines the implementation of the appropriate adult safeguard.

Constructing the Code C definitions

At the time of research, a vulnerable suspect, according to Code C, was someone considered 'mentally vulnerable' or 'mentally disordered' or below the age of 18.[2] Where an adult suspect was considered 'mentally vulnerable' or 'mentally disordered', the appropriate adult should have been called (Code C: para 3.5; Note for Guidance 1G). However, the responsibility for implementing this safeguard is left with the custody officer (*ibid.*). When interviewed, custody officers were asked for their interpretation(s) of these terms.

The most common characteristic of 'mental vulnerability' was either learning disabilities or difficulties (often used interchangeably), low intelligence, or both: the category was said to 'include people suffering from mental illness or it could include people with learning difficulties' (CO20-W Interview) or 'somebody possibly with learning disabilities' (CO30-M Interview). This did not mean that all individuals with mental illness, learning difficulties or learning disabilities *were* mentally vulnerable; rather that they *could be* mentally vulnerable. Ostensibly, 'mental vulnerability' could also be distinguished from mental illness and it could also be separated from learning difficulties, as the quote (CO9-W Interview) below illustrates:

> It's difficult to put it into words. If somebody's got a mental illness … like schizophrenia or paranoia or something, then that comes under the umbrella of mental illness. But mentally vulnerable, I suppose, if somebody's really not understanding what's happening, they've got learning difficulties, maybe they struggle to read and write. Whether you class that as mental vulnerability or just vulnerability, I don't know.

It is unclear whether the custody officer was making the point that learning difficulty is a mere vulnerability but not a mental vulnerability or whether he was unsure; the addition of *'I don't know'* would suggest the latter.

One custody officer explicitly stated that 'we don't have guidance as to what mentally vulnerable means' (CO18-W Interview). Such statements were also implicit in other interviews. A statement to this effect may suggest that the custody officer *was* aware of the guidance under Code C but such guidance was insufficient in order for custody officers to operationalise vulnerability, or it could mean that this custody officer (and potentially the other custody officers, inferred from their responses) was not aware of the Code C guidance on mental vulnerability (see Dehaghani 2017b). It also suggests that the definitions were not explored within their custody officer training or that the definitions had long been forgotten.[3] The general consensus was that Code C was inaccessible and thus deterred custody officers from reading it. Moreover, the impression was such that Code C was not necessarily written with the custody officer in mind and did not deal with the 'nuts and bolts' of the day-to-day work. That said, whilst clear and concise definitions of 'mentally vulnerable' were absent, custody officers had some idea of what it meant (*ibid.*).

Whilst custody officers had a vague notion of what 'mentally vulnerable' denoted, the definition of 'mental disorder' seemed even more problematic. As highlighted in Chapter 5, 'mental disorder' is something which is purely innate. Since 2018, a reference to the MHA Code of Practice is included within Code C. This may encourage custody officers to consult the guidance (if, indeed, they read Code C). Whilst an improvement on the earlier versions of the Code, the current (2018) version nevertheless requires custody officers to consult the MHA 1983 Code of Practice in order to know how 'mental disorder' links-up with recognised conditions (Dehaghani 2017b). The version of the Code at the time of observations and interviews included a brief reference to the MHA but did not include any references to the MHA Code of Practice. Thus, custody officers may have been unaware of this guidance.

Custody officers neither mentioned the phrase 'any disorder or disability of the mind' when asked to explain mental disorder nor at any other point during the interview. The term 'mental disorder' seemed to cause confusion and hesitancy for many, almost as if it was unheard-of. There was, however, a general awareness that mental health problems and/or learning disabilities could constitute a mental disorder, albeit there was some hesitancy in the responses. The typical response referred to mental health or learning difficulty but not necessarily disability. CO22-M (Interview) was adamant that learning disability was not included under the definition of mental disorder, stating at interview: 'define mentally disordered, there's such a variety of what it could be, such a misunderstanding of what it means … people equate learning disabilities into mental disorder and it's *not*' (emphasis added). In fact, he himself was confused as to how the two terms were related. Whilst it is true that learning difficulties are neither mental health problems nor fall under 'mental disorder', learning disabilities *are* included within the definition of mental disorder under the Code of Practice of the MHA 1983.

Custody officer responses also included references to medication and diagnosis as well as behavioural problems and cognitive impairments. Moreover, whilst it is true that an individual with mental disorder could have also been mentally vulnerable (i.e. the mental disorder can make the suspect mentally vulnerable), the two could also be mutually exclusive. Custody officers, however, seemed to conflate the two, as the following quote (CO22-M Interview) illustrates:

> Mentally disordered and mentally vulnerable, if a person has mental health issues generally I would see them as being mentally vulnerable. I don't really know. I'm not a doctor. But I would suggest that they're very, very similar. Mentally vulnerable, I would suggest that just means that they have very, very high learning issues.

Whilst the foregoing discussion gives insight into how custody officers understand (or rather do not understand) the terms under Code C (as per the pre-2018 iterations), it does not give any insight into what the custody officers were looking for when deciding whether the appropriate adult safeguard should be implemented.

Constructing the 'appropriate adult vulnerable' suspect

Custody officers did not necessarily 'need' to have the Code C definitions in mind when attempting to identify whether the appropriate adult safeguard is required. Indeed, a lack of knowledge of the terms under Code C was not necessarily an 'obstacle' to implementation, at least not for the custody officer. This is because they had their own perception of what 'vulnerability' means for the appropriate adult safeguard. Being vulnerable, in a broader sense, does not mean that the suspect, according to the custody officer, requires an appropriate adult. This holds true even where vulnerability derives from a mental disorder, as the following quote (CO3-W Interview) illustrates:

> I think when you're dealing with what people recognise as bi-polar and schizophrenia and paranoia, they are areas of vulnerability. Because they have a vulnerability due to mental illness, does that mean that they need an appropriate adult? I'm sure that people that I've dealt with have those issues,

> [those] who say 'I'm bi-polar' or 'I'm schizophrenic'. I don't just automatically tick 'Need an appropriate adult' if that's where you're running to.

Whether this was intentional or not, CO3-W commenced with 'what people recognise', which could suggest that he was sceptical about these diagnoses. Being in possession of a mental disorder did not necessarily qualify the suspect for receiving the appropriate adult safeguard. Rather, the vulnerability arising from schizophrenia or bi-polar disorder may be considered for the purposes of care in, or release from, custody; the suspect may be vulnerable in terms of 'health' or 'risk' but not vulnerable for the purposes of the appropriate adult safeguard. For the appropriate adult safeguard, custody officers had ostensibly produced and set their own benchmark.

'Symptoms' not condition: presenting as vulnerable

According to custody officers, 'appropriate adult vulnerability' was a result, not of the condition, but of the symptoms of that condition, or the impact of circumstance on that condition resulting in particular symptoms. The suspect must therefore display the symptoms of his or her condition and must perform his or her vulnerability (see Brown 2015): even when someone had a 'mental health diagnosis [which means that] you're dealing with a diagnosed mental condition [this] doesn't necessarily mean that they need an appropriate adult [because it comes down to] how they are when they're actually presented in front of you' (CO4-W Interview). As CO4-W (*ibid.*) went on to explain, such presentation can occur 'particularly if somebody isn't taking their medication [which means that] they're much more likely to display symptoms, behaviours that are different that would cause concern than somebody who is'.

The notion of presentation and performance appeared frequently. For example, for a suspect who had schizophrenia (which is classed as a mental disorder) who has recently had a

> depo-injection that they take two weekly [and] said that 'well, I had my injection yesterday' and they present well and I would never had known that they had schizophrenia hadn't they told me, I'd probably go ahead with an interview rather than [get an appropriate adult].
>
> (CO13-W Interview)

Rather than relying on the suspect's report of his or her illness, the custody officer relied on how the suspect presented and the fact that medication had been taken. The suspect's inability to adequately perform vulnerability, caused by the use of medication, could therefore challenge the perception that he or she was vulnerable. Conversely,

> if someone came in with schizophrenia and they hadn't taken their medication, they probably would be displaying something and that to me would be a

> stone bonker [sic] that they need someone to sit and make sure that they know what's going on.
>
> (CO22-M Interview)

As CO22-M suggests, the presentation of the suspect could therefore alert the custody officer to the fact that he or she is vulnerable and the presentation of vulnerability may be more apparent when the suspect had not taken his or her medication. Such indicators may be particularly useful where the suspect had not disclosed something that would constitute a vulnerability and where no such other information was available. However, the fact that someone was unable to perform their vulnerability by virtue of having taken medication, or otherwise, should not, in and of itself, be used as justification to dispute that they may be vulnerable. For example, and as Brown (1997: 212) has highlighted, Colin Lattimore (one of the 'Confait Three') 'presented well'.

Normality/abnormality: a vulnerability dichotomy

Vulnerability was, in some sense, viewed as the antithesis of normality, and such depictions are also true for the appropriate adult safeguard. The words such as 'normal' and 'abnormal' were frequently deployed to describe or articulate 'vulnerability', particularly in reference to the appropriate adult safeguard. For example, CO11-W (Interview) stated that he would not obtain an appropriate adult 'if they present normally to me, even if they have mental health issues'. CO12-W (Interview) explained that he would obtain an appropriate adult if the suspect did not '[act] how you would expect a normal person [to act when] booked in. Normal's [sic] not quite the right word but I can't think of another one'. Similarly, attending 'a school for people with issues' rather than 'a normal school' (CO2-W Interview) could provide some indication that an appropriate adult was required (although Bradley (2009) has highlighted how this is an inaccurate measure because of the tendency towards education in mainstream schools). Discussions of the interplay between medication and the need for an appropriate adult was also steeped in rhetoric of 'normality' and 'abnormality'. Having one's illness 'under control' (CO33-M Interview) meant normalisation. However, some behaviour that could be considered 'unusual' did not always lead to the implementation of the appropriate adult safeguard. For example, an appropriate adult was not provided to a suspect who 'had two knives in his hands and … was stabbing himself and … turned on us [referring to the arresting officers] with the knives. Straight away you're starting to think "That's not normal behaviour, there's obviously some issues there"' (CO28-M Interview). The severity of someone's condition, and therefore their need for an appropriate adult, could, however, be indicated by previous sectioning: 'we had a chap in yesterday who … had been sectioned previously and when I visited him when I came on duty, was literally paced up and down in his cell, almost skippy [sic], hopping around, screaming and shouting and swearing' (CO11-W Interview).

Connections were also made between abnormality and childlike characteristics; where the impairment was severe, the suspect was not deemed to be fully 'adult'. Such a comparison is interesting as it would suggest that 'appropriate adult vulnerable' suspects are viewed akin to child suspects:

> It's childlike, in so much as the kids can happily be sat at school now but if you walk into the classroom in the school round the corner and then they'll say, 'Me, me, me' because you've suggested that [they go for ice-cream] and they'll sort of acquiesce and go along with whatever you're saying and that is that understanding issue. People here will say 'Yes boss!' and they'll nod their heads a lot.
>
> (CO16-W Interview)

The comparison was based upon the suspect's capacity: for example, someone with 'learning difficulties … might have a mental capacity that isn't of an adult, it might be more in the juvenile range (CO3-W Interview). An adult with the mental age or capacity of a child or teenager may be viewed as 'appropriate adult vulnerable': 'if you've got a 25-year-old man stood in front of you, "I've got the mental age of a 12-year-old" – 12-year-old, juvenile, appropriate adult, vulnerable' (CO24-M Interview). Conversely, being unable to read and write was not necessarily an indicator, 'because they can be mentally sharp enough to be an adult in the normal sense of the word, without an appropriate adult' (CO12-W Interview). The 'vulnerable' suspect therefore had to be imbued with childlike characteristics; those behaving in a childlike manner fell within the category of suspects in need of protection, however, those who were able to 'perform' adulthood were not. This juxtaposition between 'adult' and 'child' meant that custody officers took the view that adults who were, for example, capable of raising a family were also capable of withstanding a police interview without an appropriate adult. For example, CO16-W (Interview) stated 'because a person has reading problems, doesn't mean they need an appropriate adult. [It] could be their upbringing and they've survived perfectly fine and they've a family, perfectly good job and everything else'. A similar sentiment was echoed by CO21-M (Interview) who stated that he would not

> get somebody an appropriate adult if, say it's somebody for example living on their own. Or it could be a family man, who has one or two problems with reading and writing but he holds down a full time job and he's raising a family. Why should that person need an appropriate adult?… The kids are always going to need an adult…. And he's acting in that role already, in his current position as a family man.

Such statements neglect the fact that a 'family man' may not always be an 'appropriate' appropriate adult (*DPP v Blake* [1989] 1 WLR 432; *R. v Morse* [1991] Crim LR 195). Such statements also suggest that the appropriate adult is there to protect the childlike suspect, in a similar manner to which a parent would protect their child (see Palmer and Hart 1996).

Those who are genuinely vulnerable are unable to fend for themselves; they are helpless and may be vulnerable to exploitation. An ability to survive in the outside world, by contrast, suggests that the suspect was not vulnerable. Capability and adulthood were therefore viewed as the antithesis of vulnerability. Yet, not all suspects who possessed childlike characteristics would be provided with an appropriate adult, as the following observation (Interaction 76-M) illustrates:

> Suspect has been arrested on suspicion of assault. She is alleged to have bitten her boyfriend's neck during a fight. She is visibly upset and is crying incessantly. She keeps screaming that she does not want to be 'locked away'. She makes no attempts to wipe away the tears and nasal mucus running down her face, her hair is matted and she is upset that she has to take her hair-tie out of her hair (she is screaming and sobbing while she is repeatedly asked to remove the hair-tie). She has sustained a head injury during the fight with her boyfriend and she discloses physical injuries, manic depression and self-harm. She states that she last self-harmed by cutting herself and had to be admitted to hospital as a result. I ask CO31-M about his decisions in relation to the suspect; he states that she will be placed on 30 minute visits due to her head injury but does not require CCTV as her method of self-harm would not be possible in custody. There is no mention of obtaining an appropriate adult for the suspect.

Of course, her behaviour may have been as a result of the head injury, because she was deeply upset having had a fight with her boyfriend, or because she was upset or frightened at having been brought into custody (all of which could have, nevertheless, made her vulnerable). However, she did disclose manic depression, which is a mental disorder. Any of these factors could have been taken into account when implementing the appropriate adult safeguard but it seemed, even in their totality, nothing was enough for an appropriate adult to be called.

Understanding: knowing 'what's what'

The predominant focus for the appropriate adult safeguard was capacity, comprehension, and/or understanding. Custody officers relied on whether the suspect 'understood' particular aspects of the custody process and the criminal process in order to ascertain whether he or she was 'appropriate adult vulnerable' (see also Palmer and Hart 1996). For example, 'vulnerable is anyone who for any reason has a lack of understanding as to their circumstances, why they're being investigated, why they're under arrest and the processes that we go through during investigation whilst they're in custody' (CO33-M Interview). The suspect must have little to no understanding of what is going on to be considered 'appropriate adult vulnerable'. This can be ascertained in a number of ways. For example, the suspect may not understand the reason and circumstances of arrest, the fact he or she is being detained, and the fact that he or she will be questioned. If the suspect's 'understanding of consequence is a little retarded' (CO27-M Interview) then he or she may have been provided with an appropriate adult. Of course, if the suspect failed to understand these particular aspects of the process then it could certainly be argued that he or she has been unable to invoke, whether fully or partially, his or her due process rights. By contrast, if the suspect was to invoke his or her due process rights, he or she would not be viewed as 'appropriate adult vulnerable' as he or she would be deemed to understand the process sufficiently, as the following three quotes (CO9-W Interview, CO14-W Interview, and CO28-M Interview) illustrate:

> When you go through their rights they say, 'Yes, I'd like a solicitor' or they appear to be fully engaging with you, I would say they don't need an appropriate adult because they fully understand what's happening.... They know why they're here, they understand the booking-in process, and they'll be able to understand questions in interview.
>
> The main thing that I'm looking out for is to be able to protect them ... what we're going through from a police point of view.... And I think you make sure that they fully understand what they're saying, what they're not saying, and the impact that will have on the investigation, and what happens from a criminal point of view, whether they are charged, cautioned, no further action, whatever it may be.
>
> All those questions in themselves are giving you feedback as to what their level of understanding is like. It doesn't have to be a specific question about that area, it can be anything. You get an idea of this person's level of understanding.... To me vulnerable is someone who doesn't understand what's going on, they have very limited awareness or understanding of why they've been brought to a police station.... I mean the most obvious way of answering it is when you say to someone, 'You can be detained at this police station'. It starts off 'Do you know why you've been arrested?' and they'll tell you. And then you say 'You're going to be detained here,' and they'll say 'Why am I going to be detained here?' and straight away the alarm bells are ringing.

The suspect's understanding of the criminal process could also be gleaned by his or her previous contact with, or experience of, the criminal process. For example, 'recidivists' are deemed to possess greater knowledge than 'first timers' (Kemp and Hodgson 2016 in relation to young suspects. See also Dehaghani 2017c). Capacity, comprehension, and/or understanding can therefore be conceptualised as general or specific to the criminal process. In the following quote (CO2-W Interview), a suspect who was deemed to lack capacity, in a general sense, and had schizophrenia (which is a mental disorder), was deemed not to require an appropriate adult as it was believed that he had sufficient understanding of the criminal process:

> This person had had an awful lot of contact with the police and had been through the process of being arrested and dealt with quite a number of times and had quite a number of convictions. So I was quite comfortable with that

> decision. But if someone had very few dealings with the police then I would probably have an appropriate adult. But that would be purely because I would be concerned about their level of understanding of what was going on.

Fenner, Gudjonsson and Clare's (2002: 90) findings would challenge this perception: those who are 'old hand' are not necessarily better at, for example, understanding the revised police caution. This is arguably so because the law is often complex and arcane.

Other suspects, such as those with Autism Spectrum Disorder (ASD) (a mental disorder), did not necessarily avail of the appropriate adult safeguard as the following quote (CO4-W Interview) illustrates:

> I have a friend who's a consultant anaesthetist who's on the autistic [spectrum], his son's at Oxford University doing languages. You would say that their behaviour sometimes is a bit, hmm, is bit, how they talk, that's a bit different. But does that make them different? No.... There are degrees and I think they show themselves when you talk to people, I think. It's a judgment call. The Autistic Society – is it the Autistic Society? – recommend that everybody has an appropriate adult. Do they? Does my friend who's a consultant anaesthetist need one for interview? I'd say not. So, you know, everyone has to be dealt with individually. You can't just sort of say, blanket, across the board, that everybody needs an appropriate adult.

When asked to explain this approach CO4-W (Interview) stated, 'because they know the difference between right and wrong, they know why they're here'. CO4-W's rationale was that someone of a high intellect, such as a consultant anaesthetist or someone who attends Oxford University, would not be in need of an appropriate adult because they were sufficiently (or very, as his example suggests) intelligent. Those with ASD were not provided with an appropriate adult because they, like the experienced suspect, were taken to understand what was going on. This rationale is similar to that of the courts in *Law-Thompson* ([1997] Crim LR 674), as discussed in Chapter 5. Thus, custody officers endeavoured to cognise the suspect's mental capacity and his or her ability to communicate effectively, in addition to his or her understanding of the world and of the criminal process. They did not, or did not wish, to appreciate how a suspect who seemed to understand what's going on may nevertheless fail to appreciate the long-term consequences of his or her actions, or, when placed under pressure, may be prone to falsely confessing (see Gudjonsson 2003). Obstacles may be greater where the suspect failed to 'perform' as 'autistic', or where such traits were not obvious, as the following quote (CO13-W Interview) illustrates:

> Autism at different ends of the spectrum is quite apparent to see or not. People present really, really well and they say 'I'm autistic' and if you hadn't have told me that you were autistic, I would never have known and I would've gone ahead and said 'Right, go to interview straight away'. And if

> people present well to me and they seem to know what is happening then I put them through I say 'Right, go to interview'.

Not all custody officers took this approach, however. Both CO9-W and CO10-W commented that 'anything on the autistic spectrum' would warrant the appropriate adult safeguard. CO9-W explicitly provided his reasons, stating that 'anyone that is anywhere on the autistic spectrum, our rule-book says "They will have an appropriate adult"' (CO9-W Interview).

The 'negative' case: two vulnerable women

Whilst it has thus far been suggested that custody officers did not implement the appropriate adult safeguard where the suspect did not fit their definition of 'appropriate adult vulnerable', there were two explicit instances mentioned where the appropriate adult was called where it was felt that the suspects did not meet these criteria. The first of these cases concerned a 'nineteen-year-old, female, teaching assistant' who, when she arrived in police custody 'was sound as a pound, could converse with you here' yet 'by eleven o'clock it was, "You've got to get the officers here. I don't want a solicitor. I just want to admit it; I'll admit it all"'. CO16-W recognised that her desire to 'admit something she's potentially not done' had been brought about by 'the stresses and strains of being here' even though 'she can happily deal with thirty little kids running round'. The suspect was 'somebody who's never been in trouble before' but who, after being 'in for twelve hours' was ready to (potentially falsely) confess. In the 12 hours that she was in custody 'she [couldn't] see that [confessing was] going to affect her for the next eighty years of her life'. The decision was therefore taken to obtain an appropriate adult for her. CO16-W went on to note,

> the officers weren't happy with it because they wanted to go to interview at that point. So we ended getting an appropriate adult, which happened to be her partner, which she was happy with, she's nineteen, the partner was twenty-something.

The presence of the appropriate adult was seen to radically change the outcome for this nineteen-year-old – 'she's had a solicitor and she ended up being bailed as opposed to, yesterday, when she would've been cautioned or charged straight off'. CO16-W's (Interview) rationale was that:

> Clearly she did need an appropriate adult and it was from a communication point of view because she had to communicate what was going through her mind. It's not for her to admit it to me, she needs to communicate what's going through her mind and if she says, 'No I haven't done this but I need to get out of here' then that's what she needs to communicate to the appropriate adult, who in turn can then say, 'Look, let's get a solicitor and we'll go from there'.

The suspect, whilst not known to be 'mentally disordered' and not initially considered 'mentally vulnerable' (nor actually considered 'appropriate adult vulnerable'), was nevertheless provided with an appropriate adult. The custody officer's rationale was that, at the point at which the suspect had been in custody for 12 hours (although, from the context it seems that she had been in for either four or 15 hours), she wanted to admit something she potentially had not done. She was, therefore, placing short-term gains (i.e. being allowed to go home) over long-term implications (the outcome of the case and, potentially, her liberty and livelihood) and was unable, at that point, to think in a manner which was pursuant to her own best interests (see Gudjonsson 1993: 121). Other factors, such as the fact that it was her first time in custody (see Kemp and Hodgson 2016; Dehaghani 2017c) and her gender (see Brown 2015: 92), may have also had an impact on CO16-W's recognition of her vulnerability. It also possible that the severity of the offence may have had a bearing on CO16-W's decision-making (see Chapter 8).

The second case, also mentioned by CO16-W, also concerned a suspect who was not vulnerable under the Code C definition, according to CO16-W. Whilst I had been present when this suspect was booked-back from interview, I had neither been present during the booking-in process nor during the point at which the decision was taken to obtain an appropriate adult. CO16-W (Interview) used this example to highlight what he perceived were the flaws with Code C:

CO16-W: There was a person just at the desk there who I was sorting out just before speaking to you and there is nothing in Code C that would identify her as a vulnerable person but to speak to her and to listen to the way that she lives and functions she clearly is. So I think that safeguarding is false. I think people go through, they tick all the boxes, don't need an appropriate adult and it doesn't cover them.

R: So what were her issues and how does Code C not deal with that?

CO16-W: It sounds a bit stereotypical, when you talk to her and she lives independently, she doesn't get any help or support to manage on a day-to-day basis but when she starts telling you all about her cats, she clearly is very vulnerable. The way she will tell you about police officers, she's got a very high appreciation of the police to the point where whatever a police officer says is right and she's there just to please the police officer and she might not give an honest answer – she will give you an answer that will make you happy which in turn could land her in all sorts of trouble. So I think her views and her upbringing, even though they aren't identified as having any learning difficulties or things like that. Her lifestyle just makes her easily manipulated and the accounts and the things that she will say to you won't always be true but they'll be what she thinks you want her to say.This quote from CO16-W describes acquiescence (see St-Yves 2006: 98 citing Clare and Gudjonsson 1995; Gudjonsson 1993; *R. v Ham* ((1997) 36 BMLR 169, *The Times*, December 12, 1995)); such characteristics would undoubtedly have placed this suspect under the 'mentally vulnerable' category. Again, the suspect's gender may also have a bearing upon the recognition of her vulnerability

(Brown 2015: 92). It is also possible that she had no prior experience of custody and she may have been arrested under suspicion of a serious offence. CO16-W, whilst recognising that childlike acquiescence fell within the remit of Code C (discussed above), failed to connect childlike acquiescence with his perception of, at the very least the latter of, these two women and their vulnerabilities. CO16-W's perception – or, perhaps more accurately, recognition – of vulnerability is more accurate than he ostensibly realised. Therefore, whilst there were, of course, instances where custody officers implemented the appropriate adult safeguard for suspects who were not 'appropriate adult vulnerable', this was undoubtedly the exception rather than the rule.

Disproving vulnerability: not actually vulnerable

Whilst custody officers were required to implement the appropriate adult safeguard where there was doubt as to the mental state or capacity of the suspect (Code C 2017: Note for Guidance 1G. See also Code C), there may have been opportunities to dispel this suspicion (Code C 2017: para 1.4. See also Code C). Custody officers may therefore have pursued lines of inquiry so as to ascertain or disprove vulnerability. They were, however, more inclined towards the latter than the former, as the quote from CO22-M (Interview) exemplifies:

> And if I ask someone if they can read and write and they tell me that they can, it's extremely rare that I ask them to read, extremely rare. But if people say to me that they can't read or write then I'll give them the piece of paper like the white piece of paper that gives the rights and entitlements, I'll ask them to read the top line for me and that then gives me a measure of whether or not this person can in fact read or write. Quite a lot of people will say, 'I really struggle' and you'll say, 'Can you read that for me?', 'You're entitled to a solicitor free of charge', 'Well, you've not really got a big issue with reading or writing. Perhaps someone down the line told you that you're not very good at it but it's more than adequate for what you need in custody'.

Diagnoses and medication

Attempts to disprove vulnerability did not only arise in relation to a suspect's ability to read or write, custody officers also sought to disprove vulnerability in relation to mental disorder. They did so through various means, such as asking whether the condition was self-diagnosed or medically diagnosed; as a marker of vulnerability – the latter was significantly more convincing than the former. Custody officers failed to appreciate that some suspects or detainees may be reluctant to seek a medical diagnosis or may be so paralysed by their mental ill health that they would not feel capable of seeking medical advice or assistance. Where the condition was self-diagnosed this was usually enough to disprove vulnerability entirely. For example, CO30-M (Interview), when explaining why he would not obtain an appropriate adult for someone who has 'self-diagnosed that they've got depression' said that he would ask, '"Have you seen anybody about it?"' and if the suspect responded 'No', CO30-M 'wouldn't necessarily bother with an appropriate adult because … there's no definitive diagnosis'. It did not matter that the suspect had depression, or at the very least felt depressed. The definitive diagnosis is key – it was enough to dispel the notion of vulnerability.

A low dosage on prescription or absence of a prescription may have indicated that the suspect was not sufficiently vulnerable so as to require an appropriate adult. However, a low dosage may have also indicated, to the custody officer, that the condition was either unworthy of attention or, further still, 'not really an illness', as the quote from CO16-W (Interview) indicates:

> You're just struggling with life like most people do and because you haven't got much else to do, you go to your doctors, and your doctor's a very busy person and they think, 'if I put you on these low level little anti-psychotic tablets, these little low level anti-depression tablets, at least it gets rid of you for a few months and it might even have that mellowing effect of you deciding that your depression's all dealt with'.… You can probably pre-empt most of the answers that they'll give you on the risk assessment in relation to which GP they're under, which medication they're taking.

In addition to suggesting that the vulnerability was merely a fabrication, a low dosage of medication could also cast doubt upon the validity of depression as a worthy mental illness and on the reliability of the prescription practices of the GP. Such scepticism (see Reiner 2010: 121–2) may result in a blanket, uniform approach to all suspects who see the same GP or are treated within the same catchment area.

Once it was established that the suspect had a genuine medical diagnosis and had been prescribed medication, the custody officer may have then sought to ascertain whether the suspect was taking his or her prescribed medication or otherwise complying with his or her regime. The reason for this was simple – if a suspect had been diagnosed and was taking prescribed medication then he or she was effectively 'cured' of the condition; it had no ill-effect, he or she was not in the middle of an episode and was thus, by the custody officer's logic, not vulnerable, as the quote from CO30-M (Interview) indicates:

> I don't know what kind of condition, say schizophrenia, for example or depression. If somebody has been diagnosed with that and they're being treated for it medically and they're up to date with all their medication and they can function normally in society then I wouldn't necessarily say that they were vulnerable.

Appearances can be deceiving

Whilst it has been highlighted that the use of drugs or alcohol can mask a vulnerability (Cummins 2007; Bradley 2009), custody officers seemed not to fully recognise this. Instead, it was felt that drug and/or alcohol consumption could result in the *appearance* of vulnerability; this appearance of vulnerability would then be removed through the sobering-up process. A distinction was made between a 'genuine mental health issue or [whether] they're under the influence of drink and drugs' (CO13-W Interview). Whilst this caused difficulty, custody officers nevertheless sought to ascertain whether the drugs, or alcohol, 'impact[ed] on their [the suspect's] behaviour' (*ibid.*). Questions were also raised with regard to whether the mental health issue is 'drug-induced, or alcohol-induced ... where it came from and whether the person is managing it' (CO14-W Interview). Custody officers therefore saw the use of drugs or alcohol as a means of disproving vulnerability. The inclusion of the warning in Note for Guidance 1GC (see Chapter 5) may serve to further complicate matters whereby custody officers may now be even more dismissive of the vulnerability of those who are under the influence of drugs or alcohol. However, it is possible that someone who is drug or alcohol-addicted, i.e. physically or psychologically dependent, may require the assistance of an appropriate adult. Ostensibly, the only exception was where drug or alcohol use resulted in a severe, permanent condition such as brain damage. Suspects who had suffered permanent cognitive damage as a result of sustained substance misuse would be recognised 'appropriate adult vulnerable'. Such an example was given by two custody officers (CO11-W and CO13-W): this suspect was so impaired, allegedly through years of cannabis use, that custody officers doubted whether he would be able to communicate, even with the assistance of an appropriate adult.

Detention in custody was also thought to exacerbate a suspect's condition and so custody officers attempted to ascertain whether the suspect would exhibit this vulnerability when outside of custody. Because custody is 'quite a stressful environment ... if somebody's got mental health issues we're probably seeing the bad side of it ... and how the stress side of it makes them angry or anything else' (CO1-W Interview). CO1-W (Interview) further explained:

> Perhaps seeing them [vulnerable people] in their own environment whether that is in hospital or somewhere like a day centre or something, perhaps you'll be able to recognise the signs of people who are vulnerable because of mental health rather than just when they're coming in kicking and shouting and screaming.

They therefore attempted to disprove that the vulnerability arose from something innate and prove that it was 'merely' circumstantial. As CO28-W (Interview) highlighted, in addition to the various issues that person may be dealing with,

> you've got all the other factors to consider, you know, the stress of being at the police station, the medication that they're on that's not to do with mental health issues because they may have other health issues, alcohol, drugs.

However, being detained in custody, and all the feelings, thoughts, and emotions associated with this, could have caused the suspect to become situationally vulnerable; detention in custody should not be used as a factor in disproving vulnerability. The cause of the vulnerability is insignificant; what is imperative in these circumstances is the suspect's mental state (or potential mental state) during his or her time in custody.

Reliability and choice

Custody officers expressed, whether explicitly or implicitly, that suspects were guilty and untrustworthy, even when I highlighted that not every suspect or detainee was factually guilty. Following on from this presumption of guilt, deceit, and dishonesty, some suspects were thought not to be genuinely vulnerable, particularly those who were labelled 'criminal', and therefore information by such individuals to the custody officer regarding, inter alia, their mental or physical state or condition was thought to be unreliable. Suspects were viewed as 'playing on' (CO1-W Interview) their condition rather than it being 'a genuine sort of thing' (*ibid.*). It was thought that

> a lot of [suspects] use it [saying that they have a condition] as a control strategy by saying 'Well I have this condition and I'm in control in so much as you don't know what it is and you're not a healthcare professional'. And again I have to take their word for it until I have it verified.
>
> (CO28-M Interview)

This form of power-play was also seen to be 'purely … given off the back of being an alcoholic or, sorry, being drunk or being under the influence of drugs' (CO3-W Interview). Or, as CO3-W (Interview) also highlighted, it could be 'somebody who is just being goddamn bloody minded who says, "I've got everything"'. There was therefore an awareness that the 'people in front of you aren't always telling the truth'. Although the approach could be to 'go risk averse and if anybody's got any level of mental illness, have an appropriate adult', CO3-W did not think this was the right approach to take.

It was also felt that some suspects had chosen to be 'vulnerable'. For example, travellers would not be provided with an appropriate adult because they had made a *'lifestyle choice'* (CO22-M Interview) not to read or write (and were also typically viewed as *'astute'* (*ibid.*)). Such an approach was also apparent in relation to suspects who had depression: it was also deemed to be a lifestyle choice or something that was merely circumstantial and therefore of insufficient severity, i.e. it did not impact sufficiently upon the suspect's daily life. Many custody officers felt that suspects claimed that they were depressed due to an inability to cope with life events or felt depressed out of boredom – for example, 'the lifestyle of the individual will be a big clue as to why they're depressed' (CO18-W Interview); or the suspect will '[say] that [they]'ve got depression because [they]'re not taking great steps to cope with life and [they]'re saying "Woe is me" and that's why [they] keep going out and shop-lifting instead of getting a job' (CO16-W Interview. On this point see Loftus 2009: 95). Depression was also viewed as synonymous with being 'just pissed off, fed up, whatever you want to call it' (CO1-W Interview). Custody officers tended to view depression as a turn of phrase and/or something which was overused, a condition that 'everyone has these days', or something that someone fabricates to avail of social welfare support, as the following quote (CO29-M Interview) illustrates:

> Speaking as a police officer, not just a custody sergeant, I've been doing this job for a long time now and one of the reasons people get themselves classed as being depressed is so they can go on medication and get their benefits. I have been round at people's houses to get their medication on occasion and they have boxes and boxes and boxes of unopened medication. They collect their prescription every week and don't use it.

Depression was also viewed by custody officers as a way for suspects to express their frustration with having been caught. For example, CO22-M (Interview) stated that 'the vast majority of people that come in will say that they're depressed.... It isn't because they're suffering from a medical or mental condition of depression, it's because they've been caught and are in custody'. He went on to add, 'if we had an appropriate adult for every time some said they were depressed, we would have an appropriate adult for virtually every person that comes through the door'. The perceived widespread nature of depression meant that those with depression were almost automatically excluded from the category of 'appropriate adult vulnerability' and, potentially, 'vulnerability'. Whilst custody officers tended to be most critical of depression and anxiety (and those who had such conditions), they also discounted the vulnerability of those with other mental disorders, albeit in a less critical manner. Mental disorder was largely disregarded as a distinct category. For example, as CO33-M (Interview) explained, 'I've one in custody at the moment [that has] got bi-polar. That in itself wouldn't necessarily mean that an appropriate adult is needed'. Even if a suspect came 'in with schizophrenia [or] psychosis ... they know the difference between right and wrong, they know why they're here' and therefore were deemed not to require an appropriate adult (*ibid.*). 'Appropriate adult vulnerability' was ostensibly connected with deservingness (Brown 2015: 32) and a lack of agency (Goodin 1985: 129); those who made 'choices' were perceived as blameworthy for their misfortunate. This interaction between choice and perceptions of 'deservingness' have been well-documented (Christie 1986; Brown 2015; Katz 2013; Wacquant 2009). Those who have exercised agency or choice are responsibilised (see Garland 2001) and their vulnerability denied (see Dehaghani 2017c, for examples).

To be considered 'appropriate adult vulnerable', the suspect must typically exhibit serious issues with understanding, capacity, and/or comprehension. The approach taken towards adult suspects contrasts quite significantly with that taken towards young suspects who, whether perceived as neither 'appropriate adult vulnerable' nor 'vulnerable', were provided with an appropriate adult (CO33-M Interview):

> We will have people at 15 years come in who are very bright and clearly don't need appropriate adults, they understand exactly what is going on, they've been through the system so many times, it's incredible. They've probably spent as much time in a police station as I do, a lot of our recidivists.

Defining the role of the appropriate adult

The role of the appropriate adult can be ascertained through a range of sources, however, much ambiguity nevertheless remains (see Chapter 2). Whilst this role is undoubtedly subject to the construction of, amongst others, the custody officer, relatively little is known about how custody officers interpret the role of the appropriate adult. Yet, such insights are incredibly useful when unpacking how custody officers construct vulnerability.

An ally, a guide, a support

Custody officers recognised that appropriate adults were 'there to help and guide the person that they're there to assist' (CO11-W Interview). Appropriate adults thus provided 'the support of having someone there that they know, from their side' (CO28-M Interview). The appropriate adult was also viewed as 'somebody there to act in [the suspect's] interests' (CO24-M Interview) or someone that 'will give you [referring to the suspect] an honest answer of what is going on, what will happen, a friend' (CO29-M Interview). In contrast to the largely self-interested legal representative (however, see Chapter 8) or the police officer whose role may be perceived as one of discipline, punishment or instilling fear (see Kemp and Hodgson 2016: 164; Jessiman and Cameron 2017), the appropriate adult was seen as someone who was kind, caring and without motive (other than their goal of 'looking after' the suspect). The appropriate adult was considered 'an ally for a suspect in custody' (CO13-W Interview) because:

> It's a harsh environment, particularly if you've never been in custody before, and it can be forbidding. The appropriate adult is someone that's, I suppose, going to be on their side and as much as they can, look out for their welfare. They're going to talk to them first before they're interviewed, to an extent going to gain their confidence, and someone who the [suspect] is going to be comfortable with in custody.

Such interpretations could suggest that the appropriate adult was not impartial but instead exists so as to protect the suspect (rather than the police). However, the provision of support could also be considered as something that puts the suspect at ease, which, in turn, helps the police with their investigation. The support was not seen simply as an emotional one; the appropriate adult was also *'there to support the person in making sure that they understand the process, what's going on, what's being asked of them, that they understand their rights and entitlements, that they know what they are, what they can do'* (CO24-M Interview).

The appropriate adult may also perform a protective or welfare function. This protective function was viewed as somewhat synonymous with that of a carer or parent – i.e. 'to be what a parent is to a child … as a crutch really' (CO4-W Interview), or 'to act as a parent would with a teenager, as much as they may not [understand] some of the technicalities of the law, some of the processes' (CO18 Interview). This comparison is unsurprising, given the comparisons made between 'appropriate adult vulnerability' and childlike characteristics. The welfare function of appropriate adult's meant not simply assistance with the process, but also a means through which to ensure other rights and entitlements (CO24-M Interview; CO28-M Interview):

> That that person is being cared for, that they understand that they can have food, drink, they can go outside. So basically they can understand what they are allowed to do through PACE, what we should be giving them, how they should be looked after, they should be reviewed, all that sort of stuff, that they have been reviewed. It's there to make sure the rules, the regulations, and how we look after them are being abided by and that person understands.
>
> The appropriate adult is there to ensure that their rights other than their legal rights… and any concerns that they have are being met by the police when they're in custody. That they are eating and drinking, have they ever had access to food and water [and] medical attention.

Facilitating communication, obtaining information and ensuring compliance

The predominant function of the appropriate adult was to facilitate communication between the suspect and the police and to ensure that the suspect understands what was being asked of him or her. For example, it *was* important to ascertain from the suspect 'whether or not you think they can form an opinion and give you their side of the story adequately enough' (CO17-W Interview) – the 'appropriate adult will explain things in layman's terms. And just be there to assist the reading and writing, almost' (*ibid.*). The appropriate adult could 'ensure that they [suspects] have an understanding of the processes that they're going through, the interview questioning side of things so that they're not being, arguably, oppressed and starting to just say something' (CO3-W Interview). However, the 'appropriate adult … should not answer questions on behalf of the client but they should make sure that that client understands the question fully before they answer it' (CO21-M Interview). As CO14-W (Interview) highlighted, the appropriate adult can:

> [M]ake sure the person being interviewed understands what's going and sometimes clarify what they say … make sure that the person understands what's going on and they're able to put across what they want to put across in the most effective way possible. That's what I think that the appropriate adult is there for.

The predominant focus was on the interview rather than other elements of the process. This communicative function was helpful, not only for ensuring that the suspect could impart his or her account most effectively or reliably, but also for ensuring that the police could obtain the information that they required and thereby conduct their interviews effectively and efficiently (although CO16-W felt that the appropriate adult was not always able to do so – see Chapter 10). The 'appropriate adult … might be the sort of person to say, "Well, this is the opportunity to talk to the police about why you've been arrested and this might, this might help you, with what issues are there in the first place"' (CO1-W Interview). The appropriate adult could also enable custody officers to obtain information required to conduct the risk assessment, as CO16-W (Interview) highlights:

> The appropriate adult also needs to get relevant information for me so whilst they're not telling which doctor they're seeing, which psychiatrist they're seeing, which medication they're on – they don't want to tell me that but whilst they're not telling me that, it's going to mean that they're here for longer, we can't get them interviewed, we can't get them dealt with and it's just delaying their release from here. And that appropriate adult has got to find out what's made them land in here.

The appropriate adult could therefore assist with the obtaining information for both the custody officer and the police investigation. This is unsurprising given that the main focus of the RCCP was on minimising the risk of an unreliable or false confession and very little else. The appropriate adult could also be used to ensure suspect compliance (see Choongh 1997; 1998) with the various procedures such as 'the samples side of things, because fingerprints, photographs and DNA can be taken by force if necessary. Again they're there to sort of facilitate communication between us and the detained person so they understand that "We will be taking your fingerprints, please comply"' (CO30-M Interview). Appropriate adults were viewed, although less commonly so, as a means through which to placate the suspect, such as calming a purportedly volatile suspect who had schizophrenia (Interaction 14-W. See also Bean and Nemitz 1995: 47).

Exercising independence and ensuring fairness

The appropriate adult was also, but less commonly, viewed as 'someone who isn't wearing a uniform; [they] haven't got that "them and us"' (CO28-M Interview). The appropriate adult could act as a check on the police and 'ensure that procedures are conducted fairly and undue pressure isn't placed on the person who is potentially vulnerable that is going to blurt out something that they ought not to be saying, that's going to incriminate them wrongly somehow' (CO8-W Interview). As CO4-M (Interview) highlighted, the appropriate adult could 'make sure that the vulnerable person's comfortable, and isn't pressurised or anything like that' rather than ensuring that 'the police officer [who] is interviewing … [gets] the answers that they want'. Thus, and as Code C eludes to, the appropriate adult's presence could mitigate against false confessions or otherwise misleading information. Yet, CO16-W (Interview) felt that this was:

> old fashioned in the sense of pre-PACE and trying to make sure cops did things right, then you would, for your ... vulnerable people, you would have someone coming in to make sure the cops didn't make the person write the statement and then sign it. And it was more correct in those days, making sure the cops were doing things properly, lawfully, correctly, and they were looking after the vulnerable but also checking up on the police.... They're here to ensure that the police are treating them right and they'll do that bit. And to be honest nowadays, the cops are so scared of losing their jobs, there's that much audio, there's that much CCTV around, the cops would be doing it anyway.

He therefore felt that, at least this function of the appropriate adult, was relatively pointless. Whilst it is feasible to suggest that the police are no longer oppressive and coercive (at least in the same manner that they were in pre-PACE era), it is undoubtedly changes to law and guidance that have resulted in a less coercive (although not coercion-free) approach. Moreover, the appropriate adult is not simply there to detect obvious oppression or ill-treatment, but also to identify more inconspicuous or 'softer' signs of oppressive or corrupt behaviour. The appropriate adult is also present to ensure that the suspect understands what is happening, can enforce his or her rights, can give best evidence, and can act in his or her best interests (see Chapter 2). The appropriate adult is supposed to provide resilience.

Conclusion – Code C or custody officer criteria?

To be recognised as vulnerable, the suspect had to 'perform' vulnerability (see Brown 2015); such vulnerability differed depending on purpose but, whilst having a gendered dimension, most certainly excluded factors such as race and sexuality. For the appropriate adult safeguard, the suspect must have performed in a child-like manner and must exhibit clear and often unambiguous issues with communication, capacity and/or comprehension. Custody officers held their own interpretation(s) of what vulnerability and the appropriate adult safeguard mean. Such interpretations were not entirely aligned with Code C, but could be understood when placed in the context of the wider operation of police work, the criminal justice system, and the focus of Code C. Whilst appreciating that vulnerability could be something broader and could encompass all suspects, they restricted the definition, when considering the appropriate adult safeguard, to something which focused predominantly on communication, capacity, and/or comprehension. Custody officers were therefore already, at least partly, applying the 'functional test' that has since been introduced by the 2018 version of the Code. Yet, as the data illustrate, their view of the vulnerable suspect's ability was somewhat skewed and value-laden. It remains to be seen whether changes to

Code C will result in any change to custody officer interpretation of 'vulnerability' and the appropriate adult safeguard.

Custody officer interpretations of vulnerability were supported by their view of the appropriate adult safeguard which, whilst including other functions such as oversight, welfare, support, advice and assistance, mainly facilitates communication. Rather than attempting to prove that the suspect was vulnerable or indicate some doubt, attempts were made to disprove vulnerability by illustrating that the suspect *could* understand what was happening or would happen. Yet, custody officers either failed to or decided not to recognise why suspects falling out of their (arguably restrictive) category may nevertheless require an appropriate adult. A suspect who is vulnerable (according to the 2018 or pre-2018 versions of the Code) but who nevertheless understands what is going on around him or her, may not be able to withstand pressure or adequately give his or her account pursuant to his or her best interests. The suspect may feel under attack within the adversarial interview setting after having been detained in a six-foot by eight-foot cell for between one and, potentially, 24 hours (or longer). The suspect may be unable or may feel reluctant to exercise his or her rights or ask for food, water, or fresh air. The suspect may, as a result of a low mood, anxious state, or addiction be willing to say anything to be released from custody (like one of the two vulnerable women discussed by CO16-W). The suspect may have an unwavering trust in the police and may say whatever they want to hear (like the other of the two vulnerable women discussed by CO16-W). However, provided the suspect is able to comprehend questions and formulate answers without the assistance of an independent third party, the custody officer will, in almost all circumstances, be satisfied that the suspect can move through the custody processes unaided. In order to explore the investigation of vulnerability in further depth, discussion will now turn to how custody officers identify vulnerability.

Notes

1 This is true, not simply in relation to adults, but also for young suspects (see Dehaghani 2017c; Kemp and Hodgson 2016).

2 In the current version of the Code, an adult may be vulnerable if he or she meets one of more of the criteria under para 1.13d and has or may have (although is not necessarily known to have) a mental disorder or mental health condition.

3 A small number (N = 4) of participating custody officers had recently started working in custody – two at each suite. One such custody officer (CO27-M) seemed to be aware of the Code C guidance and another custody officer (CO31-M) was not interviewed for practical reasons.

7 Identifying vulnerability in police custody

> It's only by doing some sort of scoping … not only by asking questions of the detainee or questions of the officers that brought them in, looking at whatever else is available, for example previous times they've been in custody, previous medical history to [try] and gain a picture of potential risk. And I suppose for me that is part of where the experience and my life experience, my experience in policing and my experience working here, albeit short, has led me to trust my own instincts.
>
> (CO18-W Interview)[1]

Introduction

Once vulnerability has been defined, further processes must be undergone prior to the implementation of the appropriate adult safeguard. One step in the process is the identification of vulnerability. Previous studies have highlighted the numerous difficulties with identifying whether an appropriate adult is required. Irving and McKenzie, in the first review of PACE in 1989, pointed towards the many improvements post-PACE. However, they highlighted a number of the problems with the police interview, particularly how vulnerability was identified by custody officers. Criticisms were not levelled at custody officers for their failings as they were 'working as the exigencies of the problem allow' (Irving and McKenzie 1989: 203); they suggested that if the diagnostic ability of the police could not be improved then the role of medical and social staff should take greater priority. Such findings were largely supported by Gudjonsson, Clare, Rutter and Pearse (1993: 26) who found that the most disabled and vulnerable detainees were identified by the police and the appropriate adult was called when the police considered it necessary. Whilst the researchers found a higher incidence of those requiring the appropriate adult than custody officers had identified, they noted that there were 'no obvious signs that police officers can be trained to look for' (*ibid.*: 24); particular difficulties could arise with regard to those with significant intellectual impairment who often appear to have reasonable social functioning (*ibid.*: 26). Schizophrenia was the most readily identified condition; depression was the most commonly unidentified condition. Further, almost 9% of detainees had an IQ below 70 (considered learning disabled), another 42% had an IQ between 70 and 79 (considered borderline learning disabled), and around one third of the sample were intellectually disadvantaged (*ibid.*: 24).

According to Palmer and Hart (1996: 28–9), custody officers relied on observational signs such as 'florid behaviour' and 'tangible clues' and their own 'perception', also drawing upon information from previous contact and previous records (where available). Identification was also facilitated by 'informants' such as family, volunteer groups, social workers, arresting officers, solicitors and the suspect him or herself (*ibid.*). Custody officers in Palmer and Hart's study (1996: 28) said that they usually treated all such information as reliable. Bucke and Brown's research (1997: 8) highlighted how the proportion of appropriate adults was lower for mentally disordered suspects when compared with young suspects. Phillips and Brown (1998: 55–6) ascertained that less than half of mentally disordered suspects were provided with an appropriate adult (33 out of 67), 20 of these instances involved a doctor, and, moreover, custody officers tended to await the doctor's verdict. Medford, Gudjonsson and Pearse (2003: 253) highlighted that, of the vulnerable adults brought into police custody within a month, 600 were not provided with an appropriate adult. An analysis of custody records (Bradley 2009: 43) in the East Midlands illustrated that an appropriate adult, in respect of suspects with mental illness, was only used in 0.016% (38) of the instances rather than the estimated 14% (although NAAN (2015) estimated that 11–22% of arrested adults require the assistance of an appropriate adult). According to McKinnon and Grubin (2013: 402), 39% of the detainee population had any mental health problem and 3% had a learning disability; police assessments were able to identify around 50% of those with mental health or learning disabilities. A recent NAAN (2015: 10) report found that there was inadequate identification of the need for an appropriate adult, citing issues with:

> [A] lack of effective and systematic screening, a lack of training for the police … no visual or behaviour clues … the influence of alcohol or drugs complicating the assessment, a disregard of self-reporting, the failure to use historical information … to identify learning disabilities, [suspect reluctance to disclose], [the use of standardised questions].
>
> (2015: 4. See also Hodgson 1997; McKinnon and Grubin 2010).

Appropriate adults are not, however, always called when there were suspicions regarding the vulnerability of the suspect (Brown *et al.* 1992: 48). As the researchers pointed out, this was because the condition was not considered of sufficient severity 'or that initial concerns may subsequently have been felt to have been exaggerated' (*ibid.*: 78). In sum, previous research highlighted deficiencies with identification: there were no clear signs to look out for, and custody officers had to rely on the manifestation of obvious signs and their own perceptions of the detainee. Such deficiencies were not, however, the fault of the custody officer. Yet, Bean and Nemitz (1995: 48) seemed to disagree with this assumption: they argued that vulnerability *can* often be identified but problems arise because of how custody officers make sense of the information provided to them.

This chapter will unpack the process of identification, illustrating how vulnerability could (or should be) identified, how it is identified, and the various obstacles to identification. After drawing upon the guidance (or, arguably, lack thereof), it will examine what custody officers said about identifying vulnerability and what was observed in respect of how custody officers identify vulnerability. The various themes examined herewith can be placed in the wider context of police-work, in both how they understand their world and how they interpret their identification role. The findings explored within this chapter share many similarities with previous research but also some key differences. Most notably, Bean and Nemitz' suspicion, above, holds true: the issue is not always whether vulnerability *can* be identified but instead how custody officers process the information available.

Identifying vulnerability: the law and guidance

Whilst neither PACE nor Code C establish how vulnerability should be identified, previous versions of Code C (Note for Guidance 1G) set out a 'benefit of the doubt' test, which required that an appropriate adult be called in the event that the custody officer had 'any doubt about the mental state or capacity of the detainee'. This was also reiterated in Annex E para 1 where it stated that a suspect should be treated as vulnerable for the purposes of the Code should an officer have any suspicion or be told in good faith that the suspect is vulnerable. This was further reiterated in para 1.4, where it also stated that a suspect should be treated as vulnerable for the purposes of the Code unless there existed clear evidence to dispel the suspicion that the suspect was vulnerable. These provisions made clear that the custody officer need not establish with absolute certainty that the suspect was vulnerable. However, the wording of these provisions could be subject to wide or narrow interpretation. For example, 'any suspicion', taken at its widest, would mean that all suspects should have been treated as vulnerable. 'Clear evidence' may be difficult to ascertain, short of a full psychological assessment of the suspect. Further, the inclusion of the term 'good faith' would suggest that a suspect should be provided with an appropriate adult where information relating to their vulnerability is provided honestly and sincerely, however, because suspects are 'untrustworthy', the information provided by them may be, consequentially, disregarded.

This latter issue seems to have been resolved in the most recent version of the Code as any: all references to 'good faith' have been removed. The 2018 iteration of the Code resolves some of these issues: reference is now made to 'reason to suspect', which is, at least on the face of it, not as all-encompassing as 'any suspicion' (Annex E para 1); the Notes for Guidance require that the person making the decision on the appropriate adult safeguard consider whether the suspect has met the functional test, compared with the previous reference to 'any doubt'; and para 1.4 also refers to 'reason to suspect' coupled with guidance on how to gather 'evidence' of vulnerability.

Usually, prior to being taken to a cell, the suspect must be booked in, a procedure that involves asking a number of questions, namely as part of the 'risk assessment'. The purpose of the risk assessment is to alert custody officers to any potential issues such as, inter alia, physical or mental ill health, learning needs or self-harm or suicide risk. The current risk assessment finds its origins in the Safer Detention guidance (ACPO 2006; 2012), which, since 2013, has been superseded by the College of Policing APP on Detention and Custody (2018).[2] Upon booking in, the suspect or detainee is the responsibility of the custody officer[3] who must '[document] and [record] the risk assessment for every detainee in the custody record in accordance with paragraphs 3.6 to 3.10 of PACE Code C' (*ibid.*). 'The arresting or escorting officer should make checks with any immediately available sources of information relevant to the welfare of the arrested person' (*ibid.*) – this may include the suspect (or detainee) him or herself, friends or relatives, the Police National Computer (PNC), the Police National Database (PND), legal representatives, HCPs, other relevant bodies, and appropriate adults (*ibid.*).

The risk assessment includes a range of questions, which may provide information through which to identify vulnerability. As McKinnon and Grubin (2010) have noted, the risk assessment questions are more likely to flag up mental illness, drug/alcohol misuse or self-harm rather than intellectual disability. The risk assessment(s) observed at Waterside and Mapletown, whilst somewhat lengthier than the College of Policing APP, broadly follow the same format. The Detention and Custody (2018a) assessment asks the following questions:

1 How are you feeling in yourself now?
2 Do you have any illness or injury?
3 Are you experiencing any mental ill health or depression?
4 Would you like to speak to the doctor/nurse/paramedic (as appropriate)?
5 Have you seen a doctor or been to a hospital for this illness or injury?
6 Are you taking or supposed to be taking any tablets or medication? If yes, what are they and what are they for?
7 Are you in contact with any medical or support service? If yes, what is the name of your contact or support worker there?
8 Do you have a card that tells you who to contact in a crisis?
9 Have you ever tried to harm yourself? If yes, how often, how long ago, how did you harm yourself, have you sought help?

Such questions could enable custody officers in their identification of mental disorder and/or mental vulnerability, with question one assisting with situational vulnerability, questions two and three potentially highlighting mental disorder, and question 7 helping to flag-up learning difficulty, in addition to mental disorder. Additional questions – not included on the APP guidance – covering special schooling, ability to read or write, and ability to tell the time may also assist in identifying learning disability or difficulty. However, such questions did not form part of the main risk assessment and were instead supplementary, thus requiring that an issue was flagged up first.

Since May 2018, the Code, for the first time (Note for Guidance E5 & 1GA), contains information on how vulnerability may be identified. This is through, for example, behaviour, mental health and capacity, self-report, information from relatives and friends, information from police officers/staff and police records, information from health and social care (including information provided by liaison and diversion), and/or information from other professionals who know or who have had previous contact with the individual concerned (including assessments arranged by the police or at the request of the individual, appropriate adult[4] or solicitor).

Identifying vulnerability: the reality

Whilst law and guidance may provide some information on how vulnerability could be identified, this is merely abstract. Rather, the realities of identifying vulnerability must be explored in order to fully understand the task faced by custody officers. The various means of identifying vulnerability will be explored herewith.

The risk assessment: answers given to self-report

The general consensus was that the risk assessment worked well to identify vulnerability and risk, and custody officers, as CO22-M (Interview) pointed out, are generally 'quite happy with the risk assessment that we do'. It was recognised that the risk assessment had 'built up over the years' (*ibid.*) as:

> [W]hen I first started in custody, the risk assessment was probably like four or five questions, in all truth, 'Have you ever harmed yourself? Do you feel like harming yourself?' and that would really be about it and then looking at very, very basic mental health. It has evolved tremendously. There [are] a lot of questions in there now.

The risk assessment was therefore recognised as being 'far more intensive than what they used to be' (CO21-M Interview) and was viewed to have 'changed in such a short period of time' (CO1-W Interview). It was also viewed as a 'good basis to work from' (CO14-W Interview) or 'good as a base-line to give you a good starter for where they are' (CO27-M Interview). The questions asked within the risk assessment, due in part to their specificity, provided a basis through which to identify vulnerability. For example, CO29-M (Interview) commented that '[t]he questions written down are quite specific and will give a broad outline of a person's health as well as mental health, if answered correctly' and CO8-W (Interview) commented that '[t]here are questions within the risk assessment that are designed to try and identify vulnerability.... So, for example, yes, you can get a flavour from talking to someone for a few minutes as to whether or not they appear to have learning difficulties'. The answers given to the questions can indicate vulnerability and often questions can trigger further answers, as CO24-M (Interview) explained: 'there are certain questions that we ask to everybody, they're almost like trigger questions that, when you ask them, they will bring, if someone's willing to tell you, what's up with them'. The efficacy of the risk assessment was evident during observations: it was seen to provide custody officers with 15 to 45 minutes during which they could engage with suspects, thus allowing custody officers to detect 'unusual' behaviour or other 'signs' of vulnerability.

History: previous appropriate adult

Custody officers, in addition to using the risk assessment questions, also used resources such as previous custody records (see Palmer and Hart 1996) and information contained on the PNC. The PNC, according to the APP (College of Policing 2018b), 'should be considered the primary reference for recording and accessing risk information'. All information was recorded electronically in both sites, with paper records used only as a last resort, e.g. in the event of a systems-failure (which happened once at Mapletown). At Waterside, the PNC records were typically checked by custody officers when the suspect/detainee was at the desk and were used as a first point of reference; previous custody records were only used if the custody officers had grave concern for the suspect/detainee's welfare (it was claimed that the custody suite was too busy to conduct these checks routinely, and indeed it was usually busy). At Mapletown, the PNC check was typically conducted by the arresting officer(s) prior to the suspect/detainee's arrival at the booking-in desk, and previous records seemed to be checked frequently (although not always).

During observations both CO31-M and CO20-W (who were relatively new to the custody officer role) identified vulnerability through checking previous records for information that the appropriate adult had been used on previous occasions. As CO18-W commented at interview: '[l]et's explore what was previously, if you've got the luxury of that. What was done previously in interview when this person's been in custody; have they had an appropriate adult before?' At both sites the use of an appropriate adult on previous occasions was often, but not always, a sign that an appropriate adult should be called in present circumstances – it was an indicator but was not pre-emptive. A suspect who had been provided with an appropriate adult would be 'more likely to have one again' (CO33-M Interview), with some suspects having 'been in custody that many times you just know … they will always have an appropriate adult' (CO9-W Interview). Typically, in such cases, it was 'quite obvious from their medical history that [the suspect] is a vulnerable person' (CO28-M Interview) and, in such cases, the more efficient approach involved calling an appropriate adult, rather than deliberating or seeking advice. The previous appropriate adult approach, as CO30-M (Interview) explained, was a 'fall-back', particularly where the custody officer was 'not too sure about it', however, this was 'only an avenue if they've been in custody before'.

Healthcare advice

Custody officers often relied on HCPs (but also FMEs and AMHPs where available) for assistance when identifying vulnerability (see also Nemitz and Bean 2001: 599). Although HCPs could provide advice to a custody officer, the ultimate decision rests with the custody officer himself (College of Policing 2018b. See also Code C: paras 3.5–3.11 and Annex G, paras 5, 7 and 8). HCPs were available on-site 24 hours a day seven days a week at both Waterside and Mapletown. During observations, Mapletown also had AMHPs on site during the day but such a resource was only introduced in Waterside a few months after observations had ended. Custody officers made referrals to HCPs for, inter alia, physical health issues, medication needs, and mental health issues. The custody officer could consult the HCP (and/or AMHP, if available) for advice on whether suspects/detainees were fit to detain, fit for interview, in need of an appropriate adult, or fit for release (see College of Policing 2018b). In relation to the appropriate adult safeguard, assistance was often only sought where an issue (although not necessarily *the* issue) had already been identified, as CO21-M (Interview) highlighted:

> As a custody sergeant, you'll make that initial assessment and you think, 'This person could do with a little bit further than this, I think I'm going to refer them to the mental health practitioners that we have in custody'. And those people can go and have a word with them. And then they'll come and report to us what their findings are.

HCPs and, where available, AMHPs and FMEs (although FMEs were typically only called for what were deemed to be more serious matters) were viewed as invaluable resource due to their expertise, as CO14-W (Interview) highlighted: '[s]ometimes, you know, you get a feeling that, "I'm going to refer them to the medical staff to assess them" and they usually, because they have skills and experience and knowledge, can often push in that direction as well'. By contrast, custody officers felt lacking in knowledge, as CO12-W (Interview) indicated: '[a]ny doubts really, it's the nurse to see them. They're the medically qualified persons, I'm not. I can't even give a paracetamol'. The recommendations of the HCPs, FMEs and AMHPs were, more often than not, accepted; they could aid identification of vulnerability or implement the safeguard (or not), where the custody officer believed that the suspect was (potentially) vulnerable.

Informants: family, friends, solicitors, and other officers

As CO4-W (Interview) pointed out: '[t]he officers, the officer they've spoken to, relatives' or 'any issues at the time of arrest' could facilitate identification of vulnerability. Solicitors (see Chapter 8) and friends could also pass information along to the custody officer. As CO4-W (Interview) further reiterated, 'a lot of the time … it's down to the officers who are making the arrests who are aware because they've arrested the person at home so the family have told them'. Custody officers might have a lot of information prior to the suspect arriving at the custody suite, as CO28-M (Interview) indicated:

> Very rarely does somebody come up to the desk where we're not pre-loaded. We know a lot of information about them. Even if it's the officer who's coming, 'What are the circumstances of arrest?', 'Well, yeah, he had to knives in his hands and he was stabbing himself and he turned on us [the arresting officers] with the knives'. Straight away you're starting to think 'That's not normal behaviour, there's obviously some issues there'. Call it mental health issues.

The suspect in question was not provided with an appropriate adult, but knowledge of his mental health problems was used to make others decisions (Interaction 107-W):

> Suspect has been brought in for affray. Police arrived at his home and he was self-harming (using knives). When officers tried to help him, he allegedly ran at them, waving the knives. Arresting officer advised that suspect has no pain threshold (due to mental block) and has a tendency to bite. He has previously stabbed himself through the arm and leg. Suspect has visible self-harm marks and had been hospitalised for this prior to being brought into custody. He appears quite distant but gives very clear and detailed answers. CO28-M explains that he will make him an appointment with a nurse. Suspect claims no difficulty with reading and writing but has mental health issues. CO28-M states 'So you understand everything? Yeah', but did not give suspect a chance to respond. Suspect is allowed to keep earrings and rings but advised that if he starts to self-harm these will be removed. CO28-M requests that HCP assess suspect for fitness to detain and fitness for interview. Suspect is placed on constant observations (camera). No appropriate adult was provided.

Whilst it may be only used for the purposes of ascertaining risk, information provided by informants (amongst other sources) can be vital. Whilst this was a non-PACE matter and did not require an appropriate adult, these interactions (Interactions 142-W and 145-W) indicate how important information from 'informants' is (it also serves to indicate some of the challenges custody officers face when identifying vulnerability or risk):

> Detainee has been brought in for a failing to appear at a magistrates' court (elsewhere in England). CO4-W carries out the risk assessment, to which the detainee reports no issues. The detainee's answers are accepted by CO4-W and he is placed on Level 1 observations (60-minute visits only). In my own estimation, the detainee appears dishevelled, disoriented and withdrawn. He is avoiding eye contact during the booking-in procedure. I inquire from CO4-W how he came to this decision and he explains that, whilst previous records

> show that the detainee suffered from depression, this was 18 months ago and he therefore does not wish to rely on this. Later the detainee's family come into custody to advise that he has serious mental health issues and should not be left alone in a cell. As a result, the observation level is changed from Level 1 to Level 3 (CCTV and 30-minute visits).

In this case, CO4-W either ignored or failed to recognise the risk.

Whilst Palmer and Hart's study (1996: 28–9) seemed to suggest that informants played a considerable role in assisting with the identification of vulnerability, during interview in this study only four custody officers mentioned relying on information from officers or friends and family. There were also only three occasions where information from informants was used to identify vulnerability so that the appropriate adult safeguard could be implemented. With the increase in risk assessment questions and a greater presence of HCPs (and, albeit to a lesser extent, AMHPs and FMEs) in the custody suite, informants are not as vital in aiding identification of vulnerability, when compared with some 20 years ago when Palmer and Hart conducted their study.

Observation

Whilst custody officers may conduct 'some sort of scoping… not only by asking questions of the [suspect] or questions of the officers that brought them in [but also] looking at whatever else is available' (CO18-W Interview), they heavily relied on their own interpretation of the suspect. Given that custody officers rely on the performance of vulnerability and on aspects such as comprehension, capacity and/or understanding, it logically follows that they would rely predominantly on observation as a means through which to identify vulnerability. The reliance on observation makes more sense when placed in historical context: prior to advances in the formal risk assessment, custody officers were mostly dependant on observational methods when identifying vulnerability (as ascertained through informal conversations with legal representatives who had previously worked as custody officers; see also Palmer and Hart 1996: 29).

When considering the appropriate adult safeguard, the risk assessment is beneficial, not because of the answers given, but because of the opportunity to interact with the suspect. As CO22-M (Interview) and CO29-M (Interview) highlighted, 'risk assessments aren't just about asking questions, it's what you see as much as what you ask' and 'sometimes it's the way that [the risk assessment is] answered, gives you clues as to their state of mind'. The assessment of vulnerability relied on

> the sort of personal interaction with the person that you're talking to. And sometimes just pick up on the sort of comments that they've made or some phrasing of some answers or the time it's taking them to answer some questions.
>
> (CO1-W Interview)

Similarly, although there were questions asked, 'there are obviously those people who come in who overtly display behavioural issues, mental health issues, learning difficulties' (CO4-W Interview). The word 'demeanour' was also used frequently: 'you've got to look at how that person's demeanour is' (CO21-M Interview); '[i] t's all about their behaviour, their demeanour, and some clear mental health illnesses' (CO3-W Interview); and '[i]t's not just the words; you've got to look at people whilst you're doing this risk assessment. You're assessing people's demeanour at the same time, it's not just the answers they give you' (CO21-M Interview). 'Appropriate adult vulnerability' was therefore something physical: '[i]t becomes apparent when you see them' (CO28-M Interview).

Picking up on clues: 'sniffing out' vulnerability

Custody officers also alluded to, or expressly mentioned, looking out for clues or relying on *'gut feeling'* (CO14-W Interview). Such clues included, inter alia, unusual behaviour, the interaction of the suspect, and/or the reason for arrest, for example:

> [t]o go to the extreme, if they're running around with no clothes on through traffic or been shoplifting but they're not very a good at it, you know, forever getting caught and you think, 'What you've done just seems strange'.
>
> (CO18-W Interview)

In line with being a characteristic of appropriate adult vulnerability, perceived 'abnormality' could alert the custody officer to the fact that an appropriate adult was needed. Other clues such as physical appearance, signs of paranoia and how the suspect signed his or her name could also indicate 'appropriate adult vulnerability', as CO27-M stated:

> [i]t's physically [how] they are, how their behaviour is physically, how they're standing, whether they're looking around them all of the time, very paranoid sort of behaviour ... could be how they sign their name, how quick is that action, how slow is that action.

Other factors such as being unable to tell the time, not living independently, and/or having a support worker could also be taken into account, as could the nature of the illness, whether the illness was being treated, and the type and dosage of medication.

Barriers to identification

Whilst there are ways through which to identify vulnerability, there are also many challenges or barriers to identification. In their 1996 research, Palmer and Hart (1996: 29) highlighted how 'practical difficulties', 'differences among custody officers' and 'differentiating symptoms displayed between suspects' could create difficulties for custody officers when they were identifying vulnerability. Some 20 years later, Cummins (2007: 20–1) reported challenges such as the public nature of the environment, the masking effect of alcohol or drugs, and the custody officer's lack of training. Such challenges were evident in this study, but additional difficulties emerged, emanating from, inter alia, the risk assessment, custody officer distrust of suspect reliability, the expertise (or lack thereof) of HCPs, AMHPs, FMEs, and custody officers, and the reliance on the 'extreme case'.

Limits to risk assessment and records

Despite its utility, the risk assessment is not without its drawbacks. As a starting point, the risk assessment questions, whilst able to aid the identification of mental health issues, may be limited when identifying learning disabilities or difficulties (McKinnon and Grubin 2010: 211). Questions aiding the identification of issues such as learning difficulty, additional educational needs, and cognitive impairment are largely absent from the risk assessment. Therefore, unless the suspect considers his or her learning difficulty, additional educational need, or cognitive impairment to be a 'mental health problem', he or she may be unlikely, on the basis of the questions asked, to report this issue to the custody officer. As Clare and Gudjonsson (1993a: 6) found, only 35% of detainees with intellectual difficulties believed they should tell the police. Questions such as whether the suspect went to a 'special' school (contained within the optional questions on the risk assessment) is not only potentially offensive but will also inappropriate as many individuals with, for example, learning disabilities, additional educational needs, and cognitive impairments, attend 'mainstream' schools (Bradley 2009). The risk assessment was therefore only as good as the answers provided – for example, as CO30-M (Interview) commented,

> I think the questions on the risk assessment as they stand, it gives the person the opportunity to disclose any medical or mental health issues; whether they choose to or not is entirely up to them, I can't force them.

Even when specific questions are asked, the suspect may either be unaware of why such information should be disclosed, may be distrusting of the police and, relatedly or not, may be unwilling to disclose sensitive information. The suspect's willingness to provide information was viewed as a major barrier to identifying 'appropriate adult vulnerability' – custody officers were not 'sure that the questions [asked] are answered frankly by all the detainees' (CO13-W Interview). The reluctance to answer questions is undoubtedly increased by the layout of the custody suite, which does not typically lend itself to privacy and confidentiality. This is further compounded by the background noise in the custody suite, the length of time the custody officer spends with the suspect (see above; see Chapter 3; see also Palmer and Hart 1996: 32), and the presence of individuals other than the custody officer (such as arresting officers and detention officers). Whilst custody officers, usually before conducting the risk assessment, explained to the suspect/

detainee that they were going to ask a few questions relating to health and well-being and further explained that this was being done so that the suspect/detainee could be looked after properly, they did not provide an explanation of what the outcome may be should such information be provided, such as the provision of the appropriate adult safeguard. Moreover, even if informed, suspects may fail to appreciate the significance of the appropriate adult safeguard or may be offended that such 'safeguarding' is required (see, for example, Jessiman and Cameron 2017). They may be unwilling to disclose this information out of embarrassment, shame, or stigma, as CO16-W (Interview) highlighted:

> The first question you ask them is going to make some people lie because people won't want to admit to the fact that they can't read or write, people won't want to admit to the fact that they've got dyslexia, certain problems with their reading and writing. So I think they go straight onto their back foot and they start to lie to you straight away.[5]

The suspect may not hide simply one condition – he or she may disguise them all. In such circumstances, unless the suspect was observationally vulnerable, custody officers may not have necessarily established that the suspect should have been provided with an appropriate adult (and such observations may be flawed). The questions asked may also have been limited when identifying mental vulnerability, where such vulnerability was not innate but situational. The 'previous appropriate adult' approach was limited – in part because it could only be used if the suspect had previously been in custody, but also, as was recognised, because the suspect's condition could improve or worsen between spells in custody. Previous records also ostensibly guided decisions on how best to minimise death or (serious) injury more so than on the question of whether to implement the appropriate adult safeguard.

Custody officers also felt that the risk assessment was limited because suspects may not give truthful answers. Therefore, whilst suspects may fail to provide information, they were also viewed as prone to fabrication or exaggeration or, in the words of CO14-W (Interview), 'funnily enough, people lie to the police'. Such distrust, which was more apparent in relation to the 'usual suspects' than the first timers, may act as a barrier to identifying that an appropriate adult is required if the custody officer chooses to discount the information. Because custody officers distrust suspects, they (the custody officers) are disregarding answers that would otherwise lead to the implementation of the appropriate adult safeguard. Yet, such answers were typically only disregarded where the suspect disclosed something, rather than when the suspect did not disclose any information. Distrust of the suspect was therefore a barrier both in my eyes and in the eyes of the custody officer, but for very different reasons. Such distrust may lead custody officers to take steps to disprove vulnerability but rarely will this encourage them to take steps to ascertain vulnerability (where such vulnerability was not already apparent), such as the approach of CO22–2 (Interview):

> If I ask someone if they can read and write and they tell me that they can, it's extremely rare that I ask them to read, extremely rare. But if people say to me that they can't read or write then I'll give them the piece of paper like the white piece of paper that gives the rights and entitlements, I'll ask them to read the top line for me and that then gives me a measure of whether or not this person can in fact read or write. Quite a lot of people will say, 'I really struggle' and you'll say, 'Can you read that for me?', 'You're entitled to a solicitor free of charge', 'Well, you've not really got a big issue with reading or writing. Perhaps someone down the line told you that you're not very good at it but it's more than adequate for what you need in custody'.

Adequate healthcare expertise?

HCPs may not always be experts in mental health, mental disorder, learning disabilities or difficulties and so on and may fail to identify the need for an appropriate adult. Indeed, there is no requirement for them to be trained on learning disability or mental health (JUSTICE 2017). Three custody officers at Waterside explicitly recognised the shortcomings of relying on medical or healthcare advice, however, no criticisms were levelled at any of the healthcare or medical professionals at Mapletown. This was likely because AMHPs were seemingly willing to help identify whether an appropriate adult was required. Whilst this provision was implemented in Waterside later, the consensus amongst custody officers was that the presence of AMHPs had not made the job of the custody officer any easier as AMHPs were unwilling to advise on whether the suspect (or detainee) posed a risk to themselves (either as a result of physical or mental health) or others, or whether a suspect required an appropriate adult (although it is worth noting that this was not within their remit anyway). In Waterside, it was felt that whilst some HCPs 'come from mental health background; others don't … they may come from, say, a paramedic background' (CO18-W Interview) (see also McKinnon and Grubin 2014; Laing 1995). Those coming from a 'mental health background are able to give you a better steer on how to treat and how to deal with the detainee' (CO18-W Interview). The expertise of the FME was also highlighted:

> [s]ome of the FMEs and some of the nurses are more savvy [sic] with mental health issues. I think the training that they had will be in the mental health field or won't be. So in that respect it's a bit hit and miss in respect of what service the detainees get when they're here.
>
> (CO13-W Interview)

Whilst not mentioned by custody officers, the CJJI report (2014: 5) has highlighted how healthcare and medical professionals may also lack knowledge of learning difficulties. Thus, the specific expertise of HCPs and FMEs could have a bearing on whether innate vulnerability is identified. But this may not translate into implementation of the appropriate adult safeguard as HCPs, FMEs and

AMHPs may not necessarily have an in-depth knowledge of the Code C requirements (Norfolk 1996). Advising on the appropriate adult safeguard is not within the contractual remit of the AMHP and so, when they are used for this purpose, they may, understandably, have little to no knowledge regarding the requirements. FMEs, HCPs, and AMHPs may fail to recognise the significance of innate or situational vulnerability (the latter is undoubtedly more difficult to ascertain as it may manifest internally). Confusion may also arise between the requirements for fitness for detention, fitness for interview, and the appropriate adult safeguard. FMEs, for example, have been found often declare an individual fit to be detained or fit to be interviewed whilst forgetting or ignoring the appropriate adult requirement (Southcott 1999 citing Bean and Nemitz 1994). Indeed, conversations with custody officers indicated that HCPs, AMHPs and, when called, FMEs, would consider whether the suspect was fit for interview. In such instances, the appropriate adult safeguard would be deemed unnecessary or simply would not be mentioned.

Such shortcomings did not seem to deter custody officers from using these resources – whilst some desired something better, they pragmatically accepted that limited or flawed assistance was better than no assistance at all. Moreover, it seemed that this resource was not necessarily problematic in terms of identifying vulnerability and making decisions on whether to implement the appropriate adult safeguard, rather it served its purpose well-enough in this regard. Instead, the concern was ostensibly in relation to physical or mental harm. It must also be recognised that not every custody suite has 'in-house' HCPs or AMHPs and, as such, advice may not be readily sought.

Training, knowledge and abilities: differences between officers

Custody officers may also vary in their knowledge and, when drawing upon what vulnerability means and how it should be identified, will undoubtedly draw upon professional and experiences, in addition to training. Whilst the custody officers in Waterside and Mapletown received training on how to manage the risk of death or (serious) injury caused by or caused to the person (otherwise referred to as 'Safer Detention') at least once a year (either through group face-to-face training or online modules), such training did not seem to encompass vulnerability for the purposes of the appropriate adult safeguard. As Coppen (2008: 82) has noted, training can differ between forces – it is often a 'postcode lottery'. Moreover, training on mental health, intellectual/learning disabilities and other innate vulnerabilities is inadequate (Cummins 2007: 21). In addition to finding it difficult to express what the terms 'mentally vulnerable' and 'mentally disordered' meant, having a tendency to discuss learning difficulty in the same vein as mental health, custody officers readily admitted being insufficiently qualified to ask questions about and ascertain whether a suspect was experiencing mental health problems or disorders. This is highlighted by the following statements:

> I'm not by any means an expert on mental health but you get bi-polar, schizophrenic, psychotic. There are other ones as well, which I can't quite remember.
>
> (CO12-W Interview)

> We can be bamboozled with all sorts of terms and phrases and medication that people are taking … you know, I'm not an expert in that field.
>
> (CO28-M Interview)

> I sometimes think that some of the mental health stuff that we're dealing with these days, I don't feel qualified for it and I'm asking questions of people on a mental health assessment which I don't think I should be asking.
>
> (CO21-M Interview)

They felt that mental health was not their *'area of expertise'* (CO13-W Interview), adding that they were 'not mental health practitioner[s]' (CO18-W Interview). Such lack of expertise or knowledge may explain, in part, why many suspects who can be considered 'mentally vulnerable' or 'mentally disordered' are not provided with an appropriate adult (see Dehaghani 2017b). This finding may also cast doubt on the ability if the custody officer and other police officers to carry out the functional test introduced by para 1.13 of the 2018 iteration of the Code.

Custody officers, as with all individuals, undoubtedly exhibit different strengths and weaknesses. Some valued personal experience and believed that it made them more attuned to the needs of some suspects/detainees. For example, three custody officers mentioned during informal chats or interview that they had children with learning disabilities or additional educational needs. Two of these officers explicitly stated that this provided them with a better understanding and appreciation of vulnerability and felt that it enabled them to deal with individuals in a more appropriate manner. It was, however, abundantly clear that these 'skills' were more useful in terms of minimising risk to the person (in terms of death or (serious) injury) when compared with assessing whether someone required an appropriate adult. Moreover, a greater appreciation of certain conditions did not seem to correlate with a better, more general understanding of, for example, mental disorder.

Interestingly, even though custody officers shared the same interpretation of vulnerability for the purpose of the appropriate adult safeguard (although there may be subtleties in how this is operationalised), they did feel that differences in 'personal opinion' could result in differing interpretations of vulnerability – the identification of vulnerability was seen as *'quite a subjective thing'* (CO3-W Interview). They highlighted how it was 'down to personal opinion and experience and you could present the same person to two sergeants and one would say, "This person needs [an appropriate adult]" and one would say, "No, they're OK with that"' (CO18-W Interview). As such, there may be some sort of 'custody officer lottery' whereby the outcome of the interaction (and potentially the outcome of arrest and detention) *could* vary from one custody officer to the next –

> [i]t's a bit hit and miss ... I could do it at risk assessment from somebody who says they've got depression and another sergeant can do it and they might take a completely different tackle. You're never going to get the same.
>
> (CO1-W Interview).

Custody officers were insufficiently trained in mental health issues or learning disability or difficulty and therefore do not know what 'traits' to look-out for when identifying vulnerability (and undoubtedly still are). This is even more problematic as appearances can be deceiving or may not manifest observationally (see Clare and Gudjonsson 1993a; Gudjonsson *et al.* 1993). This may also prove problematic for the functional test under the new iteration of the Code. A reliance on observations may alert custody officers to a situational vulnerability, however, their definition of 'appropriate adult vulnerability' was ostensibly premised upon a medical condition and a lack of capacity, comprehension and/or understanding (and therefore arguably required that the suspect be 'mentally disordered' *and* 'mentally vulnerable'). As with innate vulnerability, situational vulnerability may not manifest observationally. Not every vulnerable suspect is so severely impaired that he or she does not understand the world around him or her; mental disorder or mental vulnerability would not necessarily equate to abnormality (although the fact that the word 'disorder' means an abnormality or disturbance may be misleading for those with little knowledge of what it actually encompasses). Prior to the advancements in the risk assessment tools, observation may have been the main, or sole, method by which a custody officer could identify the need for an appropriate adult. However, given the developments in the risk assessment tools, there is much more information available to the custody officer and therefore observation is not the only means of detecting vulnerability. Moreover, it must be recognised that some symptoms may only appear in certain situations. As such, reliance on mere observation may result in an inaccurate assessment of the suspect's vulnerability. It remains to be seen how vulnerability will be identified now that the category of 'mental vulnerability' has been removed from the Code and the functional test introduced.

Identifying vulnerability – an investigation?

> Interview techniques, questioning, body language, signs that they give off, their eyes... There are signs that people will give off but you have to be able to pick up on, or should be able to pick up on... I think the main crux that you [referring to the researcher] perhaps won't see when we ask the questions, is what's going on in the head of the custody sergeant and the copper's nose and that copper that sniffs out a crime, can sniff out an issue. Just that penny drops

or the light bulb moment. There's just something not quite right. I'm not happy that this person doesn't have an appropriate adult and should.

(CO24-M Interview)

Custody officers believe that their experience gained through years 'on the job' enables them to correctly identify vulnerability through investigative and interrogative measures (although, as the quote above illustrates, they are unable to locate their suspicion (see Loftus 2009: 123)). The identification of vulnerability, an arguably mundane and unimportant task, can be elevated to the status of something which is exciting and requires intuition or skill, such as the police investigation. Investigations can be conceptualized (see Tong and Bowling 2006) as either 'craft' (see Hobbs 1988; see also Willis and Mastrofski 2016), 'science' (Tong 2009), or 'art'. The first of these 'competing perspectives' (*ibid.*; see, however, Bayley and Bittner 1984) – the 'craft' – views detective work as something which 'emerg[es] from experience on the job, an understanding of the suspects, victims and police involved in the process of crime investigation and an ability to craft or organise the case in a manner considered suitable to the detective' (Tong 2009: 7–8). According to Tong, the craft transfers 'the reality of police work to the courtroom context in a manner that meets the crime-control objectives of the police' (*ibid.*: 8) whereby manipulation and negotiation are key. Paperwork, in particular, is manipulated to '"fit" the official presentation requirements' (Tong *et al.* 2009: 176) or '[cover] one's ass' (*ibid.* citing Ericson 1993). By contrast, the '"art" of detective work concerns intuition, and instinctive feelings and hunches regarding problem-solving in an investigative capacity' whereby the detective can successfully demarcate the false from the genuine and identify 'the effective and creative lines of enquiry' (Tong 2009: 8). As Tong (*ibid.*) highlights, this can be done through 'reading' criminal behaviour or 'reading' the alleged perpetrator or witness; those practising the 'art' of detective work can also 'read' the 'considered motivation and strategies to avoid detection'. In marked contrast with the 'detective as artist', the 'investigator as scientist' sees the investigation based, not on instinct, but on scientific approaches that have been learned through instruction and advancement in knowledge (*ibid.*: 9).

Whilst it is doubtful that the identification of vulnerability and risk through the risk assessment sparks the same excitement and suspense that is associated with investigating a serious crime, there are some clear similarities, at least in relation to how custody officers view this task. The custody officer 'reads' the behaviour of the suspect when determining whether he or she is vulnerable relying on a hunch (art) or on the skills acquired 'on the job' (craft). There may also be some similarities, beyond the conceptual, between the identification of vulnerability for the purposes of the appropriate adult safeguard (and risk) and a typical police investigation.

As with a criminal investigation, custody officers may seek 'evidence' of vulnerability such as the use of medication or the presence of a recognised medical condition. They may, similarly, look for clues such as, inter alia, unusual answers, failure to understand questions asked, or failure to understand the reason for arrest. Informants in the vulnerability investigation are akin to witnesses (Stelfox 2009: 86–7. See also Innes 2007; Tilley *et al.* 2007), although some – such as HCPs and fellow police officers – are undoubtedly more reliable and trustworthy than others, such as suspects and family members and friends. Consultation of HCPs and FMEs, if deemed experts, may also be likened to 'forensic examination' (Stelfox 2009: 88–9). As with a criminal investigation, where detectives and other investigators may attempt to build a picture of the case through reading the case file and consulting information such as 'fingerprints, CCTV, documents, items left at or taken from the scene, and DNA' (*ibid.*: 91), custody officers may check the PNC or previous custody records to uncover more information about the suspect. The most striking similarity, however, is the custody officer's assertion that he is able to detect lies, particularly where he believes the suspect is feigning vulnerability. The reliance on a 'hunch' can be problematic – Kassin, Meissner and Norwick (2009: 211) highlighted how research has consistently shown that, whilst the police assume that they are 'highly accurate judges of truth and deception … there is little if any evidence to support this claim' and, further, the police are no better than lay people when detecting truth and lies.

CO33-M (Interview) explicitly recognised the difficulties with what is perceived as the skill to 'sniff out' an issue:

> At the end of the day, the flipside to that is that these questions are, whilst we're doing a risk assessment, untrained in terms of any sort of medical training, we're asking questions and they're sort of set questions and we don't have the skills to recognise whether they're being truthful or not, in that. I just think the risk assessment questions need reviewing really.

Custody officers do not trust suspects to tell the truth and, as a result, may attempt to disprove vulnerability; officers are trained to 'assume nothing, believe nothing, challenge everything' (Stelfox 2009: 167) except where vulnerability is not reported.

Overcoming barriers?: concluding remarks

Awareness of mental disorder and other mental health issues has undoubtedly improved and increased over the last 20–30 years. Diagnostic capabilities within, for example, the mental health and learning disability arenas are improving, thus increasing an individual's awareness of his or her own condition. Public knowledge seems to be improving, along with public discussion – mental health, for example, is being much more widely discussed (Henderson *et al.* 2016). Further, the expanding risk assessment may enable a great deal of information to come to the fore allowing suspects an opportunity to self-report, with such information later being recorded on to PNC and custody records for future reference. However, custody officers were often distrusting of this information, particularly where it derived from the suspect, and instead placed greater trust in their own assessment of the suspect. Vulnerability may not always be easily identified, particularly where questions are not worded to prompt the 'right' answers, where the suspect is unwilling to come forward with the information or where the suspect does not realise what information should be divulged. Nevertheless, information *was* often provided to custody officers and it was instead what they chose to do with it that affected whether the appropriate adult safeguard was implemented.

Custody officers lacked knowledge of the vulnerability definitions and how these corresponded with recognised medical conditions or, further, how circumstance may have rendered a suspect vulnerable. Despite (or because of) a lack of knowledge, custody officers relied on their own observations of the suspect in order to identify whether an appropriate adult was required. The answers to the risk assessment may also be limited in ascertaining situational vulnerability (i.e. mental state) and, although questions that attempt to ascertain how one is feeling may provide information on one's emotional or mental state, the risk assessment tended to focus predominantly on medical conditions. In this sense, observations may have been useful in identifying traits such as fear or anxiety (provided these were observable). Custody officers were, however, seeking more than this – vulnerability was required to be, typically, both innate and manifest physically. Rather than the threshold for identification being lower than 20 to 30 years ago, it is now considerably higher – previously custody officers had to rely on observations only, thus producing false-positives (i.e. where they thought that the suspect met their criteria but the suspect actually only appeared to), whereas now they can marry their observations with the answers to the risk assessment and use these answers to 'disprove' vulnerability.

As required by the (then in place) 'benefit of the doubt' test, custody officers should have implemented the appropriate adult safeguard where there was any doubt and should only have continued without an appropriate adult where there was 'clear evidence' to dispel the notion of vulnerability. Therefore, where there was anything that suggests that the suspect *could be* vulnerable (whether that be the appearance of the suspect, a self-report, information from informants, previous records, or information from the healthcare team), the appropriate adult safeguard should have been implemented. Whilst custody officers were ostensibly open to seek 'clear evidence' (or at least not prevented from seeking such evidence), mere distrust of the suspect or of other sources of information should not have been enough to dispel vulnerability. Custody officers seemingly relied, to a great extent, on their policing skills, but such reliance could lead to erroneous outcomes. It will be interesting to see whether the introduction of the functional test is considered by custody officers when identifying vulnerability and, if so, how, given their limited capabilities to identify vulnerability, this is operationalised. Yet, identification, as this chapter has shown, is not always the problem. It is rather, as Bean and Nemitz (1995: 48) have noted, 'more a question of what [the custody officer thinks] should happen to the [vulnerable] once detected'. The identification of vulnerability depends, at least in part, on its definition, but this does not explain the issue in its entirety. In the following chapter I will explore further reasons why the appropriate adult safeguard may or may not be implemented.

Notes

1 The terms 'risk' and 'vulnerability' were often used interchangeably. Individuals were seen as 'vulnerable' because of physical or mental health such that their condition could result in death or serious injury.

2 N.B. This had not been updated in light of the changes to Code C by the date of access (25 June 2018).

3 Prior to such times, he or she is the responsibility of the arresting or escorting officer (College of Policing 2018b).

4 The inclusion of the appropriate adult here is unusual – surely if he or she is present then he or she should not be asking for the person to be assessed for the safeguard.

5 The first question on the risk assessment in Waterside asked whether the detainee had difficulties reading or writing.

8 Implementing the appropriate adult safeguard

It's just belt and braces, ain't it?

(CO9-W Interview)[1]

Introduction

One obstacle to implementation remains. Custody officers may, for various reasons, be incentivised or disincentivised to implement the appropriate adult safeguard. They may attempt to justify their decision not to implement the safeguard. They work, not in an ideal world, but within a set of constraints that determine or dictate, at least to some extent, how they go about their work. They receive various messages from inter alia, the law, the guidance, their superiors and the courts, and they must make sense of this information. They are told to prioritise some areas of work over others; they are told that some things are unimportant. Decisions must be made within certain confines and in a manner that best makes sense. This chapter, building upon the previous chapters, focuses on what may persuade or dissuade the custody officer when making a decision on the appropriate adult safeguard. To place custody officer decision-making in a broader context, this chapter will also briefly examine how the appropriate adult safeguard is implemented for young suspects and how custody officers approach decisions on risk. These various threads will then be tied together in Chapter 9.

Calling an appropriate adult: dissuasive factors

The identification of 'appropriate adult vulnerability' did not necessarily lead to the implementation of the appropriate adult safeguard; there were instances where the suspect would have met the custody officer's requirements, and such requirements have been identified by the custody officer, but the suspect would not have been provided with an appropriate adult. The reasons for this will be explored herewith.

'Solicitor' as substitute

Whilst Code C makes it clear that solicitors (or other legal representatives) cannot act as appropriate adults, custody officers took the approach, similar to that of the courts, that they can; the presence of a solicitor (or other legal representative) negated the need for an appropriate adult. Although custody officers were somewhat critical of solicitors (although notably less so about other legal representatives) and viewed them as goal-oriented and self-interested, they also believed that solicitors or other legal representatives could act as appropriate adults. This was evident from CO2-W's interview when asked about the appropriate adult safeguard:

> The appropriate adult's motives are purely from a welfare and health perspective, to make sure that that person's OK and understanding everything and I would argue that solicitors' motives and we, as the police, motives are not wholly that. We have other motives and we have other issues that we are trying to address as well.

As Blackstock, Cape, Hodgson, Ogodrova and Spronken (2010: 345) have highlighted, the role of the lawyer was seen as someone through which 'to get the client off' or to obstruct justice. The appropriate adult, by contrast, was largely viewed as independent. Yet, because solicitors or other legal representatives could act an 'ally' (CO8-W Interview), they were suitable appropriate adult replacements. The solicitor was also seen to provide 'back-up' (CO11-W Interview) or a 'someone giving them another perspective and safety net from that, being led down the avenue that the police might lead them down should they be easily persuaded or other things' (CO2-W Interview). The solicitor was also able to facilitate communication and may have been able to explain that '"Yes, it's OK to sign that. It's just … the label for the disk"' (CO9-W Interview) or otherwise assist with reading and writing. Thus, when a solicitor was not present, 'then perhaps I'll consider an appropriate adult purely to help them with their reading and writing' (CO22-M Interview). The appropriate adult, like the solicitor, could also ensure that the interview was being conducted properly and that 'the person doing the interview is behaving appropriately and not oppressively or anything' (CO28–2 Interview). Whilst there was a recognition that both the appropriate adult and the solicitor could prevent oppressive behaviour, not all custody officers felt this way. CO22-M (Interview) expressed dissent with the notion that a solicitor can replace an appropriate adult because the appropriate adult was

> someone to reassure them, not necessarily to guide them but for that physical reassurance so it's not just you and the cops. I don't think, and perhaps I'm speaking a little bit out of turn, but I don't think that the solicitor gives that reassurance whereas the appropriate adult tends to.

However, a solicitor's presence was likely to tip the balance where the custody officer was unsure, as CO2-W (Interview) pointed out:

> I would also argue that there are sometimes that once I know someone's having a solicitor, if I'm in a little bit of a grey area and I'm a little bit unsure and know that they're having a solicitor, sometimes that decision that they're fit for interview without an appropriate adult might be swayed by them having legal representation.

Cost: Time and Money

It is no great surprise that custody officers considered matters of 'efficiency' when deciding whether to call an appropriate adult. Whilst many areas have appropriate adult schemes in operation, these schemes do not typically operate 24/7 and, even where these schemes are in operation, appropriate adults may not always be readily available or arrive promptly at the custody suite. The NAAN report, citing other research studies, has already highlighted the deficiencies in the availability and commissioning of appropriate adult services. As they noted (2015: 16), availability of appropriate adults 'has a direct impact on operational decisions, causes delays in investigations and leads to mentally vulnerable people [sic] being detained for longer than is necessary, including overnight, and in an environment which is unhelpful to their mental state'. This, they argue, arises from the absence of a statutory duty to provide appropriate adults to vulnerable adults (see also Perks 2010). The correlation between being pressurised not provide an appropriate adult and working in an area where the provision was lacking has already been established in respect of FMEs (Norfolk 1996: 12).

Although CO18-W (Interview) claimed that custody officers were not explicitly discouraged by their superiors from using the appropriate adult safeguard on the grounds of financial expense, calling an appropriate adult most certainly requires additional resources. It requires that the custody officer make additional calls and record additional information and that the suspect is re-read his or her rights (with the appropriate adult present). It may also delay the investigation and the suspect's release from custody and, inadvertently, re-direct police resources towards the custody suite and away from 'the streets' (where it is 'needed' most). Whilst family members and friends do not receive remuneration for their presence at the custody suite, those requested from the scheme may be paid. The quote below (CO22-M Interview) highlights this:

> When we bring in an appropriate adult, the person is paid for by the public purse and there's quite a cost involved in relation to it. Does this person need an appropriate adult in my opinion? If the answer to that is 'no' because it's very, very, very minor depression, in fact it's not even depression, they're just fed up, then I won't get an appropriate adult.... The practicalities are, if we adhere absolutely strictly to what my interpretation of PACE is, we'd basically be getting an appropriate adult for every single person that comes in and the

> practicality of that would be to slow the system down tremendously and to cost the public an absolute fortune.

CO22-M understood that he was not complying with PACE (or more accurately, Code C). Yet, instead of adhering strictly with his interpretation of the Code C requirements, he exercised his discretion. CO22-M also used some justifications – rather than the suspect being recognised as in need of an appropriate adult by virtue of having depression (a mental disorder), CO22-M instead rationalised this as being 'fed up'. It seems that he disagreed with Code C and therefore chose to circumvent or ignore it. The Code C approach is costly both to the 'public purse' and requires a time investment on behalf of those working within the system (presumably, here, the custody officer and others such as the interviewing officer (s)). Whilst the scheme is costlier, the voluntary provision is not without its drawbacks: although it may not cost money, it most certainly costs time.

As noted above, the time taken may impact, not simply upon the custody officer, but also upon other police officers. One should not forget that custody officers are police officers and, having gained experience through policing, appreciate the impact that their work may have on other police officers. This was highlighted in relation to managing the risk of death or (serious) injury (CO8-W Interview) but can equally apply to vulnerability for the purposes of the appropriate adult safeguard:

> I tend to be acutely conscious of, if a custody sergeant follows the Safer Detention guidelines to the letter, you end up sending a lot of people to hospital that may well not really need to go. As a police officer I'm acutely aware that police resources are finite and every time that you ask for every detained person to go to hospital, you're taking up two police officers off the street who could be potentially out there fighting crime for three, four, five hours whilst that person is being taken to hospital.

Taking medical/healthcare advice

According to Code C, the decision regarding implementation of the appropriate adult safeguard is the responsibility of the custody officer. Yet, it transpired from interview and observation that, not only did HCPs (and, depending on resources and call-outs, AMHPs and FMEs) play a role in identifying vulnerability, they were also key participants in deciding whether the safeguard should be implemented. Thus, whilst custody officers repeatedly reiterated that such decisions were 'a personal judgement', in reality the decision to obtain an appropriate adult is often delegated to the HCP and the outcome is then largely decided by them (see also NAAN 2015). At Waterside, HCPs were the only available healthcare resource (unless an FME was called out), whereas in Mapletown AMHPs were also available. A custody officer would typically accept the advice of the HCP, FME, or AMHP, even when such advice contradicted the custody officer's initial thoughts on the matter. At Waterside, for example, CO15-W felt that two suspects with schizophrenia should have been given an appropriate adult but, upon the advice of the HCP, decided not to call one (Interaction 21-W). Even suspects with co-morbidity (i.e. with two or more mental disorders) would be deemed fit for interview and without an appropriate adult present:

> Suspect is suffering from paranoia, personality disorder and depression and is referred to the HCP for an assessment. The HCP deems the suspect fit for interview but without an appropriate adult present.
>
> (Interaction 18-M)

A need for severity or significance was not unique to HCPs; AMHPs also seemed to require evidence of a significant impairment of understanding:

> The fella yesterday, although he wasn't interviewed … when he first came in with his mental health issues, you would probably think 'He needs an appropriate adult'. He was assessed by an [AMHP] and I asked if he needed one … and they said 'No, although he has mental health issues, he clearly understands everything that's happening and everything around him'. So he didn't need one. Normally, if I'm not sure, I'll put it over to them and take their advice on it.
>
> (CO11-W Interview)

Such requirements were also followed by FMEs. As Norfolk (1996: 12) highlighted, 70.9% of FMEs felt that an appropriate adult was required for mental disorder only when such disorder was 'significant'.

Sometimes the suspect would be sent to the HCP for a healthcare assessment and the appropriate adult safeguard would be advised on; on other occasions a brief conversation would ensue at the booking-in desk whereby the HCP would ask the custody officer whether he felt the suspect should be provided with an appropriate adult. Yet, before the custody officer could reply, the HCP would say 'I don't think he needs one, I'm happy to say that he doesn't need one, if you're happy with it', to which the custody officer would frequently reply, 'I don't think he needs one if you don't think he needs one' and they would both essentially agree not to make any mention of it on the custody record. The FME may also be involved in an assessment, albeit usually for more serious matters such as an informal mental health assessment or serious physical health issues.

Adopting a cynical view, one could argue that reliance on the HCP or other healthcare or medical professionals could absolve custody officers from blame for any errors in judgment, particularly where questions are raised at court. Alternatively, the custody officer may genuinely feel that the HCP, FME, or AMHP is better-placed to make these decisions, particularly as they were viewed as 'experts' compared to the custody officer's minimal and often dubious knowledge. Of course, there are instances where the HCP, FME, or AMHP will deem it necessary that an appropriate adult be called and custody officers are also willing to accept such advice when it is provided.

Leaving it up to the suspect

The custody officer may also leave the decision with the suspect; where a suspect 'agrees' that an appropriate adult is not needed or when the suspect states answers 'no' to the question of whether they want an appropriate adult then one will not be provided. As CO14-W (Interview) highlighted:

> [I]t's either way and you say, 'Do you want an appropriate adult?' and they say, 'No' ... if they're confident in themselves, who are we, 'There you are, this person you don't know, they're going to sit with you ... I don't want this person in my interview. Don't know them, don't want them'. We've got to go with what these people want. You can't just force an appropriate adult on someone.

This suggests that it is unfair to go against that suspect's wishes if the suspect felt that an appropriate adult was not required. It is unclear, however, whether custody officers explain the benefits of having an appropriate adult. Certainly, during my time in custody, I saw no such explanation offered during and, rather, there were occasions when the suspect was discouraged from obtaining an appropriate adult for reasons of, for example, efficiency or the suspect's capability. Custody officers, such as CO10-W (Interview), said they would

> speak to the [suspect] and ... say, 'Well, I initially thought that you needed an appropriate adult. Did you need one in the past?' and they say, 'No'. I say, 'Well, I thought you need one but the nurse says no. Are you happy to go ahead without one?'.

Questions could also be raised here with regard to whether the suspect is making an informed decision. That they would refuse the assistance, support, and advice of a third party having been adequately informed seems unlikely, although not implausible. The appropriate adult safeguard, rather than being something positive, was instead viewed as something which was thrust upon the suspect, as CO1-W (Interview) seems to suggest: '[t]hey might live independently; they might have a job and everything else. So who are we to decide almost, "Now you need someone else to tell you what to do"'. Yet, as Sanders and Young (2000: 242) pointed out, whilst the appropriate adult is foisted upon the suspect, so too is detention and questioning, and if something negative can be foisted upon them, then so too can something positive. Such is, however, the problem with the term 'appropriate adult'.

Calling the appropriate adult: persuasive factors

Whilst there are reasons why a suspect, when identified as 'appropriate adult vulnerable', will not be provided with an appropriate adult, there are also reasons why someone who is not deemed to be 'appropriate adult vulnerable' is provided with an appropriate adult. Such reasons may also provide further encouragement to implement the safeguard for those who are considered 'appropriate adult vulnerable', particularly when balancing these factors with the dissuasive factors discussed above.

Requested by the 'solicitor'

Although a solicitor or legal representative may facilitate the identification of vulnerability, their involvement may too lead to the implementation of the appropriate adult safeguard (see also Palmer and Hart 1996: 62–4). Custody officers may be encouraged to implement the appropriate adult safeguard 'if a solicitor says [that the suspect needs an appropriate adult because] there's always then going to be an issue at court' (CO10-W Interview). Whilst, initially, attempts may be made to placate the solicitor or legal representative and explain that an appropriate adult is not required, if the solicitor or legal representative insists, an appropriate adult will be obtained. The custody officer performs a 'balancing act': the disadvantages of failing to obtain an appropriate adult (questions of admissibility at a later stage or time taken to justify the decision) will outweigh the disadvantages of getting an appropriate adult (a delay to the investigation, time taken to call and secure an appropriate adult, and the time and cost associated with the appropriate adult's presence). The request may be at odds with healthcare or medical advice on the matter, and the custody officer must then make a decision as to whether to comply with the legal representative's request, or whether to 'trust' what the HCP has suggested. Such requests from the legal representative may not necessarily result in the implementation of the safeguard in such an instance, as CO13-W's interview quote indicates:

> If … the solicitor flags it up saying, 'I think we do need an appropriate adult here', I say 'Well, your client's been assessed and it's deemed not necessary'. If I'm going to go over and above the head of the medical professional, it puts in jeopardy and queries their position within the organisation and justice system. If we're not going to be bound by the decisions that they make, then why are they here?

What seems absent from this quotation is a recognition that the HCP's expertise is in the healthcare field, and not in the legal realm. Regardless, it seems whilst, legally, the decision ultimately rests with the custody officer, he nevertheless feels 'bound' by 'decision' of the HCP. Instead of countering the HCP, the custody officer would explain why the suspect does not require an appropriate adult, appealing to the decision or advice of the HCP. It is possible that this is done, not simply as to avoid contradicting the HCP, but also because the legal representative is there and everyone is 'ready' for interview, and calling the appropriate adult would ultimately delay the process, perhaps quite significantly.

Previous appropriate adult

Whilst Code C does not dictate such an approach, it makes sense that, unless the suspect's condition has improved so dramatically that he or she is no longer 'appropriate adult vulnerable', the use of an appropriate adult on a previous occasion could dictate that one should be used in the present situation. Thus, in addition to being used as to aid identification, it may also have been a persuasive factor when implementing the appropriate adult safeguard, particularly for those who were newer to the job (such as CO20-W and CO31-M). The previous appropriate adult approach improved efficiency, particularly because with

> [s]ome people, you just know, they've been in custody that many times, you just know … that they always have an appropriate adult. So you just get one because it's quicker to do it now rather than to go right round the houses only to come back to the same answer.
>
> (CO9-W Interview)

Sometimes the previous appropriate adult approach would perversely result in the safeguard being left unimplemented. This could occur when the suspect had *not* been provided with an appropriate adult on a previous occasion and would be used to justify not obtaining an appropriate adult in the present case. CO8-W (Interview) whilst expressing disagreement with this approach, admitted nevertheless that he used this method himself:

> I think that's a bit of a copout really, looking at previous records because you should, I think, base your decision on what you see in front of you at the time. And to me, if you ask a person, 'When you've been interviewed at the police station at the past, have you had an appropriate adult?', that's almost saying, 'I think you should have one'.… I'm not saying that I haven't done that myself but looking at that situation logically, if you're asking that question then clearly the question is going through your head that you suspect that this person should have one.… That's the reason why you're asking them if they had one in the past. And even if they say, 'No', that doesn't change the fact that you're looking at them now thinking, 'This person perhaps is the kind of person that would benefit from an appropriate adult'.

CO8-W understood that his approach is flawed, but adopted it regardless. It was recognised that some caution should be exercised with this approach as:

> They can come in two days later on, if they've had a relapse or suffering a bit more… something's affected them, perhaps being arrested two days earlier has had an effect on them, [then] they may then need that appropriate adult to make them aware, to look after them, to make sure they know what is going on.
>
> (CO24–2 Interview)

The previous appropriate adult approach could be said to serve merely as an indicator (as stated by CO1-W at interview) or may increase the likelihood of an appropriate adult being used again (as stated by CO33-M at interview) rather than acting as a definitive decision-making factor.

Seriousness of the offence

The seriousness of the offence (see also Palmer and Hart 1996: 88) and, connectedly, the venue for trial and the demands placed on the suspect are also taken into account when custody officers make their decisions. An appropriate adult may not be obtained where the custody officer feels that the case is straightforward, i.e. where the offence is minor, where there could be a clear admission, where the suspect was caught red-handed, or where investigation would result in no further action, a caution, or a fine. Indeed, and as noted earlier, some cases are never intended to be progressed beyond the police station (Choongh 1997). A suspect who was alleged to have committed murder or rape may have been more likely to be provided with an appropriate adult than someone who was suspected of, for example, shop-theft (the most commonly cited 'straightforward' offence). Custody officers explained that the line of questioning would be more complex in a more serious case, the investigators would likely 'tie the [suspect] up in knots' (CO30-M Interview), or there may be questions surrounding the requisite *mens rea*. What custody officers failed to recognise, or chose to ignore, was that questions regarding *mens rea* may also be important for less serious offences. It is not, as McBarnet (1981) argues, that certain offences are uninteresting and unproblematic, it is instead that they are treated as such by the police, the courts and the legal profession. Yet, it must be recognised that whilst, for custody officers, the magnitude of loss is greater with a murder or rape case, it is, rather, the likelihood of breach detection – such as the court at which the case will be tried and the chance that a legal team will be instructed to peer deeper into the collection of evidence – that operates more heavily on his mind. Admissibility challenges tend only to be heard in the Crown Court (Sharpe 1997: 4–5); defendants who are tried in the magistrates' court are therefore at a disadvantage. As CO8-W (Interview) highlighted: 'if it was a case that was particularly serious and was going to end up being heard in the Crown Court and questions were going to be asked'. In such circumstances, an appropriate adult may be called for a suspect who does not otherwise fit the 'appropriate adult vulnerable' requirements, such as someone with mild depression. The custody officer considered the consequences of non-implementation and the potentiality for loss if questions were later asked:

> Because for a shop-theft, if we didn't have an appropriate adult present and they went to court and at court they said, 'Actually, I'm not admitting to that now. I wasn't very well and they didn't have an appropriate adult for me'. The consequence is a shop-theft that you lose at court. GBH, murder, obviously it's the serious end. That, I think, we would be so heavily criticised that why we didn't have an appropriate adult present for those offences... If it's at the

higher end, you should have an appropriate adult. Just to safeguard, if not to negate any defence at court, but also to ensure that their needs are met whilst they're at the custody suite.

(CO28-M Interview)

Basically it's safeguarding them in that respect because obviously in the interview situation, if I was to ask you 'You went into the shop, what did you do?', you say 'Well, I went into the shop, picked up this, put it in a bag and walked out', 'Did you pay for it?', 'No', 'Did you attempt to pay for it?', 'No', 'Had you got means to pay for it?', 'No'. What else am I going to ask you? Whereas say a very serious offence, you're going to be asking a lot more about background, relationships between yourself and the victims, there's an awful lot more that can trip people up on, be likely to contradict themselves which, those contradictions, those mistakes that they might make, could then be used in court and that could then sway the case one way or the other with the jury. But say, with the basic theft, if you've got capacity you're not going to trip yourself up, are you?

(CO30-M Interview)

Both these quotes seem to misunderstand or misconstrue the admissibility rules – CO28-M stated that non-implementation of the appropriate adult safeguard would result in a 'defence' whereas CO30-M did not seem to appreciate that, at a trial at Crown Court, the jury may not actually see the evidence. CO30-M's statement also betrays an incomplete (or lack of) understanding of the offence of theft, which is much more complex than that expressed.

Benefit to the suspect

Custody officers suggested, as CO30-M has, that the appropriate adult was more beneficial to the suspect in a more serious case. The appropriate adult may also be useful, as CO28-M (Interview) has suggested, in ensuring that the suspect's 'needs are met whilst they're at the custody suite'. Whilst this may have been a mere after-thought or added so as to portray some sense of benevolence, it may also, or alternatively, suggest that custody officers, when implementing the safeguard, had in mind genuine concerns for the suspect's welfare and well-being. This was true when suspects performed vulnerability. This quote from CO9-W (Interview) further exemplifies this:

It's all about making sure that we do it fairly, isn't it? If somebody's in custody and they're vulnerable, yes they might have committed a crime but if we're going to investigate that crime, we've got to be fair to everybody. So there's no point getting an interview done with somebody and the interview's

> not fair, that they feel pressurised in the interview, you know they haven't got any support.

The standards of fairness and notions of welfare are likely to extend only to those deemed worthy.

In more serious cases, the absence of an appropriate adult, according to the custody officer, was more unfair to the suspect and puts him or her at a greater disadvantage. Less serious offences could also often be problematic, in part because they are *treated* as unproblematic (McBarnet 1981). Although the punishment may not be as severe, the process can be the punishment (Feeley 1992). A suspect in custody under suspicion of a 'low level' offence may be easily persuaded or tricked into confessing (McConville *et al.* 1991: 70–1) or may be encouraged to deal with the matter outside of the courtroom (see Chapter 1). It is not so much that the suspect under suspicion of a 'low level' offence will not face disadvantage and more so that the police will not face scrutiny for not providing an appropriate adult in such instances.

Comparing different decisions

Whilst both young suspects and adult suspects are included under the Code C guidance on vulnerability and the appropriate adult safeguard, the vulnerability of young suspects was often disputed:

> A lot of the juveniles are effectively wrong people who have done something and basically they want their parents here out of choice … the difference with the juvenile is that they're not vulnerable necessarily unless they're vulnerable juveniles. But if you take a normal juvenile, just by virtue of their age, they are deemed vulnerable by law, but they're not necessarily vulnerable by nature.
>
> (CO18-W Interview)

However, decisions in relation to young suspects are not subject to the same level of discretion as those about adults are, or, rather, subject to discretion at all. The vulnerability (or purported lack thereof) of the young suspect is immaterial:

> There are juveniles that you wonder whether or not really do need somebody sat with them. But we have no discretion on that. Adults, you do have that subjective discretion of whether you think they need one or not. And it purely comes down to the individual custody sergeant … that makes that decision.
>
> (CO3-W Interview)

In addition to making decisions regarding the appropriate adult safeguard upon booking-in, custody officers were also required to decide upon an appropriate care plan for the detainee (suspect or otherwise) whilst he or she was in custody. As with vulnerability, the risk of death or (serious) injury could be identified at least in part by the risk assessment tools (see Chapter 7). Decisions should be taken in accordance with the guidelines set out in the College of Policing's (2018a) APP on Detention and Custody. The detainee could present a risk to self, through self-harm, suicide, or physical ill health or injury, and/or drug or alcohol addiction; or to others, through violent or aggressive behaviour or possible transmission of infectious diseases. Depending on the risk assessment, some detainees will require hourly visits, some need visited every thirty minutes; some will need to be roused, others merely checked; some will be monitored by way of CCTV, some will be largely left alone in the cell and a small minority will require constant observation (a police officer will sit by the door of the cell) (ibid). For CO30-M (Interview), as with other custody officers, the main aim within custody was to ensure that 'everybody that comes in leaves alive'. Further, compliance with the risk procedures takes precedence over compliance with PACE – whilst the aim in years gone by was 'to make sure that we didn't lose investigations and that things were done properly … now … the greater focus and greater priority is care of these people whilst they're in detention' (CO2-W Interview).

Custody officers also received annual training on 'Safer Detention' (ACPO 2012; see also College of Policing 2018a) and this particular element of the job features heavily in the initial custody officer training course. By contrast, there was no annual training on vulnerability for the purpose of the appropriate adult safeguard. Moreover, whilst custody officers thought this was covered during their initial training, they could not remember the content. The only exception to this was CO22-M who had recently trained new custody officers on their training course and was therefore somewhat aware of the Code C requirements. Whilst custody officers could explain and appreciate risk, as with vulnerability, it could be difficult to identify. What matters was not that the custody officer ***actually identified*** the risk but that he followed the steps in doing so, recorded the required information, and acted according to the information available:

> No amount of questions you ask on risk assessments are going to stop someone from fitting because they are withdrawing from alcohol or stop someone harming themselves because they suffer from schizophrenia and the voices are telling them to do it.… But the important thing is we do identify the people who are liable or at risk of doing that so we can put the control measures in place.
>
> (CO4-W Interview)

Concluding remarks

Not every suspect who had been identified as 'appropriate adult vulnerable' would be provided with an appropriate adult safeguard and not every suspect who fell short of this threshold would move through the process unaided. There were various factors that the custody officer would take into account when deciding to call an appropriate adult; these factors would persuade or dissuade him from implementing the safeguard. The presence of a solicitor or other legal representative could, for example, have both a positive or negative influence on whether an appropriate adult is called. On the one hand, a solicitor or other legal representative could be seen to fulfil the role of the appropriate adult and therefore calling an appropriate adult in instances where a solicitor or legal representative was present was deemed pointless. Yet, on the other hand, if a solicitor legal representative was present and demanded that an appropriate adult was called, the custody officer may have decided to do so. This may have implications for healthcare or medical advice, another factor taken into account by custody officers. Where the HCP (or FME or AMHP) believed that an appropriate adult was unnecessary then one would not be called. However, where the demands of the solicitor or legal representative were in conflict with what had been suggested by the HCP (or FME or AMHP) the custody officer would have to decide how to manoeuvre around this.

The suspect, if deemed worthy of protection, may have been provided with an appropriate adult. However, appealing to notions of autonomy, the custody officer may have given the suspect a choice of whether to have an appropriate adult or not. Often, if the case was one of great seriousness, the custody officer, if he had not done so already, may have decided to call an appropriate adult on the request of a solicitor or legal representative for fear of an admissibility challenge later at court. He sought to protect the case from any challenges at court and would weigh up (although not in an accurate and scientific manner) the chances of a challenge being raised and such a challenge being successful with the time and/or money taken to secure an appropriate adult. Such challenges are certainly more likely in serious cases that go to the Crown Court and will involve a team of solicitors and barristers than in 'run of the mill' cases that may not even make it to the magistrates' court and will be, at best, dealt with by swiftly and routinely by an overworked and underpaid legal representative or solicitor (see Newman 2013; see also Dehaghani and Newman 2017). In the serious cases the stakes are higher for the police and the suspect, who may also have a role in whether an appropriate adult is made available. Yet, in cases that are not designated for the criminal process, the appropriate adult safeguard will remain unimplemented. Such cases, which are intended for social discipline only (Choongh 1997), will never progress beyond the custody suite and therefore do not call for the use of an appropriate adult.

Thus, a fuller picture of the implementation of the appropriate adult safeguard emerges: it is not simply about deficiencies with identification; the appropriate adult safeguard is also left unimplemented because vulnerability is constructed in a particular manner and the decision to implement the safeguard is influenced by various factors. To draw attention yet again to Bean and Nemitz's (1995: 48) contention: it is not so much a question of identification but more so 'a question of what [the custody officer thinks] should happen to the [vulnerable] once detected'. It remains to be seen whether the Home Office changes will result in any changes to custody officer practices and, if so, what these changes will be. Within the following chapter I will examine why custody officers think, interpret and construct in the manner explored within these last three chapters, placing this too in the context of the earlier chapter.

Note

1 The 'belt and braces' approach means utilising double security. This is arguably in reference to implementing the safeguard in conjunction with recording everything on the custody record. It also suggests that measures may be taken purely in the interests of security.

9 Comprehending the custody officer approach

Introduction

Straightforward and simple explanations of the gaps between the law in books and the law in action – between how the appropriate adult safeguard is supposed (or purported) to be implemented and how it is actually implemented – do not exist. Rather, the translation of the law in books to the law in action is rather complex. Legal rules are 'flexible and fluid' and whilst

> carefully prescribed … inevitably … cannot and perhaps should not provide a formulaic answer to the diverse and idiosyncratic range of circumstances and settings that the police encounter and in which the police are called on to make decisions and to act.
>
> (Skinns 2012: 226)

Laws are subject to interpretation by a range of actors and may be ignored or circumvented when necessary. The law may be rendered unimportant or may be used simply as last resort (see Hawkins 2003). This chapter, building upon previous chapters, will examine how these complex interactions can be understood through the lens of criminal justice and policing theory (but see also Bottoms and McClean 1976; Choongh 1997; King 1981; Sanders *et al.* 2010). As will become evident throughout this chapter, the complexity of law in action cannot be fully captured by the application of any one single theory. This chapter provides the penultimate piece of the appropriate adult puzzle, with the final slot being filled by Chapter 10.

Modelling the criminal process

According to Herbert Packer (1968), the criminal process can be conceptualised through the two dichotomous value models of crime control and due process. These models, rather than accurately describing any one system, represent two positions on opposite ends of a spectrum. In reality, a criminal justice system will generally display some compromise between the competing demands. The value systems also share some 'common ground' (*ibid.*: 154–7) in four assumptions: a distinction between the definition of criminal conduct and the identification and handling of criminals, a requirement that the criminal process is invoked by those furnished with the responsibility to do so, a demand for law enforcement officials to be subject to scrutiny and control, and a recognition that the alleged criminal is an independent actor is permitted to compel the 'operators of the process' to prove to the independent adjudicator that the defendant is guilty.

Crime control

The crime control model focuses on the repression of crime as its primary function. Through the repression of crime, law and social order are reinforced. However, in order to do so, the system must achieve a high percentage of apprehension and conviction and thus must operate efficiently at all stages (detection, apprehension, prosecution, conviction, and disposal). Such efficiency requires that a high number of offenders are processed using limited resources and this, in turn, demands a degree of informality but also a standard, routinised procedure whereby judicial processes, 'ceremonial rituals' and legal challenges are shunned. The process operates extra-judicially where possible; quality control and a 'screening-out' of the innocent are left largely to the police and the prosecution within whom great trust is placed. Efficiency also demands that the system operate on the presumption of guilt whereby efficient screening ensures that those who are probably guilty progress quickly through the process. Mistakes too are tolerated, and safeguards are minimal so as to promote trust and confidence in the efficiency of the system. The crime control value system has been conceptualised as an 'assembly-line conveyor belt' (*ibid.*: 159) which carries a continuous stream of standardised cases to the workers who stand at their assigned station performing the task to bring the product closer to completion.

In a crime control system, the police are provided with the opportunity to interrogate the suspect, who is viewed as 'the best source of information' (*ibid.*: 187; see also *ibid.*: 186–90). The suspect must remain psychologically vulnerable and, to do so, should not be afforded an opportunity to rally outside forces (see also Gudjonsson 2003). Whilst indefinite detention is not permissible, the rules should be flexible and allow the police to consider the relevant factors such as the gravity and complexity of the crime and the ingenuity of the suspect. The suspect should not, without justification, be held incommunicado and, whilst his or her family are allowed to know of his or her whereabouts, they are prevented from conversing as they may impede the police investigation. Although rules allowing coercive tactics, illegal arrests, and unreasonable searches may be forbidden, illegally obtained evidence need not necessarily be excluded and neither would a conviction necessarily be quashed if the rules were breached. The onus is on the suspect to prove that the confession was elicited through coercion and that, as such, it is unreliable.

Due process

The due process value system, by contrast, places limits on state power and presents obstacles that impede the further continuation of the criminal justice process. This value system is distrusting of the state, casts doubt on the morality and utility of the criminal sanction, and places the individual suspect at the forefront of the process. The ideology of due process is best explained through a contrast with crime control: due process does not oppose the repression of crime but rather it queries the crime control method of doing so; it casts doubt on the ability of police and prosecution to effectively screen-out cases and instead prefers adjudicative, adversarial, formal fact-finding processes. Due process rejects absolute efficiency where this interferes with reliability, permits a reduction in quantitative output, and allows for scrutiny and challenge. At its purest, this would leave open the opportunity for appeal provided there is an allegation of factual error. The due process system is distrustful of the state and requires that the state prove the case against the accused beyond reasonable doubt, in accordance with the procedures proscribed by law and by the authorities acting within their prescribed power to do so. It sees value in penalising those who circumvent or breach the rules and would therefore permit acquittal of the accused where evidence is illegally obtained. At its forefront lies the presumption of innocence; it thus permits the establishment of legal guilt only where the rules and the 'integrity of the process' (Packer 1968: 166) are adhered to. As a fair trial requires equal justice, the due process system would also compel the state to ensure that limited financial resources do not prevent the accused from submitting an effective defence. Due process is essentially a negative model, placing limits on the exercise of state power.

In a due process system, a valid arrest is one based only on probable cause or reasonable suspicion, made so that the suspect may answer the case against him or her, and is not for the purposes of case construction. Once arrested, the suspect must be told his or her rights, including the right to remain silent and the right to legal counsel, and must be brought before a magistrate 'without unnecessary delay' (*ibid.*: 190) and given an opportunity to contest the legality of the arrest. During this period the suspect cannot be interrogated by the police and any self-incriminating statements made during the period between arrest and presentation before a magistrate are excluded if the police failed to inform the suspect of his or her rights (unless expressly waved them), if the confession was given after exceeding the period of necessary delay, or if the confession was produced as a result of coercion. Rather than focusing upon reliability, these rules place a burden on the state to compile its own case whilst also providing suspects with the privilege against self-incrimination.

The utility of Packer's models

Packer's value systems, like any theoretical framework, are not without their limitations (see Ashworth and Redmayne 2010; Duff 1998; Macdonald 2008; McConville *et al.* 1991, 1997; Roach 1999; Smith 1997). Whilst serving as useful heuristic tools through which to analyse the decisions made and actions taken within the criminal process (Ashworth and Redmayne 2010: 39–40; see also Aviram 2011), they are nevertheless limited in their explanatory power. They can, however, help explain aspects of the criminal justice process in operation such as the due process obstacles of the presumption of innocence, the evidential standard of proof beyond reasonable doubt, reasonable suspicion for arrest, detention authorised only if 'necessary', the right to legal advice and the granting of legal aid for defence. They are also useful when examining the evidentiary standard of proof beyond reasonable doubt, the crime control influences of adverse inferences from silence, the deployment of detention to achieve reasonable suspicion, the role of instinct in stop and search, and the use of plea bargaining (Sanders *et al.* 2010: 27). The English criminal justice process, for McConville and Baldwin (1981: 153), fails to uphold even the minimal requirements of due process and instead favours an 'extreme demonstration' of crime control where the 'routine processing of cases assumes ascendancy over safeguarding individuals' rights'. More recent political rhetoric has been steeped in crime control, with a desire to 'rebalance' the criminal justice system to favour the police, victims and witnesses (see Zander 2007) whilst promoting efficiency and effectiveness. Developments such as online courts (Bowcott 2017) further add to the conceptualisation of the English criminal process as being about efficient processing, which is intrinsic to crime control. Summary and swift justice is fast becoming normalised within England and Wales. For example, the Sentence Discount Principle (under the Criminal Justice Act 2003) has generated a mass of guilty pleas (Alge 2013), and the system is readily focused on efficiency, economy and effectiveness (see Auld 2001). These developments, considered alongside the Criminal Procedure Rules (CPR) and the imposition of case management requirements on the defence, have further solidified swift and summary justice (see Ministry of Justice 2012). Managerialism has tightened its stranglehold on criminal justice; the updated CPR further seeks to encourage guilty pleas through intensified case management requirements. Furthermore, and as outlined in Chapter 1, neo-liberal ideology has resulted in new public management, civilianisation and privatisation, 'workforce modernisation' of defence lawyering, and multi-professionalism (Skinns 2011: 13–16; see also Ellison and Brogden 2010). These developments all smack of crime control.

PACE is the perfect example of due process and crime control values enshrined in one piece of legislation, at least on paper. The replacement of the 'voluntariness' requirement with that of 'reliability' (see s 76 PACE) was a step toward due process: pre-PACE, a false confession provided voluntarily could still be admitted, whereas, at least in the abstract, such a confession would post-PACE be deemed unreliable and therefore inadmissible. The role of the custody officer and the requirements for a custody record and tape-recording of interviews in addition to greater rights for suspects could also be viewed as due process developments. However, along with greater rights came enhanced police powers. Whilst Williamson (as cited by Dixon 1999: 66) asserted that PACE created 'a new climate…in which there is strict adherence to the rules' (see also Maguire 2002: 92), others have been critical of the (in)effectiveness of PACE. According to McConville, Sanders, and

Leng (1991: 189), additional safeguards have been 'easily absorbed' by the police. Further, as Quirk (2017) has pointed out, greater safeguards have been met with retaliatory crime control measures such as the decimation of the right to silence.

Bureaucracy

The bureaucratic model places rules at the centre and approaches individuals with uniformity and impartiality, each being subjected to the 'same rational assessment' (King 1981: 22). Whilst not dissimilar to due process in that the bureaucratic model too requires 'a framework of substantive and procedural norms binding upon and serviceable to both the government and the governed' (*ibid.*: 21 citing Balbus 1973: 4), the bureaucratic model is premised upon standard, closed system of rules operating 'independently of political considerations and regardless of who is in the dock' (King 1981: 22). The courts are required to manage conflict whilst remaining neutral, applying the law equally to all regardless of age, race, sex, colour, creed, social status or political beliefs. Elements of the crime control system can also be seen in the bureaucratic model: both strive to minimise costs and maximise efficiency by avoiding duplication to the greatest extent possible between criminal justice actors.

Understanding police behaviour: the interpretation of rules

> The view that policing behaviour is chiefly shaped by rules may well be wrong. Because a rule exists, it does not follow that it automatically and rigidly governs day-to-day policing behaviour. At the extreme, a rule may be universally ignored and never invoked to discipline anyone.
>
> (Smith and Gray 1983: 169)

PACE and its accompanying Codes can be seen as a series of rules setting out, and setting boundaries on, police powers and procedures. However, the existence of a rule or set of rules on paper does not equate with the exercise of such rules in practice, nor does it necessarily promote or ensure conformity. Decisions are not always subject to scrutiny, owed in part to low visibility, collegial solidarity, and a lack of direct supervision. It may be difficult to ascertain whether the police have followed the rules and adherence is not always conducive to 'doing the job well' (*ibid.*: 170). The way in which rules are interpreted helps explain why the appropriate adult safeguard may often be left unimplemented.

Discretion and the function of rules

In the United Kingdom, the police are not necessarily compelled to enforce the law (Steer 1977). Discretion is therefore an essential component to understanding the law in policing in both theory and practice and understanding how these differ (Westmarland 2008: 255). Policing is unusual as, in contrast with most other jobs, discretion typically *increases* as one is moving *down* the hierarchy (Wilson 1968:

7). Discretion is an inevitable part of police work; it may be delegated or may stem from a lack of supervision or insufficient supervision (Skolnick 1966). It arises because police officers are 'free to make choices among possible courses of action or inaction' (Davis 1969: 5; see also Klockars 1985: 93) and can decide who to stop, arrest, question and detain (Westmarland 2008: 255). Discretion may arise for one of three reasons (see Liebling and Price 2002: 80–1). The first reason relates to the vagueness of rules: a rule cannot align perfectly with a situation or action; some cases fall very clearly within the core of the rule whereas others sit somewhere within the penumbra (see Hart 2012). The second reason is concerned with the variation between situations and the reality that rules cannot 'cover every imaginable situation' (Liebling and Price 2002: 81). Third, organisations are often unclear with regards to their expectations and therefore aims and objectives may be confused or in contradiction (*ibid.*; see also Hawkins 2002). As Klockars (1985: 97–102) highlights, discretion may be necessary when: the law is too broad in scope, police resources are limited and prioritisation is therefore required, enforcement does not make sense (i.e. the law is 'bad law'), or fulfilling the purpose of the law requires the exercise of discretion. Decisions must therefore take account of the 'broad environment, particular context, and interpretative practices: their surrounds, fields and frames' (Hawkins 2002: 189; see also Hawkins 1992; Dworkin 1977). The law is 'merely one set of restraints upon, or guidance for, individual action among a varied array of social forces' (Hawkins 1992: v; see also Campbell 2005). The decision-maker will take account of 'the role of decision objectives, the incentives or disincentives to forms of behaviour, questions of socialization or training, or the importance of organizational routines' (*ibid.*). Decisions may also be subject to 'interpretative judgement' (Bronnit and Stenning 2011: 321); whilst decisions involving discretion will almost always involve interpretation (before discretion is exercised, the officer must interpret the situation), discretion only comes into play once an officer is satisfied that the circumstances require the enforcement of the rule. Whilst the law is therefore not the only motivating factor, and will not always have the effect of producing conformity, it is not unimportant.

Rules can have the effect of creating compliance (see Ericson 2007); this depends, argue Smith and Gray (1981: 171), on the function, interpretation, usage, and interaction of the rules with the 'norms and objectives of working groups of police officers'. Rules may be internalised, discourage behaviour where a breach is likely to be discovered, or 'give an acceptable appearance to the way that police work is carried out' (Smith and Gray 1981: 171). The first set of rules – working rules – are agreed-with or adopted into consciousness, are more 'likely to have a far more consistent controlling influence' (*ibid.*: 170), and will guide an officer's actions. The second type of rules – inhibitory rules – are not internalised but will be taken 'into account when deciding how to act' (*ibid.*: 171) but will discourage behaviour only where a breach is likely to be discovered. The third type of rules – presentational rules – place a 'gloss on policing behaviour so as to make it acceptable to the wider public' (*ibid.*), derive, not from the police but from the law, and 'are part of a (successful) attempt by the wider society to deceive itself about the realities of policing' (*ibid.*). As Smith and Gray (*ibid.*) highlight, 'the same rule may perform more than one function, or may be used differently by different officers or at a different time'. For Dixon (1997: 8), however, this assertion is understated: he argues that there was a 'need to consider the cumulative effect of groups of rules' and further highlighted that the non-self-executing nature of rules, i.e. that "an apparently 'presentational" rule may be made to work in an inhibitory way'. Smith and Gray's typology, according to Dixon (*ibid.*), could also be further expanded to include reactive rules ('created by the police hierarchies in response to specific incidents') and routinized rules (those that have become ritualized). Dixon's (*ibid.*) conceptualisations of the law in policing, which has provided more detail on how one can understand the police interpretation of rules, will be examined below.

A fault with the law: the legalist approach

The legalistic-bureaucratic (hereafter legalistic) is a 'legal or jurisprudential way… of looking at the world' (Lacey 1992: 362) and one which is closely tied to the idea that police organisations operate as 'effective bureaucracies' (Dixon 1997: 5). This approach posits that police actions and decisions can be directed by 'training, policy statements and internal regulation' (*ibid.*: 8). It is a firm favourite with policymakers and legislators who assert that a gap between the law in books and the law in action is caused by ambiguities in the law and that the gap can be closed with 'clearer interpretations or further legislative or quasi-legislative action' (Lacey 1992: 362; see also Dixon 1997: 1–8). The legalist responds by clarifying and codifying police powers (Dixon 1997: 1); the implementation of PACE and Code C, in response to the 'inadequacies' of the Judges' Rules, was a typical legalistic response. This particular approach suits the police – as Dixon notes, 'if problems in policing arise, it is the law which has become unrealistic and inadequate' (*ibid.*). The rules are 'blueprints, guides to a possible reality, an abstract and partial account of how things could or should be done, rather than an account of how things are' (Dixon 1997: 5 citing Bradley, Walker and Wilkie 1986: 121). The police organisation, in this conceptualisation, is a well-oiled machine that, given the right instructions, can operate accordingly.

Culturalism: a pervasive police culture

For culturalists, or interactionists (see Holdaway 1979; 1983; 1989; Fielding 1989; Manning 1977; Punch 1983), this machine has its own characteristics or traits which can influence its modus operandi. These characteristics or traits have been identified as a sense of mission, action, cynicism, pessimism, suspicion, isolation/ solidarity, machismo, racial prejudice and pragmatism (Reiner 2010: 119–32). The world of the police officer is often troublesome; regularity and predictability help to make sense of this world (Skolnick 1966). There are, however, differences in how culture operates or manifests in policing; as Reiner (2010: 132) points out, 'police culture is not monolithic, and there is both structured and individual diversity'.

Differences – to the extent that one cannot speak of 'police culture' but rather 'police cultures' (Westmarland 2008: 253) – have been found between rural and urban forces (Cain 1973), depending on rank and type of job (Hobbs 1988; Reiner 1991; Reuss-Ianni and Ianni 1983; Young 1991), between geographical location (Hobbs 1988) and between what is said in the canteen and what is done in the street (Campeau 2015; Waddington 1999b). Culture also cannot be separated from the wider socio-political and historical context (Chan 1997), which may have a bearing on how it materialises. This is not to say, however, that police officers are passive carriers of culture; indeed, they may have 'an active role to play in developing, reinforcing, resisting and transforming cultural knowledge' (*ibid.*: 74–5. See also Ewick and Silbey 1998: 39).

Whilst there are indeed differences, similarities should not be ignored (Paoline 2003) nor should the differences be exaggerated. Loftus (2009: 125), for example, whilst finding cultural differences between two stations in the same force, argued that these were subtle and, as such, concluded that there was more or less a universal police culture. Whether culture varies significantly or not, there are some constants within police occupational and canteen culture, and such characteristics may influence how the police interpret rules. The culturalist may, however, dispute the effect of rules on practice. As Dixon (1997: 9) has highlighted, the rules may indeed be devalued, whereby the law is seen as 'at best, marginally relevant and, at worst, a serious impediment to the business of policing'. The culturalist therefore views the 'formal rules [as] primarily presentational' (Reiner 2010: 189) and seeks to explain police action through subculture alone. This 'extreme rule scepticism' (Reiner 2010: 209) within culturalism has attracted criticism as it is neglectful of the role of law and structure (Dixon 1997: 14–15; see also Paoline 2003; Reiner 2010). That said, the formal rules are not defunct as 'interactionist studies themselves point to some impact of formal rules, for example in the emphasis on rank-and-file solidarity aimed at shielding deviant practices from the senior ranks, and the need always to have a good story to "cover your ass"' (Reiner 2010: 189). Police culture thus has an influence on how police officers interpret rules and how they exercise discretion (Westmarland 2008).

Structuralism: a flawed system?

Structuralists view the gap between the law in books and the law in action as something which derives from the broader political and judicial discourse and decision-making. The RCCP, for example, did not provide any clarity surrounding the role of the appropriate adult and what was permissible for the police to do during interview, and deliberately so. As Baldwin and Kinsey (1982: 208) have highlighted, much of the discourse surrounding the RCCP adopted a pro-police stance and thus endorsed 'much of existing police practice'. For Baldwin and Kinsey, legal rules are important as they send a signal to the police regarding what is expected of them. Yet, such rules may be breached or ignored, police practice may be condoned by the courts, and rules can be impacted upon by circumstance and situation, as well as geographical location (see Dixon 1997: 22). The strength of a rule can be influenced by factors such as 'status, sanctions, degree of specificity, procedure and enforcement practice' (Baldwin 1989: 166). Grimshaw and Jefferson (1987: 290) have similarly urged that structural determinants – 'law, work and democracy' – be considered in order to understand how the police operate.

Legal regulation, whilst able to help bridge the gap between law and practice (Dixon 1997: 26), is insufficient alone and must be supplemented with 'principles of justice' (Grimshaw and Jefferson 1987: 284). McBarnet's structuralism posits that it is not necessarily police practice which deviates from the 'ideals of legality' (1981: 31), rather the formal law also neglects the due process safeguards (see also McBarnet 1978a; 1978b; 2004). McBarnet (1981: 8) argues not for a focus on 'petty officials' such as the police but instead on the judicial and political elite. She urges that the criminal process be considered within an account of the state as a whole, considering firstly whether the judicial and political elite implement due process rhetoric and secondly whether such rhetoric is embodied within the law. This, she argues, should be done before postulating whether the police undermine due process rhetoric. The 'Warwick School' (see Dixon 1997) of McConville, Sanders and Leng (1991:11; see also Dixon 1997: 41) also adopt a structuralist approach but combine this with interactionism in their social constructionist account of the law in policing. Such 'social construction takes place within structural contexts, and it is these which determine outcomes' (Dixon 1997: 44).

The role of law in policing and the appropriate adult safeguard

Custody is not necessarily low visibility (see Newburn and Hayman 2002), at least not when compared with 'beat' policing, but discretion nevertheless exists, at least in part, because these decisions are rarely (and perhaps unsuccessfully) scrutinised and/or because the law lacks clarity. These factors mean that custody officers are largely left to their own devices when making decisions. In the context of the appropriate adult safeguard, custody officers may be conferred discretion because the guidance under Code C relating to vulnerability and the appropriate adult safeguard is unclear or open to 'interpretative judgement' (Bronnit and Stenning 2011: 321), because not every suspect is the same and nor are the facts of the case the same (thus also allowing for 'interpretative judgement'), and/or because organisational objectives are unclear or absent (or focussed instead on managing death or serious injury). Custody officers may also be conferred 'discretion' because of how the broader criminal process operates. Police culture then influences how decisions manifest (but is not determinative of such discretion). Each of these aspects, building upon previous chapters, will be teased-out in turn below.

A problem with the rules?

The legalist would explain the 'gap' between law and action as something which manifests because of ambiguities or inconsistencies in legal regulation: Code C does not provide the definitions for adult vulnerability until later in the guidance, these definitions are neither clear nor comprehensible, and custody officers may often struggle with operationalising the definitions. Comparing young and adult suspects, whilst age is undoubtedly easier to identify (although not problem-free),[1] the identification of vulnerability in adult suspects is not always hugely problematic. Instead, it is how custody officers define vulnerability and how they choose to use the information which impacts upon the implementation of the appropriate adult safeguard. The young suspect, whilst not always recognised as 'genuinely vulnerable' (see Dehaghani 2017c; Kemp and Hodgson 2016), must nevertheless be provided with an appropriate adult because the term '17 and under' is not open to 'interpretative judgement' (Bronnit and Stenning 2011: 321). This can be contrasted with the terms for adult vulnerability contained within Code C – 'mentally vulnerable' and 'mentally disordered' under the pre-2018 iteration and 'mental disorder' and 'mental health condition' under the current iteration – which can be subject to quite significant 'interpretative judgement'. Where guidance *is* sufficiently clear (and not open to 'interpretative judgement'), an appropriate adult may be obtained for an adult suspect regardless of other factors (see Dehaghani 2016), at least by some custody officers. For example, CO9-W (Interview) stated that '[a]nyone that is on the autistic spectrum, our rule book says, "They will have an appropriate adult" so... no matter how serious or mild you would get an appropriate adult'. However, the same custody officer also stated,

> [i]f somebody booked into custody said that they suffered from schizophrenia, I wouldn't automatically say, 'Right appropriate adult for you then', because it might be that they suffer from schizophrenia but they take medication for it, they're compliant with that medication and they're fit to be dealt with.

Custody officers have a tendency to focus on the suspect's capacity when deeming him or her 'appropriate adult vulnerable'. For the legalist, this may be due to flaws in the guidance, as a great deal of the Code C guidance lends itself to a capacity-based approach (see Chapter 5).

Not only are the ambiguities in the guidance, the rules are also less authoritative for adults when compared with young suspects. The pre-2018 guidance on adult suspects was contained later in Code C, predominantly in the Notes for Guidance. The definition of vulnerability under the 2018 iteration of Code C is scant: the term 'mental health condition' is not explained or explored and the term 'mental disorder' is not further elaborated on, beyond the reference to the MHA Code of Practice contained in Note for Guidance 1GB. The placement of the rules may be important as the Notes for Guidance assume an even lower status than the Codes 'in terms of their authority' (Zander 2013: 369). A question could be raised as to why some aspects of the definition cannot be contained in the main guidance or, at the very least, an Annex (see Dehaghani 2016; although see Zander 2015: 343–5). More importantly, the CDA 1998 s 38(4)(a) imposes a statutory duty upon Youth Offending Teams to provide appropriate adults for all young suspects. A similar duty does not exist for adults, although such recommendations have been suggested (Jacobson 2008; NAAN 2015). The legislature in Scotland are currently considering the introduction of a statutory duty to provide appropriate adult services for all vulnerable suspects. Such provisions will also cover vulnerable victims and witnesses (Scottish Government 2018). Other solutions for the legalist (see Dehaghani 2017b) would be to fill the 'gap' with more legal regulation (either through Code C or additional internal regulation (such as the College of Policing APP (2018a)). NAAN (2015), for example, have also recommended that the Code C be revised to clarify that all adults who meet the definition require an appropriate adult. Such recommendations, whilst laudable, fail to recognise the role of 'interpretative judgment' (Bronnit and Stenning 2011: 321) and the other factors influencing police decision-making (as addressed below).

The most recent changes to Code C suggest that the Home Office have subscribed to a legalist approach. The Home Office's response to the deficiencies highlighted by 'There to Help' (NAAN 2015) was to change legal regulation without committing to improving appropriate adult provision across England and Wales. The Home Office have also neither addressed the routine police breach of the Codes nor the approach of the courts towards breaches of the Codes.

A problem with the culture?

Custody officers were often provided with information through which to ascertain whether the suspect had a mental disorder or a mental vulnerability and thus required an appropriate adult but it is what they chose to do with this information that resulted in non-implementation of the safeguard. They often viewed the suspect as an unreliable source of information and therefore discounted the information provided. Those with depression were approached with cynicism and suspicion, as were many others with mental disorder. Relying on one's own observation skills and the HCPs, FMEs, or AMHPs advice was a practical approach and one that made sense. Culturalists would highlight the influence of cultural characteristics and their role in police decision-making. It is simply pragmatic to interpret vulnerability according to an understanding- or capacity-based approach because the appropriate adult's role, according to the custody officer, is mainly to facilitate communication. Even if the appropriate adult acts as an ally or a support, such support is really only needed for adult suspects who appear childlike or who are unable to look-after themselves adequately. Taking into account the cost, in terms of detriment to other functions of policing, when making their decisions is also pragmatic; calling the appropriate adult causes interruptions or delays to an effective and efficient custodial process and should therefore be approached with caution. Code C, rather than guiding police actions, is viewed as either unimportant or a serious impediment to the function of policing (see Dixon 1997: 9). The rules are, of course, not obsolete but instead 're-worked, refracted in one direction or another' (Holdaway 1989: 65). There is also value in 'a good story to 'cover your ass''' (Reiner 2010: 209). This was clear in the following explanation from CO27-M (Interview):

> We could have a very competent child, with no other issues with them, who basically just need to make sure that everything is being done right.... I think it's just open to criticism. I think if nothing was used and it was just the police interviewing a juvenile then it could be just said that the police are coercing them, having chats, all sorts, bully them into something. And so I think it wouldn't protect the police service if the juvenile didn't have an appropriate adult. I think that's where a lot of the issues would come.

The culturalist conception may explain what influences the custody officer's interpretations and views but it does not explain why custody officers may see the need to 'cover their asses'. The need to do so can be explained when read in tandem with the structuralist approach.

A problem with the structure?

The structuralist account would situate the problem with the judiciary and political elite. For example, the exclusionary rules of evidence provide a remedy to suspects where, for example, custody officers have failed to comply with Code C. Custody officers frequently mentioned that they would implement the safeguard because

> ultimately, if a case goes to Crown Court or magistrates' court and it comes down to a technical issue of does this person understand what they were doing, and would they have said that had they had an appropriate adult sitting next to them? It could all be lost on that.
>
> (CO12-W Interview)

Yet, suspects may make mistakes when questioned in relation to purportedly 'straightforward' offences such as criminal damage (see McConville *et al.* 1991: 70–1). Custody officers consider the seriousness of the case, not simply (or perhaps at all) because of the benefit to the suspect, but because the evidence may be more likely to attract scrutiny. Serious cases are awarded greater attention, not simply because of their alleged complexity but also because of the potential for and the likelihood of loss evidence (and potentially the case) at trial. Of course, where the case is unlikely to reach the courts, or the evidence is unlikely to be effectively challenged, the custody officer may have little incentive to implement the safeguard, beyond protecting the suspect.

According to Zander (2013: 369), 'judges have often been prepared to rule that a breach of a provision in a Code results in evidence being held to be inadmissible or results in the conviction being quashed'; this is most certainly evident in many of the cases examined in Chapter 5. Yet, the courts have not adopted this approach in every case. Rather, the courts have reserved criticism of the police and have, on occasion, condoned the custody officer approach. The courts do not always exclude the evidence where there has been a breach of Code C, rather they assess the reliability of the confession (if considering s 76 of PACE) or the impact of admitting evidence on the fairness on proceedings (if considering s 78 of

PACE), and nor do they always issue a s 77 direction. Code C and PACE, as Bath (2017b) highlights, were relics of the Judges' Rules, which provided guidance to police on how to conduct an investigation. Such guidance explained not necessarily how to protect the suspect but rather how to maintain the integrity of the evidence. Code C and PACE fall victim to similar problems and, as Palmer and Hart (1996: 88) have highlighted, issues with the implementation of the appropriate adult safeguard are 'compounded by judicial decisions which fail to scrutinise' the effectiveness of the safeguards. The courts are, of course, somewhat bound by the guidance provided in ss 76, 77 and 78, but they are not prevented from interpreting 'reliability' and 'fairness' widely. Similarly, with custody officers, the courts focus mostly on capacity, particularly when assessing reliability, and have also adopted the view that a solicitor can replace the appropriate adult.

Yet, the judiciary are not entirely to blame. They must rely on the guidance handed-down to them by parliament. It was not the judiciary who placed the appropriate adult rules in a Code of Practice and neither was it the judiciary who rendered breaches of the Codes subject to the exclusionary rules of evidence (rather than holding an officer liable to civil or criminal proceedings (PACE, s 67 (10)). The courts did not fail to place the appropriate adult safeguard for adults on a statutory footing, similar to that for young suspects, and nor have they, since 1986, largely failed to provide further guidance on the terms contained within Code C. The fault for these elements lie with the political, rather than judicial, elite.

The Home Office response to 'There to Help' is further evidence that the political elite are responsible for the disregard of the appropriate adult safeguard. The Home Office did not resolve the issue with patchy provision (see Chapter 2). It also did not introduce a statutory duty (see Jacobson (2008) and NAAN (2015)) to provide appropriate adults to adult suspects. It did not commit to encouraging forces to implement improved (or, arguably in some cases, any) training on vulnerability and the appropriate adult safeguard. It also created new guidance without a full and considered approach: the Home Office Working Group, of which I attended twice, did not discuss the matters set out on its agenda and, upon conclusion, had not discussed the issues that required addressing. The draft that was put forward for public consultation was not, to my knowledge, constructed through consultation with the Working Group members (indeed, I was invited to submit our comments on a draft, to which I never received a reply). The draft was then adapted in light of the public consultation but it appeared that some definitional issues and ambiguities still remained. I was given the opportunity to further comment on the draft and had detailed conversations with a contact at the Home Office. Through these conversations it appeared that the draft (and later drafts) were rushed; indeed, I noted a number of inconsistencies when commenting on the post-consultation draft. As with previous versions of the Code, anomalies and oddities remain or have been introduced.

However, even if the political elite were to remedy some of the above issues, the operation of the criminal process makes it so that many cases do not reach the courts. Thus, the practical functioning of the criminal process also produces obstacles to the effective implementation of suspects' rights, creating, in turn, a further lack of accountability (see also Choongh 1997: 209). This argument is further bolstered by the relative dearth of cases where evidence, because of non-implementation of the appropriate adult safeguard, is challenged; admissibility, because of the practical functioning of the criminal process, is an ineffective enforcement mechanism. It is thus, to echo McBarnet (1978a; 1978b; 1981; 2004), not simply the law in action that undermines due process; the law in books also undermines its own due process rhetoric. Although perhaps PACE and its accompanying Codes were never destined to embody due process safeguards for suspects; it is clear from the rhetoric surrounding PACE and the Codes that they were designed as instructions to the police so that they may protect the integrity of evidence.[2] Thus, to echo Kendall (2018), the safeguards were crime control from their very inception; they were not intended as due process and therefore, in this sense, due process could not be said to be for crime control.

Vulnerability and risk: explaining the 'why'

Custody officers prioritise the identification and management of risk of death or (serious) injury, over the identification and safeguarding of vulnerability; keeping detainees safe has overridden concerns with Code C and PACE (assuming that Code C and PACE were ever of huge concern). Risk and discourses surrounding risk have become central to policing (see Ericson and Haggerty 1998). The first factor to note here is that the College of Policing guidance assumes an even lower position than that of Code C or PACE. But it is not the hierarchical status of the rules which matter, instead it is the implications for breach: a failure to implement the appropriate adult safeguard can result in exclusion of evidence at trial, whilst a failure to identify risk and adequately 'manage' the detainee could result in injury, illness, or death:

> Worst case scenario is that somebody dies in custody, which is probably the worst thing that can happen to a police force and anybody that's involved with that person. So it's important to identify what risks you're dealing with as early as you can so you can put something in place to try and mitigate that risk or manage it.
>
> (CO20-W Interview)

The main aim for custody officers is to ensure that 'everybody that comes in leaves alive' (CO30-M Interview). The greater onus on risk is motivated, officially speaking, by a desire to prevent deaths in custody *and 'to make sure that we, the police service, were looking after people better'* (CO2-W Interview). However, as CO17-W (Interview) highlighted, unofficially, the identification and management of risk is motivated by a desire to avoid blame:

> The job [the police force] is absolutely scared of a death in custody. They are absolutely bottling it. There's been one or two occasions recently where

> people have self-harmed, that were going to self-harm anyway, and the job's absolutely petrified of it because they won't stand up and say, 'Well, this person is mentally ill' or 'This person was going to self-harm anyway'. And the blame will always come back to the staff and not to the person who's responsible for their own actions.

This was reiterated by CO24-M (Interview):

> If we don't identify any risk, we can't care for these people properly. You want to avoid, without tempting fate, touching wood, a death in custody. Or any issue, or anybody coming to harm in custody. It's why we identify risk.... I don't want anything to happen [to them] that is going to get me in trouble. So [their] care is [of] paramount importance.

Deaths in police custody attract negative publicity and may result in the custody officer being suspended from duty pending investigation (see also Police Federation undated. See also Angiolini 2017). Moreover, if the custody officer had erred in judgement, he may, in theory, lose his job or be held criminally liable for the detainee's death (see CPS undated; BBC 2016). The custody officer must take steps to ensure that he does as much as possible to prevent a death in custody and must express concern for the detainee, in an attempt to obtain full and accurate information regarding the detainee's mental and physical well-being. Where a detainee indicates or states that he or she may have a particular ailment, it is the responsibility of the custody officer to find out more. For example, if, when asked about physical health conditions, the detainee informs the custody officer that he or she suffers from asthma, the custody officer will ask about the medication he or she takes, the dosage, whether this medication is on his or her person or at home, if he or she experiences asthma attacks and if so, when was the last. He or she will also be seen by the HCP. Custody officers were less likely to dismiss as unreliable information provided by the detainee because of the implications associated with a death or injury in police custody. A death or serious injury in police custody can be a 'pension killer' (Wooff and Skinns 2018). The hierarchy of guidance is largely unimportant; instead it is the implications of non-compliance which are central to custody officer decision-making (see Chapter 10).

Conclusion

Custody officers take a range of factors into account when deciding whether to implement the safeguard but it is worth recognising that rules may have varying functions and their use may depend, inter alia, on the wider context of the case, how the police view the rules, and/or how clear or effective that rule is. Custody officers chose not to adhere to Code C because it would involve providing an appropriate adult for basically every suspect who passed through the doors and 'the practicality of that would be to slow the system down tremendously and to cost the public an absolute fortune' (CO22-M Interview). In other words, the rules for adults were viewed as over-inclusive (see Hawkins 1992: 8) and would impede efficiency. Custody officers did not wish for greater clarity as this would render Code C 'too prescriptive' (CO27-M Interview). Indeed, Code C was praised for its flexibility and for not 'constrain[ing] [custody officers] by definites' (CO28-M Interview). The ambiguity of the rules therefore allowed custody officers to exercise discretion.

The legalist, culturalist, and structuralist accounts all hold some explanatory power. Legalism explains, at least in part, the differences in approach between young and adult suspects. Culturalism helps illuminate the characteristics influencing custody officer decision-making and also assists with understanding the custody officer's approach to how vulnerability is defined and identified. Structuralism assists in explaining the definition of vulnerability and custody officer decision-making. However, these perspectives are also somewhat limited in illustrative value: legalism fails to consider that a 'gap' arises not simply because of ambiguities or inconsistencies in the law, culturalism does not fully explain why custody officers need (or, rather, do not need) to cover their asses, and structuralism does not explain why custody officers are cynical, suspicious or pessimistic. A social constructionist (see McConville *et al.* 1991) account, combining culturalism and structuralism, enables us to understand why custody officers interpret the rules in a particular manner and why they are permitted to do so.

Police behaviour is affected by the approach of the judicial and political elites (Dixon 1995). Custody officers adopt the safeguards pursuant to their own objectives (which are predominantly crime control or efficiency focused) and can do so because the law and the operation of the criminal justice process permit this. To echo McConville, Sanders and Leng (1991: 55), custody officers can most certainly be viewed as 'facilitators' rather than 'doorkeepers', in that they facilitate the police objective of interviewing and evidence-gathering more so than protecting the suspect's due process entitlements (supposing that the law actually confers such safeguards). Due process and bureaucracy are not obsolete but are far from primary considerations. Custody officers are not necessarily reprimanded for non-implementation, but instead are largely left to self-regulate. Discretion is necessary in many instances but what is problematic is how discretion is deployed. The final chapter will examine how police decision-making can be understood through a (new) theoretical lens and how discretion can be reduced or removed in relation to the appropriate adult safeguard.

Notes

1 During observation there was one occasion where a young suspect was initially thought to be an adult. She gave both a false name and date of birth, which placed her at 23 years old. After being booked-in, she was sent to have her samples taken, at which point a warning flashed-up on PNC to say that the fingerprints matched that of another record. This other record included a date of birth, which placed the suspect at 15 years old. Whilst this may have (unknowingly) happened on more occasions, this is arguably the exception rather than the rule.

2 Indeed, rumour has it that the Home Office consulted the police, pre public consultation, on how they wanted the newest version of Code C to look and allowed that to lead their revisions.

10 Reconceptualising vulnerability?

Introduction

The implementation of the appropriate adult safeguard is complicated, nuanced and multi-faceted. The law in books is often a complex creature, but such complexities magnify when the law in books is transferred into action. It is important not to simply adopt one theoretical perspective but instead to recognise where various approaches illuminate particular aspects of the problem. This book has drawn attention to such complexities and has deconstructed and reconstructed the various threads. A picture of how custody officers approach the task of identifying vulnerability and implementing the appropriate adult safeguard, and why they approach their task in the manner explored has emerged. But the picture is thus far incomplete. In order to explore the final piece of the puzzle, this chapter will draw upon and examine the grounded theory emerging from the data. Immersion in the world of the custody officer has allowed for a full appreciation of the role and its demands. This, combined with reflections upon how other criminal process actors – the courts and the political elite – 'treat' vulnerability, allows for a more holistic understanding of the reality of the appropriate adult safeguard for adult suspects. This reality, considered alongside broader renderings of vulnerability, also holds the key to the removal of discretion. These aspects and opportunities for future study will be discussed in this chapter.

Theorising custody officer decision-making

The theories examined in Chapter 9 do not fully explain the custody officer approach to vulnerability and the appropriate adult safeguard because, alone, they are unable to fully conceptualise the realities of the role of custody officer. This is because many decisions are not made simply because of crime control, bureaucracy, police culture, the structure of the organisation or of society, or the approach of the judicial and political elites. Rather, custody officers, as explained earlier, make decisions that best suit their own personal and professional ends. These aims and objectives can encompass the various considerations of crime control, bureaucracy, police culture, or the approach of the judicial and political elites, and to varying degrees. Taking the example of vulnerability and the risk of death or (serious) injury, a picture emerges. For example, CO4-W (Interview), when discussing an occasion when he was required to change a risk-management decision, stated:

> You have to cover your back. You have to cover your back. Because that was what the family were saying, the family were saying, 'We've got these issues'. And rest assured, because this is what happens quite often, 'We have these issues and if you don't do anything and something goes wrong, we're going to be pointing the finger at you'. Our hands are tied.

Custody officers also often referred to 'walking a tight-rope' (CO14-W) or having our 'hands tied' (CO4-W Interview). Decisions were made because of accountability or, rather, the avoidance of scrutiny. Yet, at the same time, custody officers sought to minimise personal exertion and would therefore weigh the effort to be made against the benefits to be reaped. Implementing the appropriate adult safeguard costs (precious) time and may keep the suspect in custody for longer, thus increasing the time that the custody officer is responsible for him or her. Yet, where a suspect does not understand the interview process, an interview without an appropriate adult may be fruitless or, at the very least, time and energy-intensive. But where a case is likely to reach the Crown Court, questions are more likely to be asked regarding the admissibility of evidence and therefore custody officers may be more likely to implement the appropriate adult safeguard, if only to save himself and/or the police from scrutiny and to prevent the loss of an 'important' case. Where a solicitor is present, an appropriate adult may not be needed, not because the suspect would not benefit from one, and not simply but because the solicitor can perform a similar role (as this can most certainly be disputed), but because it is much easier to simply arrange for one person to be called. To call an appropriate adult, as well as a solicitor, would require an attempt at coordinating the simultaneous presence of numerous individuals. If questions were going to be raised at court, the solicitor would undoubtedly ask for an appropriate adult; if a solicitor does not make such a request, the custody officer would think it unlikely that questions of admissibility would later be raised. This may suggest the prioritisation of crime control, with the secondary consideration of bureaucracy (and the ascendancy of bureaucracy where crime control is weak). However, this does not hold true when considering decisions on how to manage the risk of death or (serious) injury.

The custody officer may be unwilling to take chances when ascertaining and managing the risk of death or (serious) injury because of the serious personal and professional repercussions that may materialise should something go wrong. When a suspect/detainee presents with a particular risk, the custody officer must put the requisite safeguards in place because, should the suspect/detainee come to harm, the police will not simply lose evidence or a case at court. If the custody officer fails to appropriately respond to risk, he may be suspended from duties pending investigation, he may lose his job (and his pension), and (although unlikely (see Inquest undated)) may ultimately face criminal sanction. The custody officer therefore needs to ascertain whether the detainee is, as Wooff and Skinns (2018) have highlighted, an 'Oscar winner' or a 'pension killer' (i.e. whether the detainee is dramatically over-emphasising any risk or pretending to have an illness or injury, or whether the detainee poses a genuine risk and where failure to act will result in loss of employment and loss of pension). In instances where the custody officer fails to identify risk of death or (serious) injury, or where the custody officer wrongly assumes the detainee or suspect to be 'playing-up', the police force may also be obliged to answer questions and may shoulder some of the blame. Yet, given the low probability of disciplinary action, it seems that custody officers overstate the risk involved. The reason that it is so prominent is perhaps because there are personal repercussions, even if such repercussions are unlikely to result from a death or serious injury in custody.

Vulnerability is also constructed in a manner that best makes sense to the custody officer; it is interpreted through his frame of reference. Essentially, vulnerability and the appropriate adult safeguard are interpreted pursuant to police objectives. Vulnerability is also identified in a way that best makes sense to the custody officer, i.e. something akin to a police investigation. Decisions on the appropriate adult are made in the easiest and most straightforward manner possible, indicating, too, a sense of pragmatism (see also Dehaghani 2017a). A desire to minimise effort may also explain why the custody officer consults the HCP for advice – it is easier to defer a decision to someone else, particularly someone with more 'expertise'. Custody officers, therefore, are not unlike other workers: as Punch (1985: 187) has noted, researchers often become 'mesmerised by the police world and attribute behaviour uniquely to its culture whereas fruitful similarities, and contrasts, abound with workers in other types of organisational setting'. Ultimately, they take a path of least resistance, prioritising personal gains and losses, and thereafter professional gains and losses. They are human beings, adopting an approach that is, to them, favourable *and* makes sense. The 'status, sanctions, degree of specificity, procedure and enforcement practice' (Baldwin 1989: 166) are important but, of greater importance is whether the sanction will affect the custody officer.

Closing or filling the gap

How custody officers approach vulnerability and the appropriate adult safeguard has been examined in the foregoing chapters. A question remains with regard to what can be done. One response would be to continue with the current approach and thus do nothing at all. However, this approach may be problematic as whilst 'discretion is lauded as not only inevitable but wise and desirable' (Reiner 1996: 1010), it is not always used in an 'equal opportunity' manner (*ibid.*). For the appropriate adult safeguard, discretion is not necessarily used in a positive manner (to safeguard suspects who would not otherwise fall under the guidance), rather it is used in a negative manner, (to remove the safeguard from suspects who are, in fact, caught by the guidance). Discretion could, however, be removed or lessened in a number of ways.

Improving the provisions

The Code C provisions could be 'tightened-up', guidance clarified and the status altered: definitions contained under the College of Policing guidance could be incorporated into Code C,[1] the guidance could be moved from the Notes for Guidance to the main Code or an Annex, and a statutory duty could be introduced for adults, similar to that which is available for young suspects (as suggested by Jacobson (2008) and NAAN (2015)). Such changes assume that custody officers understand and operationalise the definitions in the 'correct' manner, and/or require that attention be paid, by custody officers, to Code C. These changes would fail to take account of 'interpretative judgement' (Bronnit and Stenning 2011: 321) connected with adult vulnerability, as demonstrated by the research in this book, and place considerable faith in custody officers and the criminal process. It is also possible that such changes will be 'easily absorbed' (McConville *et al.* 1991: 189) by custody officers. Such recommendations – whilst potentially improving knowledge, rendering the Code more accessible, and lessening the chance that an appropriate adult will fail to attend for an adult suspect – are flawed because they fail to recognise the importance of police culture and the broader structure of the criminal process.

Increasing accountability and sanctions for non-compliance

A slightly better solution would be to require greater activity from the courts in holding custody officers accountable for their actions or inactions, with decisions more readily open to challenge. This would require an increase in the likelihood of detection along with an increase in the severity of the sanction.[2] The courts could deem every piece of evidence inadmissible where an appropriate adult was not obtained in breach of Code C. This may require either a wider interpretation or a change in the requirements of ss 76 and 78. Yet, this would require that the case reach the courts, which is a low probability event, considering that the vast number of cases do not make it that far. Such a recommendation also requires that an individual continues through the criminal justice process. Exclusion of evidence lacks severity: the most that is lost is the case. A more radical recommendation would be to render a breach of Code C subject to civil or criminal sanction, either against the police force or the individual officer. Whilst it may be more permissible to invoke civil sanction, it must be remembered that the criminal sanction should only be invoked as a last resort (see Packer 1968). More problematically, in terms of practicality, is that such a recommendation is founded-upon the certainty, or near certainty, that a breach is detected.

Accountability may also be achieved through the Independent Office for Police Conduct (IOPC)[3] complaints procedure. However, such a remedy requires awareness of the breach and an ability and/or a desire to see through the complaints process. As the Angiolini Report (2017: 28) highlighted:

> People who spend time in police custody are not generally a group who campaign collectively. Many are vulnerable or marginalised within society, for

> example, they may have mental health problems or be repeat offenders, and many feel shame and a stigma about having been in police custody. While there are community groups who campaign on particular policing issues, such as stop and search, the police custody experience is not generally the subject of widespread or sustained public debate.

Upon perusal of (the then) IPCC website, there were no recorded complaints dealing solely with non-implementation of the appropriate adult safeguard in respect of adult suspects (see, for example, IPCC 2009: Case 2.6 Bulletin 8). The practical realities of the complaints procedure may also prove difficult. Suspects may be reluctant to complain about police malpractice or violence, because they feel like it would be a waste of time, because the police would 'get away with it' regardless, because they would be specifically targeted in the future for having previously complained (Choongh 1997: 196), or because they simply wish to put the ordeal behind them. There is also a question as to whether officers take detainee complaints seriously (*ibid.*: 83).

Filling the 'gap' with ethics and training?

Whilst a 'gap' between the law in books and the law in action may be impossible to remove entirely, adoption of the 'intensely practical scheme' (Ashworth and Redmayne 2010: 37) of the ECHR, coupled with the use of ethical principles, may help fill this gap (*ibid.*: 62). Ethical principles hold an important place within the criminal process and particularly within policing (see Council of Europe 2001; Council of Europe 1979; College of Policing 2014; s 39A (5) of the Policing Act 1996 as amended by s 124 of the Anti-Social Behaviour, Crime and Policing Act 2014. See also Wright 2007). The police, by virtue of their position, have the power to radically alter the life of another and are the 'ultimate gatekeepers of citizenship and respectability' due to their 'crucial role in protecting hard-to-reach and vulnerable groups' (Neyroud and Beckley 2001: 38). As custody officers tend to act in a self-interested manner, ethical guidelines could direct them towards the exercise of positive discretion, i.e. discretion exercised in the best interests of the suspect. An ethical model could encourage compliance with the appropriate adult safeguard (although no reference is made to this in current Codes of Ethics) and may help challenge the current police perception of vulnerable suspects as 'social junk' (Spitzer 1975). Custody officers may be more willing to invest time and effort in safeguarding the vulnerable, whilst also being mindful of the detrimental implications of not implementing the appropriate adult safeguard. An ethical approach could potentially drive reform of the criminal process and successfully confront the long-standing, engrained and problematic occupational policing culture(s). It may help to strengthen disciplinary rules and procedures thus bolstering individual rights within the criminal process. Yet, it remains to be seen whether ethical principles would guarantee the implementation of the appropriate adult safeguard for every suspect who meets the criteria set out within Code C. Doubt may also arise regarding the extent to which an ethics-based approach is capable of infiltrating police culture. For example, Bittner (Wright 2007: 596 citing Bittner 1970), highlighting that prejudice is unavoidable in police work, has raised scepticism regarding the kind of ethics the police are required to adopt. Given the failure of the criminal justice process to properly embody due process principles, it seems unlikely that ethical guidelines can remedy police practices with regard to vulnerable suspects.

Another option would be to provide custody officers with training. This suggestion was advanced by Palmer (1996: 635) who proposed that 'the introduction of basic training for all police officers in the recognition of mental illness and learning difficulties will reduce the potential for breaches of the Codes'. Yet, this supposes that custody officers have little awareness of the requirements of Code C. Such an assumption is simply misguided: it is often what custody officers choose to do with the information provided that leads to non-implementation of the appropriate adult safeguard. Palmer's suggestion was made despite her recognition (*ibid.*: 639) that the appropriate adult safeguard is not implemented 'even when custody officers are aware of the illness or handicap'. It is also worth noting that custody officers, whilst receptive to the idea of more training in relation to the management of risk posed by death or (serious) injury, felt that they knew enough with regard to vulnerability and the appropriate adult safeguard. Whilst custody officer knowledge most certainly requires improvement, it is unlikely that this suggestion would lead to an improvement in the uptake of the appropriate adult safeguard, given the interplay between various factors (see Chapters 5–8).

Training guidelines or ethical principles may act merely as a sticking-plaster rather than adequately addressing non-implementation. Custody officers tend to interpret the law in a way that best suits their needs and makes sense to them. Further, as McConville, Sanders and Leng (1991 cited in Maguire and Norris 1994: 74) have noted, malpractice, an '*integral and routine* part of the investigative process in England and Wales', does not necessarily occur as a result of cultural pressures or occasional enthusiasm, rather malpractice occurs because the police are ambivalent or will or allow malpractice to happen, particularly when it fulfils a police purpose. Custody officers, rather than searching impartially for vulnerability, construct it in a manner pursuant to their own personal or professional purpose, and similarly implement the appropriate adult safeguard pursuant to their own objectives and the requirements of the investigation.

(Re)-constructing vulnerability?

There are two major obstructions to the implementation of the appropriate adult safeguard: the task of ensuring compliance is onerous, if not impossible, and an accurate assessment of vulnerability is difficult, if not impossible, given its subjective and internal nature (see Choongh 1997: 97). Even if custody officers are to adopt the Code C definition of vulnerability and implement the safeguard for every suspect who is identified as vulnerable, this requires that identification procedures are flawless (see Chapter 7). A reconceptualisation of vulnerability may resolve these issues.

Those exhibiting issues with capacity, comprehension and understanding are not the only suspects to experience difficulty understanding legal rights or providing reliable and accurate information, or to be suggestible, compliant or acquiescent. Vulnerability can manifest for a plethora of reasons. Much of the rhetoric around vulnerability, as contained within Code C, is somewhat misleading as it suggests that a vulnerable suspect is one who may provide false, misleading or unreliable information. This is further compounded by ss 76, 77 and 78 PACE. The focus is not on the suspect, but rather on preserving the integrity of the evidence (undoubtedly a relic of the Judges' Rules) and this message is undoubtedly one that is sent to, and received by, the custody officer. Code C and PACE fail to appreciate that acting in one's own best interests may not necessarily equate to avoiding the provision of false, unreliable or misleading information. Rather, it could mean not saying anything at all and/or obstructing the police interview and wider investigation. What is also omitted from Code C is an explanation or appreciation of how police custodial detention and the daunting nature of the criminal process may prompt someone to act against his or her own best interests. Vulnerability may arise through detention in police custody, the unequal power relations between the detainer and the detained, and through the police exercise of 'physical, territorial and information control' (Hodgson 1994). When viewed through the lens of police power and control, detention in police custody and custodial interrogation can be considered coercive, even with improved safeguards (Gudjonsson 2003: 25; see also Skinns *et al.* 2017). As Choongh (1997: 97) highlighted, 57% of detainees in his study experienced confinement as distressing and caused them to feel powerless.

Although there are (what are purported to be) due process safeguards available to the suspect in police custody, the nature of police custody may undermine the suspect's ability to realise or enforce his or her rights (see Rock 2007). The distress brought about through arrest and detention may destabilise a suspect to the extent that he or she experiences barriers to the comprehension or invocation of his or her rights, or is indeed unable to understand and invoke his or her rights. The suspect's rights and entitlements are typically read upon booking-in, after the suspect has been asked a range of intrusive questions regarding mental and physical well-being and has been subjected to a rather invasive search. The rights can often be read whilst the search is being carried-out, as was observed in this study (see also Sanders *et al.* 2010). The suspect is therefore, for that reason or another, pre-occupied when rights are given and those who have experience of custody may be disinterested (Brown, *et al.* 1992). Educational difficulties may further compound this issue, rendering the uptake of rights almost impossible. For example, as Rock (2007: 109) notes, 'reading in detention is particularly difficult because it necessitates reading alone', and whilst some suspects may have previously relied on social networks to facilitate reading, custody 'dismantles' the support networks in place. The provision of the appropriate adult safeguard may go some way to remedy this issue (*ibid.*: 109–10).

Supposing that a suspect can digest the information provided, the realisation of these rights may be impeded by a reluctance or inability to exercise them. This is particularly important given that the rights available to suspects, such as the right to legal advice, are 'triggered only by a *positive* request' (McConville *et al.* 1991: 50). A reluctance to exercise one's rights may stem from a fear of appearing bothersome or, more poignantly perhaps, guilty; a feeling that they have 'nothing to hide'; a desire to be released as soon as possible, or a willingness to confess (and a failure to understand the benefits of requesting legal representation) (see Kemp 2013; Kemp and Balmer 2008; Skinns 2009). Vulnerability arises, inter alia, from being brought into contact with the criminal process (Feeley 1992), being detained in police custody (see Choongh 1997),[4] having adverse inferences drawn from your silence (see Quirk 2013; 2017), having limited access to the case against you (particularly when compared with the information held by the police) (see Owusu-Bempah 2017), or being unable or unwilling to exercise your rights. On this basis, it could be argued that all suspects are vulnerable within police custody. The focus, within an adversarial criminal justice process, should not be, as Code C and PACE would suggest, on the provision of reliable information but instead on somehow restoring the inherent power imbalance and thus enabling the suspect to act in his or her own best interests. The opportunity to interact with an individual who is not at all involved in the investigation (i.e. not a police officer or solicitor) could help address this.

Reconceptualisation would also bring with it the additional benefit of removing issues with identification, definition and discretion. A reconceptualisation of vulnerability would require the widening of the appropriate adult provision to include all who are subject to police investigation under suspicion of committing a criminal offence (and would apply to suspects whether detained whilst questioned or not). Yet, this wider safeguard may not be sufficient for all suspects, considering that some may need more support than others, or a specific type of support. But, as it stands, the appropriate adult safeguard does not necessarily meet these needs (see Chapter 2). The issues with the appropriate adult safeguard were highlighted by CO16-W at interview:

> The appropriate adult: they're not medically trained; they've not worked with vulnerable adults or youths in the community or anything like that. People, they go away to uni [sic] and they do degrees on and they've studied this for years and they're developed in their field. And yet here, you've got someone coming in who likes helping people and [is] dealing with everyone's abilities and disabilities. And again, it's just not right. If someone comes in who speaks French, you don't sort of shout at them and speak slowly, you get a French interpreter. If somebody who comes in who can't hear, can't speak, you don't get somebody who can do a bit of Makaton, you get somebody who can do British Sign Language. So, if someone's got a particular issue that's making them vulnerable in custody, then I don't know why we're ignoring it and saying, 'Yeah, we'll just get this person in.' It's just saying to me, if you've got a heart problem and your GPs [does the] surgery or the local vet [does] it because they're qualified generally. You've got to have your specialists and this is why we're just ticking the boxes and doing a little bit to say that we're

> looking after vulnerable people but if we want to do it properly.... We could have specialists in these areas that you can bring in.

The problems with volunteers, as highlighted by Pierpoint (2000: 388–9), were mentioned by CO16-W (Interview):

> You've got some twenty-year-old bloke who lives with his partner and because he's got a learning difficulty... suddenly you'll get some sixty-year-old bloke that he's never seen before, that he's got no interest in whatsoever, has nothing in common with and that person is meant to help him with communication.... Some sixty-year-old [person] who knows less about the words and the slang and everything else that you use and they're meant to be helping you with your communication. The ideas for why these appropriate adults are here are good [sic] but then it doesn't work.... If it was outside the police station and he wanted some help or assistance, he wouldn't go and speak to the old boy who's in here, he would go and speak to Danny the youth worker down the road who's down with the young [people] and understands what they're going through.... They can empathise with the person. But they've got no understanding at all. So all this assisting with communication, it isn't there nowadays, it just isn't there.

On the basis of such considerations, it is time to consider whether a generic support could be provided for all suspects, with an additional tailored safeguard provided to those with capacity or comprehension issues. Here it should also be recognised that it is not simply those with learning disabilities or mental health problems who are not the only individuals who may possess issues with communication. A name change may also signal a move away from current notions of vulnerability which seem to construct the vulnerable suspect as someone lacking capacity or appearing childlike and abnormal (see Chapters 5 and 6). A specialist advocate (suggested by Palmer 1996: 641) could assist generally and an intermediary (see YJCEA 1999) could be provided for those with capacity and comprehension issues. This could, however, add additional complexity and such complexity could generate confusion for custody officers therefore making it less likely that they would follow the rules.

Along with a reconceptualisation of vulnerability, there must also be a reconceptualisation of how the role of the appropriate adult is framed: it should be one which places the suspect on an equal footing with the state, not as one which focuses on the extraction of information. In such instances, the notion of 'reasonable adjustment' under the Equality Act 2010 could be helpful. However, caution must be exercised here. Whilst the Equality Act 2010 and its requirement for 'reasonable adjustments' could be lauded as something through which to fundamentally alter how the appropriate adult safeguard is conceptualised, it also requires that the individual for which these adjustments are made possess a 'protected characteristic' (s 4 Equality Act 2010). When cross-referencing these 'protected characteristics' with Code C, one can see how the appropriate adult's role could be limited to those with mental impairment. As a result, those who fall outside of this category could potentially be denied assistance.

Practical obstacles may arise when implementing change: for example, as noted by Ventress, Rix and Kent (2008: 371), 'realistically ... it would be extremely difficult to provide an appropriate adult in all cases where somebody is "mentally disordered" within the meaning of section 1 of the [MHA] 1983'. This is most certainly a concern of the Home Office when reflecting upon its attempts to rectify the supply and demand issue highlighted by the NAAN 'There to Help' Report (2015). Rather than, as NAAN have suggested, provide more funding for the appropriate adult safeguard, the Home Office have altered the definition of vulnerability in respect of adult suspects. Another, or additional, option would be to make legal advice mandatory for those considered especially vulnerable (JUSTICE 2017). Bringing fewer people into contact with the criminal justice process would reduce cost significantly and ensure that funds be redistributed to safeguarding those who are (see, for example, the enhancement of freedom model (Sanders *et al.* 2010)).

The Home Office made a number of changes to Code C in May 2018 (see Chapters 2 and 4, in particular). These changes have failed to tackle a number of important issues: the lack of or patchy provision of appropriate adult services across England and Wales has not been addressed. Whilst improving the provision would not necessarily reduce the custody officer's discretion or 'interpretative judgement' (see Bronnit and Stenning 2011: 321) when implementing the appropriate adult safeguard, custody officers are undoubtedly disincentivised when deciding whether the implement the appropriate adult by patchy or no provision. Similarly, the introduction of a statutory provision would not remove discretion or 'interpretative judgment' but would ensure that appropriate adult services are provided where requested (and could therefore incentivise custody officers to call an appropriate adult). There are also questions as to why the definition of 'mental vulnerability' was not retained and why the term 'mental health condition' was introduced. Considering that custody officers pay little attention to the definitions contained within the Codes (see Chapter 6), it is possible that a change to the definition will result in little or no change to the implementation of the appropriate adult safeguard. The functional test also does not seem to take into account, or at least dismisses, the difficulties custody officers experience when attempted to identify vulnerability. Overall, the Home Office changes may give the impression of doing something whilst actually doing little to nothing to change the uptake of the appropriate adult safeguard. This could, coincidentally, be the desired effect.

Considerations for further research and concluding remarks

This study, by focussing on custody officers, has provided an in-depth and nuanced account of how custody officers, as those tasked with the responsibility of implementing the appropriate adult safeguard, define, identify and make decisions on vulnerability. It has also contributed to the discourse surrounding wider questions of risk in policing and, more specifically, in police custody. This study is the first to build a grounded theory of custody officer decision-making in relation to the appropriate adult safeguard, and has made theoretical, empirical, methodological, and practical advancements in how we can understand police decision-making, the implementation of the appropriate adult safeguard, and the concept of vulnerability. Whilst in-depth, it was limited to two forces, thus restricting the generalisability of the findings. Moreover, it did not involve a review of custody records. These would have been useful so as to accurately ascertain what recorded information was available on the suspect and would also have been useful when decisions were later changed (e.g. a decision not to obtain an appropriate adult was later replaced by a decision to obtain one). Whilst updates were available on an ad-hoc basis (see Chapter 3), the custody records would have been useful to ensure consistency.

It should also be recognised that, whilst the implementation of the appropriate adult safeguard is the responsibility of the custody officer, it hinges, at least in some instances, on the recommendations of the HCP or, where available, FME or AMHP. Although not mentioned in relation to vulnerability, the role of the detention officer is also viewed as important in the ongoing risk-assessment. Future studies could therefore address how the appropriate adult safeguard is negotiated by these actors, particularly to the extent that definitions and decision-making mirror that of custody officers (see, for example, Norfolk 1996). Given the call for a reconceptualisation of vulnerability, another interesting avenue for exploration would be to examine how suspects and other detainees understand and experience detention in custody and the wider criminal process, and whether they consider themselves vulnerable and why (building on the work of Choongh (1997)). Further research is also undoubtedly required to examine, in greater detail, the role of the appropriate adult and, in particular, service-users' perspectives on the safeguard (adding to the recent work of Jessiman and Cameron (2017)). Finally, as has been noted, this research was conducted in 2014 and 2015. Thus, a future research project could address whether the 2018 version of the Code have resulted in any alteration to how and why the appropriate adult safeguard is implemented. My suspicion is that the changes to Code C will result in little to no change in custody officer practice.

It must be remembered that justice is delivered (or rather, not delivered, as the case may be) as part of a process. Within this process, it is impossible to sever one aspect from the other(s). This book has considered the translation of the appropriate adult safeguard from books into action, placing this also within the context of the broader criminal justice process. A holistic approach to the criminal justice process is required if suspects and other detainees are to be adequately safeguarded. Thirty years post-PACE it is time to rethink how justice is delivered and to completely reconceptualise how vulnerability is framed. The resolution is neither simple nor impossible but does require a sea-change in policing practice, police culture and the structure of the criminal justice process. The matter is greater in magnitude than occasional or infrequent non-implementation of the appropriate adult safeguard. The policing process, whilst problematic in and of itself, also contributes to and is part of the wider punitive process. This reality is inescapable.

Notes

1 I recommended, in earlier drafts of this book, that the MHA 1984 Code of Practice be incorporated into Code C. This has, to an extent, been done in the 2018 iteration of Code C.

2 This suggestion would point towards deterrence theory.

3 The IOPC was formerly known as the Independent Police Complaints Commission (IPCC) – see Policing and Crime Act 2017.

4 See also Cesari *et al.* (2016: 206) and van Oosterhout (2016: 252) in the context of Italy and the Netherlands, respectively.

Bibliography

Adebowale, V., 2013. *Independent Commission on Mental Health and Policing Report.* London: Independent Commission on Mental Health and Policing.

Alge, D., 2013. Negotiated Plea Agreements in Cases of Serious and Complex Fraud in England and Wales: A New Conceptualisation of Plea Bargaining? *European Journal of Current Legal Issues* 19.

Angiolini, E., 2017. *Report of the Independent Review of Deaths and Serious Incidents in Police Custody.* London: Home Office.

Ashworth, A., and Redmayne, M., 2010. *The Criminal Process*, 4th edn. Oxford: OUP.

Asquith, N., and Bartkowiak-Théron, I., 2015. Policing Diversity and Vulnerability in the Post-Macpherson Era: Unintended Consequences and Missed Opportunities. *Policing*, 9(1), 89–100.

Association of Chief Police Officers, 2012. *Safer Detention and Handling of Persons in Police Custody*, 2nd edn. Wyboston: ACPO and NPIA.

Auld, R., 2001. *Review of the Criminal Courts of England and Wales: Report.* London: Ministry of Justice.

Aviram, H., 2011. 'Packer in Context: Formalism and Fairness in the Due Process Model. *Journal of Law and Social Inquiry*, 36(1), 237–261.

Baldwin, R., 1989. Regulation and Policing by Code. In M. Weatheritt, ed. *Police Research: Some Future Prospects.* Aldershot: Avebury. 157–168.

Baldwin, R., and Kinsey, R., 1982. *Police Powers and Politics.* London: Quartet Books.

Bath, C., 2017a. Personal Correspondence: 29 June 2017.

Bath, C., 2017b. Personal Correspondence: 1 September 2017.

Bath, C., 2018. Personal Correspondence: 2 May 2018.

Bayley, D.H., and Bittner, E., 1984. Learning the Skills of Policing. *Law and Contemporary Problems*, 47(4), 35–49.

BBC News, 2016. Lisburn police station: Officer and former police employee to be charged over death of man in custody. Available online at: www.bbc.co.uk/news/uk-northern-ireland-36255191 (accessed 6 June 2016).

Bean, P., and Nemitz, T., 1995. *Out of Depth and Out of Sight.* Loughborough: University of Loughborough.

Blackstock, J., Cape, E., Hodgson, J., Ogodrodova, A., and Spronken, T., 2014. *Inside Police Custody: An Empirical Account of Suspects' Rights in Four Jurisdictions.* Antwerp: Intersentia.

Blumer, H., 1969. *Symbolic Interactionism: Perspective and Method.* New Jersey: Prentice-Hall.

Bottomley, K., Coleman, C., Dixon, D., Gill, M., and Wall, D., 1991. *The Impact of Aspects of the Police and Criminal Evidence Act 1984 on Policing in a Force in the North of England*. Hull: Centre for Criminology and Criminal Justice.

Bottoms, A.E., and McClean, J.D., 1976. *Defendants in the Criminal Justice Process.* Abingdon: Routledge.

Bowcott, O., 2017. Government's £1bn plan for online courts 'challenges open justice'. Available online at: www.theguardian.com/law/2017/mar/15/governments-1bn-plan-for-online-courts-challenges-open-justice (accessed 8 September 2017).

Bradley, K.J.C., 2009. *Review of People with Mental Health Problems or Learning Disabilities in the Criminal Justice System*. London: Department of Health.

Braun, V., and Clarke, V., 2013. *Successful Qualitative Research: A Practical Guide for Beginners.* London: Sage.

Bronnit, S., and Stenning, P., 2011. Understanding Discretion in Policing. *Criminal Law Journal*, 35, 319–332.

Brown, D., 1997. *PACE Ten Years On: A Review of the Research*. Home Office Research Study No 155. London: Home Office.

Brown, D., Ellis, T., and Larcombe, K., 1992. *Changing the Code: Police Detention Under the Revised PACE Codes of Practice*. London: Home Office.

Brown, K., 2014. Questioning the Vulnerability Zeitgeist: Care and Control Practices with 'Vulnerable' Young People. *Social Policy and Society*, 13, 371–387.

Brown, K., 2015. *Vulnerability and Young People: Care and Social Control in Policy and Practice*. Bristol: Policy Press.

Bryman, A., 2012. *Social Research Methods*, 4th edn. Oxford: OUP.

Buchanan, J.M., 2005. Afraid to be free: Dependency as desideratum. *Public Choice*, 124, 19–31.

Bucke, T., and Brown, D., 1997. *In Police Custody: Police Powers and Suspects' Rights under the Revised PACE Codes of Practice*. Home Office Research Study No 174. London: Home Office.

Burns, R., 2000. *Introduction to Research Methods*, 4th edn. London: SAGE.

Butler, J., 2004. *Precarious Life: The Powers of Mourning and Violence*. Brooklyn: Verso.

Butler, J., 2010. *Frames of War: When is Life Grievable?* Brooklyn: Verso.

Cain, M., 1973. *Society and the Policeman's Role*. Abingdon: Routledge and Kagan Paul.

Campbell, E., 2005. Theorising the evidence on discretionary decision making: alternative perspectives. *Evidence and Policy* 1(1), 33–60.

Campbell, T., and Heginbotham, C., 1991. *Mental Illness: Prejudice, Discrimination and the Law*. Aldershot: Dartmouth.

Campeau, H., 2015. 'Police culture' at work: making sense of police oversight. *British Journal of Criminology*, 55(4), 669–687.

Cape, E., 2013. Designing out defence lawyers. In J. Robins, ed. *No Defence: Lawyers and Miscarriages of Justice*. London: Wilmington Publishing.

Cesari, C., 2015. Between Respecting 'Traditional' Safegards and Modern Needs of Protecting Juveniles. Country Report Italy. In M. Panzavolta, D. de Vocht, M. van Oosterhout and M. Vanderhallen, eds. *Interrogating Young Suspects: Procedural Safeguards from a Legal Perspective*. Antwerp: Intersentia.

Cesari, C., de Felice, D., and Patanè, V., 2016. Italy: Empirical Findings. In M. Vanderhallen, M. van Oosterhout, M. Panzavolta and D. de Vocht, eds. *Interrogating Young Suspects: Procedural Safeguards from an Empirical Perspective*. Antwerp: Intersentia.

Chan, J.B.L., 1997. *Changing Police Culture: Policing in a Multicultural Society*. Cambridge: Cambridge University Press.

Charmaz, K., 2006. *Constructing Grounded Theory: A Practical Guide through Qualitative Analysis*. New York: SAGE.

Charmaz, K., 2011. Grounded Theory Methods in Social Justice Research. In N Denzin and Y Lincoln, eds. *The SAGE Handbook of Qualitative Research*, 4th edn. New York: SAGE.

Choongh, S., 1997a. *Policing as Social Discipline*. Oxford: Clarendon Press.

Choongh, S., 1997b. Policing the Dross: A Social Disciplinary Model of Policing. *British Journal of Criminology*, 38(4), 623–634.

Christie, N., 1986. The Ideal Victim. In E.A. Fattah, ed. *From Crime Policy to Victim Policy: Reorienting the Justice System*. Basingstoke: Palgrave Macmillan.

Clare, I., and Gudjonsson, G.H., 1993a. *Devising and Piloting an Experimental Version of the Notice to Detained Persons (Report on the Royal Commission on Criminal Procedure)*. Research Study No. 7. London: HMSO.

Clare, I., and Gudjonsson, G.H., 1993b. Interrogative suggestibility, confabulation, and acquiescence in people with mild learning difficulties (Mental handicap): Implications for reliability during police interrogation. *British Journal of Clinical Psychology*, 32, 295–301.

College of Policing, 2014. *Code of Ethics: A Code of Practice for the Principles and Standards of Professional Behaviour for the Policing Profession of England and Wales*. London: College of Policing. Available online at: www.college.police.uk/What-we-do/Ethics/Documents/Code_of_Ethics.pdf (accessed 27 April 2016).

College of Policing, 2016. *Authorised Professional Practice, Mental Health: Mental Health – Detention*. London: College of Policing. Available online at: www.acollege.police.uk/app-content/mental-health/mental-health-detention/#appropriate-adults (accessed 25 June 2018).

College of Policing, 2018a. *Authorised Professional Practice, Detention and Custody*. London: College of Policing. Available online at: www.acollege.police.uk/app-content/detention-and-custody-2/?s= (accessed 25 June 2018).

College of Policing, 2018b. *Authorised Professional Practice, Detention and Custody, Risk Assessment*. London: College of Policing. Available online at: www.acollege.police.uk/app-content/detention-and-custody-2/risk-assessment/ (accessed 25 June 2018).

College of Policing, 2018c. *Authorised Professional Practice, Mental Ill Health: Mental Vulnerability and Illness*. London: College of Policing. Available online at: www.acollege.police.uk/app-content/mental-health/mental-vulnerability-and-illness/ (accessed 25 June 2018).

Collins, J., 2013. The Contours of Vulnerability. In J. Wallbank and J. Herring, eds. *Vulnerabilities, Care and Family Law*. Abingdon: Routledge.

Cooper, P., and Gerry, F., 2017. Vulnerability and Defences. In P. Cooper and H. Norton, eds. *Vulnerable People and the Criminal Justice System*. Oxford: OUP, 183–228.

Coppen, J., 2008. PACE: A View From the Custody Suite. In E. Cape and R. Young, eds. *Regulating Policing: The Police and Criminal Evidence Act 1984 – Past, Present and Future*. Oxford: Hart, 75–90.

Corbin, J., and Strauss, A., 2008. *Basics of Qualitative Research: Techniques and Procedures for Developing Grounded Theory*, 3rd edn. New York: SAGE.

Criminal Justice Joint Inspectorate, 2009. *A Joint Inspection on Work Prior to Sentence with Offenders with Mental Disorders*. London: HMIP.

Criminal Justice Joint Inspectorate, 2014. *A Joint Inspection of the Treatment of Offenders with Learning Disabilities within the Criminal Justice System – Phase 1 From Arrest to Sentence*. London: HMIP.

Criminal Law Revision Committee, 1972. *Criminal Law Revision Committee Eleventh Report, Evidence (General)*. Cmnd 4991. London: HMSO.

Crown Prosecution Service, 2010. *Diverting offenders with mental health problems and/or learning disabilities within the National Conditional Cautioning Framework*. London: CPS 2010. Available online at: www.cps.gov.uk/legal/d_to_g/diverting_offenders_with_mental_health_problems_and_or_learning_disabilities_within_the_national_/#a08 (accessed 19 May 2014).

Crown Prosecution Service, undated. *Prosecution Policy and Guidance, Legal Guidance, Deaths in Custody*. London: CPS. Available online at: www.cps.gov.uk/legal/d_to_g/deaths_in_custody/ (accessed 8 December 2015).

Cummins, I., 2007. Boats against the current: Vulnerable adults in police custody. *The Journal of Adult Protection*, 9(1), 15–24.

Cummins, I., 2011. The Other Side of Silence: The Role of the Appropriate Adult Post-Bradley. *Ethics and Social Welfare*, 5(3), 306–312.

Darbyshire, P., 2000. The mischief of plea bargaining and sentencing rewards. *Criminal Law Review*, 895–910.

Davis, K.C., 1969. *Discretionary Justice: A Preliminary Inquiry*. Baton Rouge, LA: Louisiana State University Press.

Dehaghani, R., 2016. He's just not that vulnerable: Exploring the Implementation of the Appropriate Adult Safeguard in Police Custody. *Howard Journal of Crime and Justice*, 55(4), 396–413.

Dehaghani, R., 2017a. Automatic authorisation: an exploration of the decision to detain in police custody. *Criminal Law Review*, 3, 187–202.

Dehaghani, R., 2017b. Custody Officers, Code C and Constructing Vulnerability: Implications for Policy and Practice. *Policing*, 11(1), 74–86.

Dehaghani, R., 2017c. 'Vulnerable by law but not by nature': examining child and youth vulnerability in the context of police custody. *Journal of Social Welfare and Family Law*, 39(4), 454–472.

Dehaghani, R., 2017d. *Vulnerability in Police Custody: Definition and Identification in the Context of the Implementation the Appropriate Adult Safeguard*. Leicester: University of Leicester.

Dehaghani, R. 2017e. Response to Home Office Code C consultation. Available online at: www.researchgate.net/publication/321875877_PACE_Consultation_2017_Response_of_Dr_Roxanna_Dehaghani_Cardiff_University (accessed 26 June 2018).

Dehaghani, R., 2018. Condemning and Condoning Non-Implementation of the Appropriate Adult Safeguard: *R. v Beattie and Miller v D. Criminal Law Review*, 8, 646–651.

Dehaghani, R., and Newman, D., 2017. 'We're vulnerable too': an (alternative) analysis of vulnerability within English criminal legal aid and police custody. *Oñati Socio-Legal Series*, 7(6).

Dehaghani, R., and Newman, D., (in progress). Constructing the case for the defence: ineffective lawyering, police impropriety and the efficacy of legal protections.

Denscombe, M., 2002. *Ground Rules for Good Research: A 10 Point Guide for Social Researchers*. Buckingham: Open University Press.

Department of Health, 2001. *Valuing People: a new strategy for learning disability for the 21st Century*. White Paper, Cmd 5086. London: TSO.

Department of Health, 2015. *Mental Health Act 1983: Code of Practice*. London: TSO. Available online at: www.gov.uk/government/uploads/system/uploads/attachment_data/file/396918/Code_of_Practice.pdf (accessed 10 November 2015).

Department of Justice, 2015. *Police and Criminal Evidence (Northern Ireland) Order 1989: Code C: Code of Practice for the Detention, Treatment and Questioning of Persons by Police Officers*. Belfast: Department of Justice.

Diduck, A., 2013. Autonomy and Vulnerability in Family Law: The Missing Link. InJ. Wallbank and J. Herring, eds. *Vulnerabilities, Care and Family Law*. Abingdon: Routledge.

Dixon, D., 1997. *Law in Policing: Legal Regulation and Police Practices*. Oxford: Clarendon Press.

Dixon, D., 1999. Police Investigative Procedures: Changing Legal and Political Contexts of Policing Practices. In C. Walker and K. Starmer, eds. *Miscarriages of Justice: A Review of Justice in Error*, 2nd edn. London: Blackstone Press, 65–82.

Drake, K.E., Bull, R., and Boon, J.C.W., 2008. Interrogative Suggestibility, Self-Esteem, and the Influence of Negative Life Events. *Legal and Criminological Psychology*, 13, 299–307.

DuffP., 1998. Crime Control, Due Process and 'The Case for the Prosecution'. *British Journal of Criminology*, 38(4), 611–615.

Dunn, M., Clare, I., and Holland, A., 2008. To Empower or to Protect? Constructing the 'Vulnerable Adult' in English Law and Public Policy. *Legal Studies*, 28(2), 234–253.

Durcan, G., Saunders, A., Gadsby, B., and Hazard, A., 2014. *The Bradley Report Five Years On: An Independent Review of Progress to Date and Priorities for Further Development*. London: Centre for Mental Health.

Dworkin, R., 1977. *Taking Rights Seriously*. London: Duckworth.

Ellison, G., and Brogden, M., 2010. *Policing in an Age of Austerity: A Postcolonial Perspective*. Abingdon: Routledge

Ericson, R.V., 2007. Rules in Policing: Five Perspectives. *Theoretical Criminology*, 11(3), 367–401.

Ericson, R.V., and Haggerty, K.D., 1998. *Policing the Risk Society*. Oxford: Clarendon Press.

Evans, R., 1993. The Conduct of Police Interviews with Juveniles. *Royal Commission on Criminal Justice Research Study* 8. London: HMSO.

Evans, R., and Puech, K., 2001. Reprimands and warnings: populist punitiveness or restorative justice? *Criminal Law Review*, 794–805.

Ewick, P., and Silbey, S.S., 1998. *The Common Place of Law: Stories from Everyday Life*. Chicago, IL: University of Chicago Press.

Fairclough, S., 2017. 'It doesn't happen … and I've never thought it was necessary for it to happen': Barriers to vulnerable defendants giving evidence by live link in Crown Court trials. *International Journal of Evidence and Proof*, 21(3), 209–229.

Fairclough, S., 2018. Speaking up for Injustice: Reconsidering the provision of special measures through the lens of equality. *Criminal Law Review*, 4–19.

Feeley, M.F., 1992. *The Process is the Punishment: Handling Cases in a Lower Criminal Courts*. New York, NY: Russell Sage.

Fennell, P., 1994. Mentally disordered suspects in the criminal justice system. *Journal of Law and Society*, 21, 57–71.

Fenner, S., Gudjonsson, G. and Clare, I. (2002) Understanding of the current police caution (England and Wales) among suspects in police detention. 12(2) *Journal of Community and Applied Social Psychology*, 83–93.

Fielding, N.G., 1989. Police culture and police practice. In M. Weatheritt, ed. *Police Research: Some Future Prospects*. Aldershot: Avebury.

Fisher, H., 1977/78. *Report of an Inquiry by the Hon. Sir Henry Fisher into the Circumstances Leading to the Trial of three persons on Charges arising out of the death of Maxwell Confait and the fire at 27 Doggett Road, London SE6*. HC 1977/78 90. London: HMSO.

Fineman, M.A., 2009. Evolving Images of Gender and Equality: A Feminist Journey. *New England Law Review*, 42, 437–460.

Fineman, M.A., 2013a. Equality, Autonomy, and the Vulnerable Subject in Law and Politics. In M.A. Fineman and G. Grear, eds. *Gender in Law, Culture, and Society: Vulnerability: Reflections on a New Ethical Foundation for Law and Politics.* Farnham: Ashgate.

Fineman, M.A., 2013b. Feminism, Masculinities, and Multiple Identities. *Nevada Law Journal*, 13, 619–639.

Garland, D., 2001. *The Culture of Control: Crime and Social Order in Contemporary Society.* Chicago, IL: University of Chicago Press.

Gibson, B., and Hartman, J., 2013. *Rediscovering Grounded Theory.* London: SAGE.

Glaser, B., and Strauss, A., 2009. *The Discovery of Grounded Theory: Strategies for Qualitative Research.* New Brunswick, NJ: Aldine.

Goodin, R., 1985. *Protecting the Vulnerable: A Reanalysis of Our Social Responsibilities*Chicago, IL: University of Chicago Press.

Goffman, E., 1956. Embarrassment of Social Organisation. *American Journal of Sociology*, 57, 264–271.

Goffman, E., 1969. *The Presentation of Self in Everyday Life.* London: Allen Lane.

Griffiths, J., 1970. Ideology in Criminal Procedure or A Third 'Model' of the Criminal Process. *Yale Law Journal*, 79, 359–417.

Grimshaw, R., and Jefferson, T., 1987. *Interpreting Policework: Policy and Practice in Forms of Beat Policing.* Crows Nest: Allen and Unwin.

Group 4 Securicor, undated a. *A Day in the Life of a Health Care Professional.* Available online at: www.g4smedicalservices.co.uk/library/files/Day_in_the_life_HCP.pdf (accessed 22 June 2017).

Group 4 Securicor, undated b. *A Day in the Life of a Forensic Medical Examiner.* Available online at: www.g4smedicalservices.co.uk/library/files/Day_in_the_life_FME.pdf (accessed 22 June 2017).

Gudjonsson, G.H., 1993. Confession Evidence, Psychological Vulnerability and Expert Testimony. *Journal of Community and Applied Social Psychology*, 3, 117–129.

Gudjonsson, G.H., 2006. The psychological vulnerabilities of witnesses and the risk of false accusations and false confessions. In A. Heaton-Armstrong, E. Shepherd, G.H. Gudjonsson and D. Wolchover, eds. *Witness Testimony: Psychological, Investigative and Evidential Perspectives.* Oxford: OUP.

Gudjonsson, G.H., 2003. *The Psychology of Interrogations and Confessions: A Handbook.* Hoboken, NJ: Wiley.

Gudjonsson, G.H., 2010. Psychological vulnerabilities during police interviews: Why are they important? *Legal and Criminological Psychology*, 15, 161–175.

Gudjonsson, G.H., and Joyce, T., 2011, Interviewing adults with intellectual disabilities. *Advances in Mental Health and Intellectual Disabilities*, 5(2), 16–21.

Gudjonsson, G.H., and MacKeith, J.A., 1990. A proven case of false confession: psychological aspects of the coerced-compliant type. *Medicine, Science and the Law*, 30(4), 329–335.

Gudjonsson, G.H., Clare, I., Rutter, S., and Pearce, J. 1993. Persons at Risk During Interviews in Police Custody: The Identification of Vulnerabilities. *Royal Commission on Criminal Procedure Research Study No 12.* London: HMSO.

Hart, H.L.A., 2012. *The Concept of Law*, 3rd edn. Oxford: Clarendon Press.

Hawkins, K., 1992. Introduction. In K. Hawkins, ed. *The Uses of Discretion.* Oxford: Clarendon Press.

Hawkins, K., 1992. Preface. In K. Hawkins, ed. *The Uses of Discretion*. Oxford: Clarendon Press.

Hawkins, K., 2002. Order, rationality and silence: some reflections on criminal justice decision-making. In L.R. Gelsthorpe and N. Padfield, eds. *Exercising Discretion: Decision Making in the Criminal Justice System and Beyond*. Cullompton: Willan.

Hawkins, K., 2003. *Law as Last Resort: Prosecution Decision-Making in a Regulatory Agency*. Oxford: OUP.

Henderson, C., Robinson, E., Evans-Lacko, S., Corker, E., Rebollo-Mesa, I., Rose, D., and Thornicroft, G., 2016. Public knowledge, attitudes, social distance and reported contact regarding people with mental illness 2009–15. *Acta Psychiatrica Scandinavica*, 134, 23–33.

Henham, R., 1998. Human Rights, Due Process and Sentencing. *British Journal of Criminology*, 34(2), 592–610.

Herring, J., 2016. *Vulnerable Adults and the Law*. Oxford: OUP.

Hobbs, D., 1988. *Doing the Business: Entrepreneurship, Detectives and the Working Class in the East End of London*. Oxford: OUP.

Hodgson, J., 1994. Adding Injury to Injustice: The Suspect at the Police Station. *Journal of Law and Society*, 21(1), 85–101.

Hodgson, J., 1997. Vulnerable Suspects and the Appropriate Adult. *Criminal Law Review*, 785–795.

Holdaway, S., 1979. *The British Police*. London: Edward Arnold.

Holdaway, S., 1983. *Inside the British Police: A Force at Work*. Oxford: Basil Blackwell.

Holdaway, S., 1989. Discovering structure. Studies of the British police occupational culture. In M. Weatheritt, ed. *Police Research: Some Future Prospects*. Aldershot: Avebury.

Her Majesty's Inspectorate of Constabulary (HMIC), 2015. *The Welfare of Vulnerable People in Police Custody*. London: HMIC.

Home Office, 2017. *Revised Code of Practice for the Detention, Treatment and Questioning of Persons by Police Officers. Police and Criminal Evidence Act (PACE) 1984. Code C*. London: Crown.

Home Office and National Appropriate Adult Network, 2011. *Guide for Appropriate Adults*. London: Home Office.

Independent Police Complaints Commission, 2009. *Case 2.6 Bulletin 8 – General*. Available online at: www.ipcc.gov.uk/sites/default/files/Documents/bulletin82.6.pdf (accessed 26 April 2016).

Innes, M., 2007. Investigation order and major crime inquiries. In T. Newburn, T. Williamson and A. Wright, eds. *Handbook of Criminal Investigation*. Cullompton: Willan.

INQUEST, undated. *Statistics, Unlawful Killing Verdicts and Prosecutions*. Available online at: www.inquest.org.uk/statistics/unlawful-killing-verdicts-and-prosecutions (accessed 4 May 2016).

Irving, B., and McKenzie, I., 1989. *Police Interrogation: The Effects of the Police and Criminal Evidence Act 1984*. London: Police Foundation.

Jacobson, J., 2008. *No One Knows, Police Responses to Suspects with Learning Disabilities and Learning Difficulties: A Review of Policy and Practice*. London: Prison Reform Trust.

Jessiman, T., and Cameron, A., 2017. The role of the appropriate adult in supporting vulnerable adults in custody: Comparing the perspectives of service users and service providers. *British Journal of Learning Disabilities*, 45(4), 246–252.

JUSTICE, 2017. *Mental Health and Fair Trial*. London: JUSTICE.

Kassin, S.M., Meissner, C.A. and Norwick, R.J., 2009. 'I'd Know a False Confession if I Saw One': A Comparative Study of College Students and Police Investigators. *Law and Human Behavior*, 29(5), 211–227.

Katz, M.B., 2013. *The Undeserving Poor: America's Enduring Confrontation with Poverty*. Oxford: OUP.

Kebbell, M., and Davies, G., 2003. People with intellectual disabilities in the investigation and prosecution of crime. *Legal and Criminological Psychology*, 8, 219–222.

Kemp, V., 2013. 'No time for a solicitor': implications for delays on the take-up of legal advice. *Criminal Law Review*, 3, 184–202.

Kemp, V., 2014. PACE, Performance Targets and Legal Protections. *Criminal Law Review*, 4, 278–297.

Kemp, V., and Balmer, N., 2008. *Criminal Defence Services: Users' Perspectives. An Interim Report*. London: Legal Services Research Centre Research Paper.

Kemp, V., and Hodgson, J., 2016. England and Wales: Empirical Findings. In M. Vanderhallen, M. van Oosterhout, M. Panzavolta, and D. de Vocht, eds. *Interrogating Young Suspects: Procedural Safeguards from an Empirical Perspective*. Antwerp: Intersentia.

Kendall, J., 2018. *Regulating Police Detention: Voices from Behind Closed Doors*. Bristol: Policy Press.

King, M., 1981. *The Framework of Criminal Justice*. London: Croom Helm.

Klockars, C.B., 1985. *The Idea of Police*. Beverly Hills, CA: SAGE.

Kraaij, V., Arensman, E., and Spinhoven, P. (2002). Negative Life Events and Depression in Elderly Persons: A Meta-Analysis. *The Journals of Gerontology: Series B*, 57(1), 87–94.

Lacey, N., 1992. The Jurisprudence of Discretion: Escaping the Legal Paradigm. In K. Hawkins, ed. *The Uses of Discretion*. Oxford: Clarendon Press.

Laing, J., 1995. The mentally disordered suspect at the police station. *Criminal Law Review*, 371–381.

Law Commission, 1993. *Mentally Incapacitated and Other Vulnerable Adults: Public Law Protection*. Law Com No 130. London: Law Commission.

Levine, C., 2004. The concept of vulnerability in disaster research. *Journal of Traumatic Stress*, 15(5), 395–402.

Liebling, A., and Price, D., 2003. Prison officers and the use of discretion. InL.R. Gelsthorpe and N. Padfield, eds. *Exercising Discretion: Decision Making in the Criminal Justice System and Beyond*. Cullompton: Willan.

Littlechild, B., 1995. Reassessing the role of the 'appropriate adult'. *Criminal Law Review*, 540–545.

Loftus, B., 2009. *Police Culture in a Changing World*. Oxford: OUP.

Macdonald, S., 2008. Constructing a Framework for Criminal Justice Research: Learning from Packer's Mistakes. *New Criminal Law Review*, 11(2), 257–311.

MacInnes, C., 1980. *Mr Love and Justice*. London: Allison and Busby.

Maguire, M., 2002. Regulating the Police Station: The Case of the Police and Criminal Evidence Act 1984. In M. McConville and G. Wilson, eds. *The Handbook of the Criminal Justice Process*. Oxford: OUP.

Maguire, M., 2008. Criminal Investigation and Crime Control. In T. Newburn, ed. *Handbook of Policing*, 2nd edn. Cullompton: Willan.

Maguire, M., and Norris, C., 1994. Police Investigations: Practice and Malpractice. *Journal of Law and Society*, 21(1), 72–84.

Manning, P.K., 1977. *Police Work: The Social Organization of Policing*. Cambridge, MA: MIT Press.

Manning, P.K., and Hawkins, K., 1989. Police decision-making. In M. Weatheritt, ed. *Police Research: Some Future Prospects*. Aldershot: Avebury.

McBarnet, D., 1981. *Conviction: Law, the State and the Construction of Justice*. Basingstoke: Macmillan.

McBarnet, D., 2004. *Crime, Compliance and Control: Collected Essays in Law*. Farnham: Ashgate.

McBarnet, D.J., 1978a. False Dichotomies in Criminal Justice Research. In J. Baldwin and K. Bottomley, eds. *Criminal Justice: Selected Readings*. London: Martin Robertson.

McBarnet, D.J., 1978b. Police and the State: Arrest, Legality and the Law. In G. Littlejohn, B. Smart, J. Wakeford and N. Yuval-Davis. *Power and the State*. London: Croom Helm.

McConville, M., and Baldwin, M., 1981. *Courts, Prosecution and Conviction*. Oxford: Clarendon Press.

McConville, M., and Hodgson, J., 1993. *Custodial Legal Advice and the Right to Silence*. Royal Commission on Criminal Justice Research Study No 16. London: HMSO.

McConville, M., Sanders, A., and Leng, R., 1991. *The Case for the Prosecution: Police Suspects and the Construction of Criminality*. Abingdon: Routledge.

McConville, M., Sanders, A., and Leng, R., 1997. Descriptive or Critical Sociology: The Choice is Yours. *British Journal of Criminology*, 37(3), 347–358.

McConville, M., Hodgson, J., Bridges, L., and Pavlovic, A., 1994. *Standing Accused: The Organization and Practices of Criminal Defence Lawyers in Britain*. Oxford: OUP.

McKinnon, I., and Grubin, D., 2010. Health screening in police custody. *Journal of Forensic and Legal Medicine*, 17, 209–212.

McKinnon, I., and Grubin, D., 2013. Health screening of people in police custody— evaluation of current police screening procedures in London, UK. *European Journal of Public Health*, 23(3), 399–405.

McKinnon, I., and Grubin, D., 2014. Evidence-Based Risk Assessment Screening in Police Custody: The HELPPC Study in London, UK. *Policing*, 8(2), 174–182.

McLaughlin, K., 2012. *Surviving Identity: Vulnerability and the Psychology of Recognition*. Abingdon: Routledge.

Medford, S., Gudjonsson, G.H., and Pearse, J., 2003. The efficacy of the appropriate adult safeguard during police interviewing. *Legal and Criminological Psychology*, 8, 253–266.

Mergaerts, L., 2017. Personal Correspondence: 1 December 2017.

Mindroom, undated. Learning difficulty or Learning disability? Available online at: www.mindroom.org/index.php/learning_difficulties/what_are_learning_difficulties/learning_difficulty_or_learning_disability/ (accessed 10 November 2015).

Ministry of Justice, 2012. *Swift and Sure Justice: The Government's Plans for Reform of the Criminal Justice System*. London: Ministry of Justice.

Ministry of Justice, 2015. *Criminal Procedure Rules*. London: Ministry of Justice.

Misztal, B., 2011. *The Challenges of Vulnerability: In Search of Strategies for a Less Vulnerable Social Life*. Basingstoke: Palgrave Macmillan.

Moonen, X., de Wit, M., and Hoogeveen, M., 2011. Mensen met een licht verstandelijke beperking in aanraking met politie en justitie. *Proces, tijdschrift voor strafrechtspleging*, 90(5), 235–250.

Morgan, R., 1996. Review Article: The Process is the Rule and the Punishment is the Process. *Modern Law Review*, 59, 306–314.

Munro, V.E. and Scoular, J., 2012. Abusing Vulnerability? Contemporary Law and Policy Responses to Sex Work in the UK. *Feminist Legal Studies*, 20(3), 189–206.

National Appropriate Adult Network, 2013. *NAAN National Standards*. London: NAAN. Available online at: www.appropriateadult.org.uk/images/pdf/national_standards_2013.pdf (accessed 14 August 2017).

National Appropriate Adult Network, 2015. *The Home Secretary's Commission on Appropriate Adults: There to Help: Ensuring Provision of Appropriate Adults for Mentally Vulnerable Adults Detained or Interviewed by Police*. London: NAAN.

National Appropriate Adult Network, 2017. *PACE Consultation 2017: Consultation Response: December 2017*. Available online at: www.appropriateadult.org.uk/images/pdf/2017_CodeC_NAAN_final1.pdf (accessed 25 May 2018).

National Appropriate Adult Network, undated a. *Our Network*. Available online at: www.appropriateadult.org.uk/index.php/about-us/naan-map (accessed 14 August 2017)

National Appropriate Adult Network, undated b. *Information: What is an Appropriate Adult?* Available online at: www.appropriateadult.org.uk/index.php/information/what-is-an-appropriate-adult (accessed 5 December 2017).

National Appropriate Adult Network, undated c. *Information: For Developers and Commissioners: Prohibited Individuals*. Available online at: /www.appropriateadult.org.uk/index.php/information/development/sources-models/prohibited-individuals (accessed 25 June 2018).

National Appropriate Adult Network, undated d. *Information: For Developers and Commissioners: Mandatory Presence*. Available online at: www.appropriateadult.org.uk/index.php/information/development/the-role-of-appropriate-adults/mandatory-presence (accessed 25 June 2018).

Nemitz, T., and Bean, P., 2001. Protecting the rights of the mentally disordered in police stations: The use of the appropriate adult in England and Wales. *Journal of Law and Psychiatry*, 24(6), 595–605.

Newburn, T., and Hayman, S., 2002. *Policing, Surveillance and Social Control: CCTV and Police Monitoring of Suspects*. Abingdon: Routledge.

Newman, D., 2013. *Legal Aid Lawyers and the Quest for Justice*. Oxford: Hart.

Neyroud, P., and Beckley, A., 2001. *Policing, Ethics and Human Rights*. Cullompton: Willan.

Norfolk, G.A., 1996. Fitness to be interviewed and the appropriate adult scheme: a survey of police surgeons' attitudes. *Journal of Forensic Medicine*, 3, 9–13.

O'Mahony, B.M., Milne. B., and Grant, T., 2012. To Challenge, or not to Challenge? Best Practice when Interviewing Vulnerable Suspects. *Policing*, 6, 301–313.

Owusu-Bempah, A., 2017. *Defendant Participation in the Criminal Process*. Abingdon: Routledge.

Packer, H.L., 1964. Two Models of the Criminal Process. *University of Pennsylvania Law Review*, 113(1), 1–68.

Packer, H.L., 1968. *The Limits of Criminal Sanction*. Stanford, CA: Stanford UP.

Palmer, C., 1996. Still Vulnerable After All These Years. *Criminal Law Review*, 633–644.

Palmer, C., and Hart, M., 1996. *A PACE in the Right Direction?: The Effectiveness of Safeguards in the Police and Criminal Evidence Act 1984 for Mentally Disordered and Mentally Handicapped Suspects – A South Yorkshire Study*. Sheffield: University of Sheffield.

Paoline, E.A., 2003. Taking stock: Toward a richer understanding of police culture. *Journal of Criminal Justice*, 31(3), 199–214.

Pearse, J., 1995. Police interviewing: The identification of vulnerabilities. *Journal of Community and Applied Social Psychology*, 5(3), 147–159.

Perks, M., 2010. *Appropriate Adult Provision in England and Wales: Report prepared for the Department of Health and the Home Office by Mark Perks Development Officer, National Appropriate Adult Network.* London: NAAN Available online at: www.gov.uk/government/uploads/system/uploads/attachment_data/file/117683/appropriate-adult-report.pdf (accessed 22 June 2017).

Phillips, C., and Brown, D., 1998. Entry into the Criminal Justice System: A Survey of Police Arrests and their Outcomes. *Home Office Research Study No 185.* London: Home Office.

Pierpoint, H., 2000. How Appropriate are Volunteers as 'Appropriate Adults' for Young Suspects? *Journal of Social Welfare and Family Law*, 22(4), 383–400.

Pierpoint, H., 2001. The Performance of Volunteer Appropriate Adults: A Survey of Call Outs. *Howard Journal of Criminal Justice*, 40(3), 255–271.

Pierpoint, H., 2004. A Survey on Volunteer Appropriate Adult Services. *Youth Justice*, 4(1), 32–45.

Pierpoint, H., 2006. Reconstructing the Role of the Appropriate Adult in England and Wales. *Criminology and Criminal Justice*, 6(2), 219–238.

Pierpoint, H., 2008. Quickening the PACE? The Use of Volunteers as Appropriate Adults in England and Wales. *Policing and Society*, 18, 397–410.

Pierpoint, H., 2011. Extending and Professionalising the Role of the Appropriate Adult. *Journal of Social Welfare and Family Law*, 33(2), 139–155.

Police Federation, 2017. Custody seen as Punishment Posting. Available online at: http://polfed.org/newsroom/4916.aspx?utm_content=bufferc47d0&utm_medium=social&utm_source=twitter.com&utm_campaign=buffer (accessed 13 September 2017).

Police Scotland, 2017. Appropriate Adults Standard Operating Procedure. Available online at: www.scotland.police.uk/assets/pdf/151934/184779/appropriate-adults-sop (accessed 30 November 2017).

Price, C., and Caplan, J., 1977. *The Confait Confessions.* New York, NY: Marion Boyars.

Punch, M., 1983. *Control in the Police Organisation.* Cambridge, MA: MIT Press.

Punch, M., 1985. *Conduct Unbecoming: the social construction of police deviance and control.* London: Tavistock.

Quinn, K., and Jackson, J., 2007. Of Rights and Roles: Police interviews with young suspects in Northern Ireland. *British Journal of Criminology*, 47(2), 234–255.

Quirk, H., 2013. Twenty years on, the right of silence and legal advice: the spiralling costs of an unfair exchange . *Northern Ireland Legal Quarterly*, 64(4), 465–484.

Quirk, H., 2017. *The Rise and Fall of the Right of Silence.* Abingdon: Routledge.

Reiner, R., 1991. *Chief Constables: Bobbies, Bosses or Bureaucrats?* Oxford: OUP.

Reiner, R., 1996. Policing and the Police. In M. Maguire, R. Morgan and R. Reiner, eds. *The Oxford Handbook of Criminology.* Oxford: OUP.

Reiner, R., 2010. *The Politics of the Police*, 4th edn. Oxford: OUP.

Reuss-Ianni, E., and Ianni, F.A.J., 1983. Street Cops and Management Cops – The Two Cultures of Policing. In M. Punch, ed. *Control in the Police Organisation.* Cambridge, MA: MIT Press.

Roach, K., 1999. Four Models of the Criminal Process. *Journal Criminal Law and Criminology*, 89(2), 671–684.

Robertson, G., Pearson, R., and Gibb, R., 1996. Police interviewing and the use of appropriate adults. *Journal of Forensic Psychiatry*, 7(2), 297–309.

Rock, F., 2007. *Communicating Rights: The Language of Arrest and Detention.* Basingstoke: Palgrave Macmillan.

Royal Commission on Criminal Procedure, 1981. *The Royal Commission on Criminal Procedure Report*. Cmnd 8092. London: HMSO.

Royal Commission on Criminal Justice, 1993. *The Royal Commission on Criminal Justice*. Cmnd 2263. London: HMSO.

Sanders, A., 2008. Can Coercive Powers be Effectively Controlled or Regulated? In E. Cape and R. Young, eds. *Regulating Policing: The Police and Criminal Evidence Act 1984 – Past, Present and Future*. Oxford: Hart.

Sanders, A. andYoung, R., 2000. *Criminal Justice*, 2nd edn. London: Butterworth.

Sanders, A., Young, R., and Burton, M., 2010. *Criminal Justice*, 4th edn. Oxford: OUP.

Sanders, A., Bridges, L., Mulvaney, A., and Crozier, G., 1989. *Advice and Assistance at Police Stations and the 24 Hour Duty Solicitor Scheme*. London: Lord Chancellor's Department.

Sandland, R., 1995. Review of Criminal process: an evaluative study. *Criminal Law Review*, 42, 679–680.

Scottish Government, 2018. Scottish Government Consultation: Establishing a statutory Appropriate Adult service in Scotland. Available online at: https://beta.gov.scot/publications/establishing-statutory-appropriate-adult-service-scotland/ (accessed 18 April 2018).

Sharpe, S., 1997. *Judicial Discretion and Criminal Investigation*. London: Sweet and Maxwell.

Skinns, L., 2009. 'Let's get it over with': early findings on the factors affecting detainees' access to custodial legal advice. *Policing and Society*, 19(1), 58–78.

Skinns, L., 2010. Stop the clock? Predictors of detention without charge in police custody areas. *Criminology and Criminal Justice*, 10(3), 303–320.

Skinns, L., 2011. *Police Custody: Governance, Legitimacy and Reform in the Criminal Justice Process*. Abingdon: Routledge.

Skinns, L., 2012. The role of the law in policing: the well- trodden path, the road less travelled and the road ahead. *Cahiers politiestudies*, 25, 225–246.

Skinns, L., Wooff, A., and Sprawson, A., 2017. Preliminary findings on police custody delivery in the twenty-first century: Is it 'good' enough? *Policing and Society*, 27(4), 358–371.

Skinns, L., Rice, L., Sprawson, A., and Wooff, A. (2017) Police legitimacy in context: an exploration of 'soft' power in police custody in England. *Policing: An International Journal of Police Strategies & Management*, 40(3). 601–613.

Skolnick, J., 1966. *Justice without Trial*. Hoboken, NJ: Wiley.

Smith, D.J., 1997. Case Construction and the Goals of the Criminal Process. *British Journal of Criminology*, 37(3), 319–346.

Smith, D.J., and Gray, J., 1983. *Police and People in London. Volume 4: The Police in Action*. London: Policy Studies Institute.

Soanes, C., and Stevenson, A., eds., 2008. *Concise Oxford English Dictionary*, 11th edn. Oxford: OUP.

Southcott, J.L., 1999. The psychiatric nurse and the 'appropriate adult. *Journal of Psychiatric and Mental Health Nursing*, 6(5), 357–361.

Spitzer, S., 1975. Towards a Marxian Theory of Deviance. *Social Problems*, 22(5), 638–651.

Stańdo-Kawecka, B., and Kusztal, J., 2015. Procedural Complexity within a Welfare Approach. Country Report Poland. In M. Panzavolta, D. de Vocht, M. van Oosterhout and M. Vanderhallen, eds. *Interrogating Young Suspects: Procedural Safeguards from a Legal Perspective*. Antwerp: Intersentia.

Stańdo-Kawecka, B., and Kusztal, J., 2016. Poland: Empirical Findings. In M. Vanderhallen, M. van Oosterhout, M. Panzavolta, and D. de Vocht, eds. *Interrogating Young Suspects: Procedural Safeguards from an Empirical Perspective.* Antwerp: Intersentia.

Steer, D., 1970. *Police Cautions: A Study in the Exercise of Police Discretion.* Oxford: Blackwell for the Penal Research Unit.

Stelfox, P., 2009. *Criminal Investigation: An Introduction to Principles and Practice.* Cullompton: Willan.

St-Yves, M., 2006. The psychology of rapport: five basic rules. In T. Williamson, ed. *Investigative Interviewing: Rights, Research and Regulation.* Cullompton: Willan.

The Guardian, 2015. Appropriate adult not available for many vulnerable people in police custody. Available online at: www.theguardian.com/society/2015/aug/26/appropriate-adult-not-available-for-many-vulnerable-people-in-police-custody (accessed 18 April 2018).

The Open University, undated. Timeline of learning disability history. Available online at: www.open.ac.uk/health-and-social-care/research/shld/timeline-learning-disability-history (accessed 18 April 2018).

Thomson, L.D.G., Galt, V., and Darjee, R., 2007. Professionalizing the role of appropriate adults. *The Journal of Forensic Psychiatry & Psychology*, 18(1), 99–119.

Tilley, N., Robinson, A., and Burrows, J., 2007. The investigation of high volume crime. In T. Newburn, T. Williamson and A. Wright, eds. *Handbook of Criminal Investigation.* Cullompton: Willan.

Tong, S., 2009. A Brief History of Crime Investigation. In S. Tong, R.P. Bryant and M.A. H. Horvath, eds. *Understanding Criminal Investigation.* Hoboken, NJ: Wiley-Blackwell.

Tong, S., and Bowling, B., 2006. Art, Craft and Science of Detective Work. *The Police Journal*, 76, 323–330.

Tong, S., Bryant, R.P., and Horvath, M.A.H., 2009. Crime Investigation in Context. In S. Tong, R.P. Bryant and M.A.H. Horvath, eds. *Understanding Criminal Investigation.* Hoboken, NJ: Wiley-Blackwell.

Turner, B., 2006. *Vulnerability and Human Rights.* University Park, PA: Pennsylvania State University Press.

Vanderhallen, M., and van Oosterhout, M., 2016. Belgium: Empirical Findings. In M. Vanderhallen, M. van Oosterhout, M. Panzavolta, and D. de Vocht, eds. *Interrogating Young Suspects: Procedural Safeguards from an Empirical Perspective.* Antwerp: Intersentia.

van Oosterhout, M., 2016. The Netherlands: Empirical Findings. In M. Vanderhallen, M. van Oosterhout, M. Panzavolta, and D. de Vocht, eds. *Interrogating Young Suspects: Procedural Safeguards from an Empirical Perspective.* Antwerp: Intersentia.

van Oosterhout, M., and Meese, J., 2015. Balancing the Need for Protection and Punishment of Young Delinquents. Country Report Belgium. In M. Vanderhallen, M. van Oosterhout, M. Panzavolta, and D. de Vocht, eds. *Interrogating Young Suspects: Procedural Safeguards from an Empirical Perspective.* Antwerp: Intersentia.

van Oosterhout, M., and de Vocht, D., 2015. Protecting Juvenile Suspects in a Pedagogical but Punitive Context. Country Report the Netherlands. In M. Vanderhallen, M. van Oosterhout, M. Panzavolta, and D. de Vocht, eds. *Interrogating Young Suspects: Procedural Safeguards from an Empirical Perspective.* Antwerp: Intersentia.

Ventress, M., Rix, K., and Kent, J., 2008. Keeping PACE: fitness to be interviewed by the police. *Advances in Psychiatric Treatment*, 14(5), 369–381.

Wacquant, L., 2009. *Punishing the Poor: The Neoliberal Government of Social Insecurity*. Duke, NC: Duke University Press.

Waddington, P.A.J., 1999a. *Policing Citizens: Authority and Rights*. London: UCL Press.

Waddington, P.A.J., 1999b. Police (canteen) sub-culture: an appreciation. *British Journal of Criminology*, 39(2), 287–309.

Westmarland, L., 2001a. *Gender and Policing. Sex, Power and Police Culture*. Cullompton: Willan.

Westmarland, L., 2001b. Blowing the whistle on police violence: ethics, research and ethnography. *British Journal of Criminology*, 41(2), 523–535.

Westmarland, L., 2008. Police Cultures. In T. Newburn, ed. *Handbook of Policing*, 2nd edn. Cullompton: Willan.

Whitaker, B., 1979. *The Police in Society*. London: Eyre Methuen.

White, C., 2002. Re-assessing the social worker's role as an appropriate adult. *Journal of Social Welfare and Family Law*, 24(1), 55–65.

Williams, J., 2000. The inappropriate adult. *Journal of Social Welfare and Family Law*, 22(1), 43–57.

Willis, J.J., and Mastrofski, S.D., 2016. Improving policing by integrating craft and science: what can patrol officers teach us about good police work? *Policing and Society*, DOI: 10.1080/10439463.2015.1135921

Wilson, J.Q., 1968. *Varieties of Police Behaviour*. Cambridge, MA: Harvard University Press.

Wooff, A., and Skinns, L. 2018. The role of emotion, space and place in police custody in England: Towards a geography of police custody. *Punishment & Society*. Available online at: http://journals.sagepub.com/doi/abs/10.1177/1462474517722176 (accessed 9 April 2018).

Wright, A., 2007. Ethics and Corruption. In T. Newburn, T. Williamson and A. Wright, eds. *Handbook of Criminal Investigation*. Cullompton: Willan.

Young, M., 1991. *An Inside Job: Policing and Police Culture in Britain*. Oxford: Clarendon Press.

Zander, M., 2005. *The Police and Criminal Evidence Act 1984*, 5th edn. London: Sweet and Maxwell.

Zander, M., 2007. Response to 'Modernising Police Powers: Review of the Police and Criminal Evidence Act (PACE) 1984, Home Office Consultation Paper, March 2007'1–2 Available online at: www.lse.ac.uk/collections/law/staff%20publications%20full%20text/zander/PACE%20-%20MZ%20Response%20to%20CP%20May%2023%202007.pdf (accessed 4 May 2016).

Zander, M., 2013. *Zander on PACE: The Police and Criminal Evidence Act 1984*, 6th edn. London: Sweet and Maxwell.

Zander, M., 2015. *Zander on PACE: The Police and Criminal Evidence Act 1984*, 7th edn. London: Sweet and Maxwell.

Index

For Product Safety Concerns and Information please contact our
EU representative GPSR@taylorandfrancis.com Taylor & Francis
Verlag GmbH, Kaufingerstraße 24, 80331 München, Germany